URBAN AMAZONS

Urban Amazons

Lesbian Feminism and Beyond in the Gender, Sexuality and Identity Battles of London

Sarah F. Green
Lecturer in Social Anthropology
University of Manchester

HQ
75.6
.G72
L664
1997

First published in Great Britain 1997 by
MACMILLAN PRESS LTD
Houndmills, Basingstoke, Hampshire RG21 6XS and London
Companies and representatives throughout the world

A catalogue record for this book is available from the British Library.

ISBN 0–333–66974–6 hardcover
ISBN 0–333–68429–X paperback

First published in the United States of America 1997 by
ST. MARTIN'S PRESS, INC.,
Scholarly and Reference Division,
175 Fifth Avenue, New York, N.Y. 10010

ISBN 0–312–16470–X

Library of Congress Cataloging-in-Publication Data
Green, Sarah F., 1961–
Urban amazons : lesbian feminism and beyond in the gender,
sexuality, and identity battles of London / Sarah F. Green.
p.   cm.
Includes bibliographical references and index.
ISBN 0–312–16470–X
1. Lesbian feminism—England—London.   2. Lesbians—England–
–London—Identity.   3. Lesbians—England—London—Political
activity.   I. Title.
HQ75.6.G72L664   1996
306.76'63'09421—dc20   96–9723
                                                                              CIP

This book is printed on paper suitable for recycling and made from fully managed and
sustained forest sources.

10   9   8   7   6   5   4   3   2   1
06   05   04   03   02   01   00   99   98   97

Printed and bound in Great Britain by
Antony Rowe Ltd, Chippenham, Wiltshire

Contents

List of Figures

List of Tables

List of Plates

Acknowledgements

I will be always indebted to Susan Benson, Esther Goody and Gill Dunne for their guidance, constructive criticism and continual encouragement.

A Research Studentship grant from New Hall, Cambridge, was one of the many forms of assistance, both financial and practical, the college has given me over the years. Were it not for the college's generosity and understanding, I would not have been able to begin this study, let alone finish it. I am also indebted to Churchill College, Cambridge, for giving me a research fellowship which allowed me to revise the text in my own time.

For their helpful comments and time given freely, I am grateful to Marilyn Strathern, Frances Pine, Barbara Bodenhorn, Teresa Brennan, Gillian Crowther and Simon Coleman. Ray Abraham's encouragement and interest was greatly appreciated. Innumerable students' comments during seminars were of immense help.

The Department of Social Anthropology at the University of Cambridge continually provided assistance, both material and practical. I would particularly like to thank Humphrey Hinton, who will be sorely missed, and Mary MacGinley for their help, friendship, generosity and patience.

Jack and Esther Goody provided me with a home and food when my funds ran out, for which I will always be grateful.

I would also like to thank Brian Gosschalk of MORI, for his understanding that I was never really cut out to be an opinion pollster.

Few things test personal friendship as much as long-term research and writing a book, and I would like to thank all those who lived through it with me, especially Helen Middleton. I hope to be able to see more of them in the near future. My mother has been unstintingly helpful and supportive, and I would like to thank my father for his encouragement.

I am also indebted to Suzanne Duvall, whose belief in me all those years ago in Dallas was the spark that gave me the courage to begin this project.

I give special thanks to the other Sarah Green, Sarah C. Green. During the research and production of the first draft of this text, she was a continual source of strength. Her faith and patience were worth much more than I could ever repay.

That this book was ever finished is due to Rebecca Boden and Dox, whose intensively caring approach gave me the courage to recognise the limited utility of seriousness.

Last, but most importantly, I would like to thank the women in London, without whose help, interest and comments this research would not have been possible. Even though the time I was in London was a difficult one of transition for the community, these women's strength, courage and determination in the face of frequently extremely fraught situations was an inspiration to me. They were and are all remarkable women. I only wish that I had that same strength of character myself.

Sarah F. Green
April 1996
University of Manchester
Department of Social Anthropology
Manchester M13 9PL, UK

Introduction

This study is about two things: a group of women living in London in the late 1980s, and what it means to be a person in the late modern age. In substantive terms, it is about women whose lives were guided by their feminist beliefs and political struggles, both with others and amongst themselves. It is a story about what happens when a theory based on making 'the personal political' is put into practice, and the often painful process of discovering that living it is far more complicated and contradictory than theorising it. Based on eighteen months' ethnographic research in London, this study describes how the contexts in which the theory was lived caught up with beliefs and ideals, questioned them and eventually began turning them into something else.

The political beliefs were based on radical and revolutionary feminist approaches towards gender, sexuality and sexual desire. These motivated some women to attempt to create a separatist lesbian feminist community in which to live and from which to campaign against what was seen as a man-made world that dominated women through sexual oppression. In practice, the attempt to create this woman-only space in the city resulted in a series of continual conflicts over differences between women, particularly concerning race and class, but later also involving female sexual desire.

I argue that the problems stemmed from two sources. First, the theory privileged personal experience, which continually emphasised the differences between women and demanded that they be acknowledged, while simultaneously emphasising the importance of the commonality of women, which denied these differences. The attempt to create a community based on this approach inevitably lived out the conflict embedded in it (a classic western cultural case of individuality versus sociality). This coincided with changes in feminist and gender theory, which began to question 'essentialist' and 'ethnocentric' models of gender. Second, the context in which these events occurred (late 1980s London) strongly influenced the direction of the debates and the interactions these women had with others. It was a decade which began with the Greater London Council (GLC), under the socialist leadership of Ken Livingstone, which fought a rearguard action against the Conservative Thatcher administration, but continued in the second half of the decade with the Government's abolition of the GLC and the fragmentation of many of the grassroots movements which had grown and developed during that period.

1

On one level then, this book concerns the creation of a lesbian feminist community, its struggles to carve out a space for itself in London, its inter-actions with other groups and the subsequent questioning of the whole basis upon which it had created itself. The research for it was carried out during a transitional period in the community. There were many threads to the changes: conflicts over differences between women, particularly in terms of race; the virtual abandonment of living in collective households; the increasing demand to discuss difficult issues such as diverse forms of lesbian sexual desire, and violence in lesbian relationships; wide-ranging experimentation with dress styles amongst younger women, using clothes rejected by earlier feminists as objectifying; the increasing trend in making lesbian films exploring previously 'taboo' issues. At the time, these threads were collectively regarded as a moment of fragmentation in the community – things were 'falling apart at the seams', as one woman put it, but no one was quite sure where it was all going, or what was going to replace it.

Today, the change is recognised as a move away from 'identity politics' and the 1970s style of radical feminism which emphasised the commonal-ity of women, and towards an emphasis on 'the politics of difference' and 1990s style theories of gender and sexuality, which emphasise diversity, and the fluidity, or at least the lack of authenticity and coherence, of sub-jective identity. The development of Queer politics, a still nascent theoret-ical standpoint combining varieties of feminist, gay and postmodernist thought, is the leitmotif of these changes.

This transition will be familiar to anyone following the trends in gender and sexuality literature, where the question of what constitutes gender and/or sexuality, let alone gender *identities* and sexual *identities*, is being critically reappraised. This study provides an example of how such reap-praisals were experienced in practice within a community which was gen-erally extremely reflexive about these issues.

On another level, the book provides a window through which to look at much wider social and political issues. The study questions the assertion that lesbian feminists are part of a 'sub-culture' or 'counter-culture', as if their culture is somehow separate from, and located beneath or beyond what is experienced by 'normal' people. Rather, I suggest that they are both a part and a reflection of the culture and city in which they exist. Short-term changes in London, such as the rise and fall of Ken Livingstone's GLC, as well as long-term social change in Britain, such as a prolonged political shift to the right, substantial changes in economic conditions, and changing attitudes towards gender, sexuality and identity, affected and were reflected in the lesbian feminist community.

The book explores such wider issues as they were experienced by lesbian feminists in London. These include: an analysis of the way grass-roots movements and local government became intertwined during the 1980s in London; the 'identity politics' and 'hierarchy of oppressions' debates; the shift from 'movement' politics to 'lifestyle' politics; and the introduction of the 'politics of difference' based on postmodernist thought. In particular, doubts about previous assumptions, particularly concerning the authenticity and fixed nature of gendered and sexual identities are explored, and the book makes use of the fact that during the research, Section 28 of the 1988 Local Government Act ('Clause 28'), which prohibits the promotion of homosexuality, was passed into law. This event brought out all the differences and some of the similarities in the arguments being put forward by different constituencies, including lesbian feminists, concerning sexuality and gender.

STRUCTURE OF THE TEXT

The text is structured in a roughly ethnographic style, mixing often detailed description with analysis. Chapter 1 describes the context, the way the study was carried out in practice, and lays out the conceptual framework for the lesbian feminist community. Chapter 2 descriptively locates the community within the city and discusses a variety of the more public and political organisations and events associated with it. Chapter 3 describes more personal aspects of community life and analyses the structure of networks of social relations. Chapter 4 then steps back to think about all this material, on the one hand comparing its findings with other studies of lesbian/feminist communities, and on the other looking at the historical roots of the concepts which formed the basis of such communities. Chapter 5 then focuses back on London, and considers how the particular development of local government politics during the 1980s became involved in structuring the community – both in terms of physical space and material resources, and in terms of concepts. This is followed, in the same chapter, by a detailed analysis of how this worked in practice during a dispute within a lesbian feminist collective. And Chapter 6 brings together all these strands, while dealing with debates over sexuality and sexual desire, which formed the focus of many conceptual conflicts. This final chapter contains the central analytical argument.

I have treated the way in which issues of gender, sexuality and identity were debated (in both literature and within the community) as culturally specific, rather than being applicable to the general human condition.

I have analysed the lesbian feminist community in London as one expression of Euro-American culture in the late twentieth century, which shares many, if not most, characteristics with the rest of that culture. My anthropological background militated against my seeing this community as if it were a separate culture. It looked entirely Euro-American to me, and not at all like the product of any other culture of which I was aware, in either form or intellectual underpinnings.

All the names of individual women have been changed to protect their anonymity. I am aware that while this will be effective in preventing those uninvolved in the community from recognising the women concerned, it will not always be effective for those familiar with the community, particularly in the case of those women mentioned who were well-known public figures. This issue has taxed me for a very long time. I delayed publishing the study for three years after completing it, to establish a temporal distance between the events and people described and the text. I have also severely limited detailed personal descriptions of individuals as I have not changed the names of any places or organisations with which they were involved, nor the locations of these places within London. This decision was based on the fact that information is publicly available about all the places and organisations actually named, and the fact that their spatial distribution is important in understanding the community's location within the city.

The result of this compromise is that it is difficult for the reader to visualise many of the women mentioned in the text, and I have made much more use of general statements than I would otherwise have done.

Finally, a note about intellectual objectivity: in keeping with most of my colleagues these days, I don't believe in it. Had someone else done the study, or had I done it at a different moment in my life, I have no doubt that different arguments would have been made. With this limitation in mind, I do want to emphasise that I have, to the best of my ability, attempted to represent the events described as they occurred, and the different perspectives women expressed in a manner that in some way approximates what they might have said themselves. This is impossible to achieve perfectly, as I will have always seen things and heard people with my eyes and ears, which are inevitably attuned to paying more attention to some factors than others in my efforts to untangle the complexity of things going on around me. This kind of limitation, however, should not stop one trying.

1 A Matter of Identities

My time in London began in December 1987, when the new Local Government Bill was entering its final drafting stages in Parliament. This would not normally have been particularly relevant to lesbian feminism, but at the last minute, a new clause was introduced into the Bill. It had the short title of, 'Prohibition on Promoting Homosexuality by Teaching or by Publishing Material.'[1] It became popularly known as Clause 28, now Section 2A of the Local Government Act, 1988 (see Appendix A).

The clause prohibited local authorities and schools under their control from teaching that homosexuality should be a positive identity or from publishing anything which suggested this. Those supporting the legislation thought such practices encouraged people to become homosexuals, and felt the promotion of 'positive images' was a tactic used by left-wing councils to undermine the fabric of British social life. With this in mind, the clause also prevented local authorities from suggesting that homosexuality constituted 'a pretended family relationship.'

Lesbian and gay groups around the country immediately mobilised campaigns against the proposed legislation, and lesbian feminists also rapidly organised separate actions of their own. As far as lesbian feminists were concerned, Clause 28 was not so much an attack on gay rights, as a direct attack against the lesbian feminist political platform.[2] Their political views, based on radical and/or revolutionary feminism, differed substantially from those of either gay liberation or other forms of feminism, and was the source of a number of antagonisms between lesbian feminists and other groups involved in sexual or gender politics, as will be seen.

In London, one of the groups formed during lesbian feminist meetings about Clause 28 was the Lesbian Stop The Clause group, later known as Lesbians Against the Clause. Ideas about direct action, in addition to demonstrations, were formulated within that group, as was the strategy of splitting up into groups of four or five women to carry out protests. Two incidents attracted national attention: in the first, four lesbian feminists abseiled into the House of Lords on February 2 1988, after a vote that the clause should remain in the Bill without amendment; in the second, another four women chained themselves to two newscasters' desks as they began presenting a live edition of the BBC's *Six O'Clock News* on May 28, 1988.

The legislation was the latest episode in an ongoing battle between the Conservative government and a number of Labour local authorities, particularly those in London. It was a battle stimulated by policies introduced by the Greater London Council (GLC) under the leadership of Ken Livingstone between 1981 and 1986, which had significantly affected the lives and political existence of lesbian feminists in the capital. The GLC itself had been abolished by the Government on April 1 1986, but a number of inner city boroughs in London, particularly Camden, Islington, Hackney and Haringey in the north, and Lambeth and Lewisham in the south (known collectively by the conservative media as the 'Loony Left' boroughs), attempted to continue the policies formulated by the GLC. And central government continued to curb their activities, not only through controlling local government funding, but also through legislation which attempted to prevent the implementation of many of their policies. Amongst these were 'positive images' campaigns on behalf of lesbians and gay men; a number of initiatives on behalf of women informed by various hues of feminism; anti-racist and anti-apartheid activities; and support for Sinn Fein (Ali, 1984, Carvel, 1987, Forrester *et al*, 1985).

What these policies had in common was a concern about identity – gay identity, gender identity, ethnic and national identity. Throughout this book, the question of identities and the inequities generated by the differences between them is always in the background. This was a time when 'political correctness' was under fire in Britain, and the debate focused on the nature of the differences between people, and what creates these differences. Do people possess authentic differences, or are they all the product of cultural, political, and/or economic conditions? Does one difference lead to more oppression than another? Even if these differences are culturally constructed, does it make them any less 'real' in practical terms?

These problems are familiar ground in theoretical debates about gender, agency, the construction of the subject and so on. In this study, I will be looking at how the debates were played out in practice. Theory was not just theory here: it deeply involved people's everyday lives, affected what they chose to do and what they thought about themselves.

The issue centrally concerned not only lesbian feminists, but also ethnic groups, gay rights groups, local authorities and the state legislature. Lesbian feminists interacted with all of these and had to share their 'space' with them – both intellectual and physical. Many of the conflicts between lesbian feminists and these others concerned the nature of identity in a world of asymmetries, both symbolic and material, and disagreements on the major causes of inequality: gender, sexuality, ethnicity or class and their various combinations and permutations.

Figure 1 Some moments from the Clause 28 campaign: two of the many articles which appeared in the tabloid press, a flier advertising a Lesbians Against Clause 28 meeting, a local authority lesbian and gay unit flier and a popular postcard resulting from the abseiling incident. The artist was Kate Charlesworth, published by Cath Tate Cards, London.

1. A MOMENT IN TIME

The study's beginning during the Clause 28 affair immediately high-lighted the importance of the historical moment and the particular place in which these things were happening. It was not coincidental that the majority of lesbian feminists in London lived and/or worked in one of the London boroughs marked off as 'Loony Left' by their opponents, nor that most of their organisations, meeting places and bookshops were also located in these areas. Nor is it irrelevant that these places contained unusually high numbers of poor and unemployed people (even though parts of Camden and Islington particularly have been in the process of 'gentrification' for some time), a high percentage of ethnic minorities and chronic housing problems, expressed both in the high proportion of homeless and in the low quality of much of the housing stock, as well as a large portion of London's artists, writers, musicians, fringe venues and the headquarters of various campaigning organisations such as Greenpeace and CND (Campaign for Nuclear Disarmament). It is not by chance that residents in these boroughs repeatedly elected strongly socialist candidates to run their councils at a time when the country at large, and even the Labour Party itself, was swinging rapidly in the other direction. It was impossible to ignore 'external' social, political and economic conditions in which lesbian feminists existed. Lesbian feminists were (and still remain) very much a part of London as a city, woven into its fabric much as most other Londoners. They were not isolated from other groups, wider conditions, the rhythms and structure of the city.

This is an important point: the lesbian feminist community was generated out of the conditions of the city, and out of Euro-American intellectual traditions, which includes both feminism and ideas about sexual and gender identities particular to those cultures. Lesbian feminist separatism was a product of its time and place (as was the so-called 'libertarianism' which challenged it). In that respect, I agree with Foucault that oppositional groups and ideas usually reflect cultural traditions as much as non-oppositional ideas.[3] For this reason, I have rejected the labels 'sub-culture' or 'counter-culture' for lesbian feminists in London. As the text will show, there are many areas where underlying assumptions about the way we are as persons are the same both for lesbian feminists and their opponents. The difference is in the interpretation of what this means, and what should be done about it. The study of these women therefore also constitutes a study of 'Euro-American' culture (for want of a better term), and the kinds of shifts and changes which are currently affecting it.

I am not suggesting that radical and revolutionary feminist perspectives did not impose their particular stamp on the situation. They also had their own internal dynamic, and one of the purposes of doing this research was to look at what happens when oppositional political theories are put into practice in everyday life, in conditions where its adherents were not isolated from that to which they were opposed. I do want to emphasise, however, that the *way* in which the approach was put into practice was substantially affected by the context in which it existed, and that the approach itself was a product of the cultural and material conditions in which it emerged: that is to say, within a 'western', multi-cultural metropolis in the late 1980s.

I will be looking at the changes under way within lesbian feminist space in London during the late 1980s in this light. It was a period marked by a shift in many lesbian feminists' understanding of the concept of difference, which was the combined result of their experiences in London and the shifting concerns within feminism. This centrally involved a reanalysis of the concepts of gender and sexuality, reflected in the development of the 'politics of difference' and the resistance such politics provoked from lesbian feminists, in particular against the strand coined 'libertarianism'. Few women who were labelled 'libertarians' would refer to themselves using that label, but many lesbian feminists identified it as anti-feminist and associated it with lesbian sado-masochism (S/M), which most 'libertarians' denied.

'Libertarianism' will be discussed in detail in Chapter 6, but briefly, the label referred to an emphasis on diversity between women, rather than their unity; and it focused on the analysis of femininity as a cultural construct, rather than focusing on the oppression of women by men, and on patriarchy. Furthermore, 'libertarianism' was regarded as distinct from the wider 'politics of difference' movement because of its strong emphasis on exploring female sexual desire and practice using an essentially postmodernist approach. Lesbian feminists accused 'libertarians' of being fundamentally conservative, and promoting the idea that women should 'do what they like and forget about feminism'. It appeared to lesbian feminists that 'libertarians' were promoting forms of sexual performance (whether in practice or as film or theatre) which had been pin-pointed as particularly oppressive for women by lesbian feminists: the kind which experimented with dominance and subordination. Hence the association with S/M.

In contrast, 'libertarians' argued they were attempting to deconstruct and reformulate the symbolism involved in the performance of difference.[4] By using 'dominant' symbolism in unexpected ways, its power is undermined. Their argument was that it is impossible to change things if you do not first undermine the cultural construction of reality. The lesbian feminist view was that it is impossible to change things if you do not first attack the concrete structures of power.

Underlying the explicit disagreements, there was a much deeper issue concerning the nature of gendered and sexual identities, which were increasingly looking fluid, flexible and much more diverse than they had done before the introduction of postmodernist thought. In practical terms, the lesbian feminist community had relied upon believing in the authenticity of both womanhood and lesbianism as a basis for creating the community, even if that authenticity was not necessary in intellectual terms. Undermining the idea that gender and sexuality are at some fundamental level real, which postmodernist approaches did do, led many women to feel that their community was fragmenting.

However, not only shifts in theories were changing things in such communities, as Faderman has also noted for contemporary lesbian and lesbian feminist communities in the USA (Faderman 1992, esp. pp. 274–284). Ironically, many of the conflicts were the result of such communities being the victims of their own success. In earlier years, when they were small, and when the only people who dared to participate were those who had little to lose – mostly young, unemployed, white women with no children, who were willing to live in a squat – there was not a great deal of diversity in the community. These small groups could develop their politics without being heavily challenged by people who felt differently. In later years, as the communities expanded and diversified, this was no longer possible.

In many respects, the community studied here was ahead of its time in more general cultural terms. Only very recently has the media picked up on there being a problem with the idea of an authentic identity in today's post-everything world – in articles about the fact that we can now change anything about ourselves, particularly our bodies; in looking at the significance of new reproductive technologies, and asking whether this will confuse ideas about gender and identity; in looking at the effects of the internet, where people can now continually disembody and re-create themselves in virtual reality, and can cross borders and boundaries seamlessly; in bemoaning the fragmentation of communities and cultures and wondering where it is all going to lead. These kinds of issues came up earlier in the lesbian feminist community, and were explored, often painfully, earlier; and, a few years after having done the research for this book, it looks like solutions are beginning to be found, also earlier.

This study therefore goes beyond the realms of a lesbian feminist community in London and the conflicts the women who were part of it in the late 1980s experienced in trying to come to terms with the changes they faced.

2. LONDON: THE CONTEXT AND THE STUDY

The lesbian feminist community was not contained within a single, continuous geographical boundary in London: lesbian feminists' homes, though concentrated in certain inner city boroughs, were scattered in amongst the 610 square miles of Greater London and its 6.6 million inhabitants, as were their organisations. Available buildings were usually shared with other women's and/or lesbian groups and organisations (Chapter 2), and most social venues used by lesbian feminists were actually run by lesbian and gay groups (Chapter 3). Further, a number of social venues were ordinary pubs or clubs for most of the time, but would periodically hold a women-only evening.

Thus the boundaries of the community existed more as conceptual markers which did not always *physically* exclude non-community space or individuals. Moreover, these markers, or representations of space, were sometimes as temporary as the two hours of a meeting. This gave the community a fluidity and a sense of continual change. Although this quality was interesting in its implications for the analysis of communities, it did not make research particularly easy. The sheer scale of activities added to the difficulties. Lesbian feminists in London produced enormous amounts of written material, both published and circulated as photocopies; they attended dozens of marches and demonstrations, ran dozens of groups, courses, organisations and staged benefits, poetry readings and so on.

I first contacted lesbian feminist organisations through women's bookshops in London. A variety of journals and newsletters produced by lesbian/feminist groups were available there, which frequently carried listings of events, and there were also notice boards giving information about groups and events, amongst other things. Listings also appeared in the widely available weekly London magazines, *City Limits* (now closed) and *Time Out*, and in the less widely available lesbian and gay weekly newspaper, the *Pink Paper*.

I then began attending events and demonstrations, at that time mostly associated with the campaign against Clause 28. I also wrote to the Lesbian Archive and Information Centre (hereafter referred to as the Archive), which was then a lesbian feminist organisation. In the letter, I explained my research and was enthusiastically welcomed by Paula, one of the Archive's workers, to come and participate as a volunteer. From these small beginnings, I quickly gained access to a wide range of activities, organisations and groups in the lesbian feminist community.

I was open from the start about the purpose of my research interests in lesbian feminist activity in London, as far as this was possible. This did

Figure 2 The darker shaded boroughs are those in which the majority of women-only and lesbian/feminist places were located. The lighter shaded boroughs are where a number existed, but not as extensively as in other boroughs. The bold line within the map represents the division between inner and outer London.

The London Boroughs

not cause many difficulties, and I often had the impression that after a time, women decided to 'forget' my reasons for being there. Occasionally, I experienced hostility and from time to time was deliberately misled, but this was rare – much rarer, in fact, than I had been led to believe, having been warned (by people I now realise did not personally know any lesbian feminists) about these 'Amazons', and having read numerous attacks against them, both in the popular media and in academic literature. For the most part, there was a great deal of interest in my work, and I was asked many times to explain not only what I was doing, but why. The searching nature of some questions helped me enormously in formulating ideas and notifying me of areas that I had not yet considered.

A substantial part of the study involved participating in lesbian feminist organisations and attending meetings and courses. There were few opportunities to research women's lives at home, as residences were scattered and strongly defended as 'private' space (see Chapter 3). I did however live with one lesbian feminist separatist (Nicola) for three months when I moved to London in May 1988, supplemented this with visits to women's homes after they had become friends and discussed home life with both interviewees and acquaintances. I moved four times during eighteen months, living north of the river Thames twice and south of the river twice, though almost all my research centred on North London, which is where the bulk of lesbian feminists I came to know lived. Figure 2 outlines the areas where the study was concentrated.

There were four aspects to the study, which varied according to the depth of the information gathered as against its breadth. The first aspect was the most in-depth, in which I spent a great deal of time with particular organisations and groups, charting their structures, day-to-day activities, interrelationships and so on. This aspect took up the bulk of my time. The second aspect involved in-depth interviews with thirty women, 26 of them taped, discussed further below. The third aspect was intended to supplement this detailed work with less intensive studies of a broader cross-section of groups and organisations, involving short periods of time working with them and/or taped interviews with members of organisations and groups. The fourth aspect was the collection of mass, but very sparse, data – such as analysis of mailing lists, which gave a few details about a large number of women and/or organisations.

My initial contact with the Archive proved to be a long-lasting one, and its two paid workers, Anne and Paula, became close acquaintances. I became a member of its collective for just under a year. Collectives constituted the major type of formal structure and indeed almost the only formal lesbian feminist structure, other than management committees and temporary organising committees. I became a member of the organising committee for a four-day lesbian feminist conference ('The Lesbian Summer School') held in the summer of 1988, and was involved in both the planning stages and the conference itself (see Chapters 5 and 6).

I gained information about other collectives from their collective members, both in formal interviews and informally, and I volunteered to work in organisations for a period, though I did not attend collective meetings, which were closed to non-members. Although all the organisations were run (at least partly) by lesbian feminists, the majority were not intended primarily for their use (unlike the Archive; see Chapter 2). Groups rather than organisations were much more frequently run by *and for* lesbian feminists. Unlike groups, all organisations required substantial resources and were funded by grants, usually from a local authority or the

London Borough Grants Scheme (LBGS), whose grant conditions required the organisation to provide a general service. Such services included legal advice, assistance with housing, help lines, women's centres and training centres. Many of these organisations were not publicly known to be run by lesbian feminists, and it would be a breach of confidentiality to name them here. Those organisations which were run primarily for lesbians or lesbian feminists included the Lesbians and Policing Project (LESPOP), the Lesbian Custody Group, Lesbian Employment Rights, Camden Lesbian Centre and Black Lesbian Group (CLC/BLG) and London Lesbian Line.

In all, I visited and/or interviewed members of 29 organisations; I worked for a period of between four to ten weeks in three. I worked in the Lesbian Archive from the beginning of fieldwork up until November 1988, when a collective dispute led to its closure for three months.

I also attended six courses run by and for lesbian feminists, and attended meetings of 13 groups, each on at least three occasions. They were usually in the form of discussion groups. In total, I attended 68 meetings, some of which were *ad hoc*, and I further attended 31 events, including marches, demonstrations, conferences, readings and social events. As a white woman, I could not of course attend 'Black Women Only' groups or events.

I supplemented the ethnographic collection of information about women, their views and their activities through in-depth, taped, semi-structured life history interviews with 26 women and four untaped interviews. They were conducted, except for three women, in their own homes, and I made one to three visits in each case to complete the interviews, which lasted between three to six hours each. I had prepared a list of 58 questions, but women were free to discuss any issues.

I tried to ensure that a broad range of opinion and experiences were represented in those I asked to interview, though this was not always easy due to the divisions existent within the community. Of the 30 women interviewed, 25 lived north of the river and five south of the river; 10 lived alone, though four of these lived in flats which were part of housing co-operatives; seven lived with their lovers and the rest shared their housing with other women. All except five had moved at least once in the last three years. Their ages ranged from 19 to 57 at the time of the interview, and they had spent between one year and almost twenty years involved with feminism and/or lesbian groups and networks in London. Levels of involvement in the community varied and had fluctuated over time for most of the interviewees. Four had been married, and six had children, one through AID. Five were from ethnic minorities (one Chinese, one Asian, two West African, all

British, and one African American); four either currently or at some time in the past defined themselves as working class; one was disabled and the remainder were able-bodied, white, self-defined middle class women, though not all were British. All felt they were lesbian feminists of some description, but there was a wide range of interpretations of what this meant, and most had changed their views on several occasions.

The core of the questionnaire was identical in all interviews, but other questions were altered and some were added, depending on my knowledge of the interviewee's particular experiences. The subjects covered are listed in Appendix B.

Finally, I was fortunate in having the opportunity to work on two films for Channel 4 on older lesbians' lives and experiences.[5] This provided invaluable comparative and historical data on the community in London since the 1930s, data which are not available elsewhere. I am extremely grateful to Suzanne Neild and Rosalind Pearson, producers and directors of the programmes, for the chance to participate in these two projects.

3. LIMITS OF THE STUDY

There were certain areas it was not possible to research as adequately as I would have liked. Although I gained a reasonable amount of information on women's lives at home, it was difficult to get as wide-ranging a knowledge of this area as I did of their more public and collective activities.

It was also difficult to visit women in their places of employment, except where they worked in women-only organisations or businesses that formed part of lesbian feminist space. The majority did not, though they were frequently volunteers in such organisations. Most of the women I knew had occupations in the social or health services, in teaching or in various manual trades (see Chapter 3).

Finally, I did not research areas involving lesbian sado-masochists ('S/M dykes'). Lesbian feminists never mixed socially with women who identified themselves as S/M dykes, and it was not uncommon for lesbian feminists to campaign to have S/M dykes excluded from venues, meetings or even marches and demonstrations. If I was going to spend most of my time within radical, and particularly revolutionary, feminist circles, I had to avoid attending any venues known to be S/M venues, and I did not get to know any women who identified themselves as S/M dykes. I did on occasion find myself at a meeting or event where several such women were present (usually indicated by the wearing of S/M clothing styles), but this was rare.

4. RADICAL AND REVOLUTIONARY FEMINISM DEFINED

There have been many ideas and approaches which have come under the labels 'radical' or 'revolutionary' feminism and separatism over the years since the terms were coined. Here, I want to concentrate on the ideas which went under these labels during my study in London, rather than attempt to cover their development and changes over time.[6] There was never any complete agreement even among the women in London, so the following is a general outline, rather than representing what any particular women believed.

Both radical and revolutionary feminism argue that women in contemporary society suffer oppression and that its roots lie within the sexual/gendered relations between men and women. However, where radical feminism concentrates on social constructions of gender in its critique of dominant beliefs and modes of existence, revolutionary feminism concentrates more on sexual practice – and in particular, violence within heterosexual relations. These relations are seen as defined by patriarchal values which place women in a position of subordination to men. Within this perspective, patriarchal values cannot be reduced to something else – for example, material relations (as most socialist feminists would argue)[7] or psychoanalytic explanations.[8]

Unequal sexual relations between men and women, which are, in this view, paradigmatic of all other relations in a patriarchal society, are seen as fundamentally bad for women, in and of themselves. Many radical and revolutionary feminist investigations have concentrated on exactly *how* bad they have been – for example, by looking into the issues of rape, domestic violence, pornography and incest.[9] Revolutionary feminism has concentrated almost exclusively on sexual violence and pornography, arguing that violence underlies the construction of patriarchally-defined sexual practice. All other violence and abuse women experience at the hands of men is viewed as resulting from the violence constructed around sexuality.[10] The radical feminist approach has taken a wider range of women's experiences into account, concentrating more on gender constructions and how these cause emotional damage in women and the suppression of both life chances and the realisation of potential – the result of women being objectified, defined and controlled by men.[11] In this view of patriarchy, men constitute subjects – persons who define themselves through themselves, and also have the right to name and define objects in the world. In contrast, women constitute objects, defined through men, or a view created by men, and they do not have the autonomy to define things independently of that view.[12]

These perspectives were seen by separatists as providing powerful motives for withdrawing from relations with men. In the revolutionary feminist view, the actual or threatened violence by men against women was the main expressed motive for separatism. For radical feminists, the view was more that unless women escape from the influence of men and male values, they cannot know their own true potential or what or who they really are as women. Therefore, withdrawal from sexual and emotional relations with men was seen as the only way for a woman to become her 'authentic' self.

Thus women must change their personal lives. They cannot continue to have any relations with men politically or emotionally and be free while patriarchy remains in place. For example, in this perspective the nuclear family is bad for women not because, as socialist feminists tend to argue, it forms a supporting arm of capitalism at women's expense, but because it traps a woman in a system of sexual relations which suppresses her, objectifies her and often inflicts physical and emotional damage on her.

The redefinition of lesbianism which arises from these approaches is a complex issue. Briefly, lesbianism in separatist theory is fundamentally a *political* identity, and sexual practice all but disappears in the definition of the term. It means being 'woman-identified', it means refusing to participate in a system which oppresses women, refusing to be defined (objectified) by men, and instead identifying with women (i.e. themselves, thus becoming subjects).[13] Since heterosexual relations are perceived as being at the root of patriarchy, becoming a lesbian pulls the system of patriarchy out at the roots – or at least allows a woman to escape the worst of its effects upon her. It also carries the potential of allowing a woman to be the most 'authentic' of women, and constitutes the most fundamental challenge to patriarchy.[14] Some have argued that lesbians throughout history have always constituted political rebels against patriarchy, even if they themselves would not have expressed it in that way.[15]

The analysis thus turns towards a concern about *hetero*-patriarchy – that is, a system of 'compulsory heterosexuality', as Adrienne Rich (1980) put it. Heteropatriarchy ensures that patriarchy remains in place, it is a system which forces women to participate in it, by making them believe they have no choice and that patriarchally-defined heterosexual relations are 'natural'. Heterosexuality here means *socially constructed* sexual relations between men and women; there is no such thing as 'natural' sexual practices between men and women within the radical or revolutionary feminist thought.

To be absolutely clear on this point, for it is frequently misunderstood, it is not argued that heterosexuality *per se* is the problem: it is argued that patriarchal ideology defines heterosexuality in such a way that women become locked into a system of oppression – it is the structure through which patriarchy operates. It is further argued that it is difficult if not impossible to know what heterosexuality would be like without patriarchy, because there do not appear to be any known examples of it.

There are two different approaches to separatism which emerge from this analysis. The revolutionary feminist approach would like to see a revolution in the form of all women becoming lesbians, defined as being woman-identified women, otherwise known as 'political lesbians' – women who choose lesbianism on political grounds. The radical feminist approach hopes that, one day, the patriarchal system will be removed, so that being a heterosexual woman will not entail a life of oppression and support for a system which oppresses all other women. In the meantime, though, both radical and revolutionary feminist separatists would argue that withdrawal from men is the only solution for women. I was *jokingly* told during fieldwork that the difference between the two feminisms is that 'radical feminists believe men are the enemy and hope that one day they'll change; revolutionary feminists believe that men are the enemy and hope that one day they'll all *die*.'

There are two important implications in this redefinition of lesbianism. First, in order to be a feminist, a woman must be a lesbian, and therefore heterosexual women are not in fact feminists, even if they say they are.[16] Second, lesbianism must constitute a challenge to hetero-patriarchy, which carries with it the implication that some women who have sexual relations with other women might not in fact be lesbians. The most common example used for that was S/M dykes: since the definition of lesbianism here constitutes a political standpoint, any woman who behaves in an anti-feminist manner is not really a lesbian. It is the character of sexual *relations* which are important to the identity, and if those relations replicate heterosexual relations as they exist within this society, or if they harm women, then they are not lesbian relations.

The key point here is that this definition of lesbianism was asserting an authentic *gender* identity, not an authentic *sexual* identity: sexual practices would reveal whether or not women had rejected patriarchal definitions of themselves and were defining themselves through themselves, not through men. Women who behaved in an anti-feminist manner – and worst of all, in their sexual practices with other women – had failed to remove internalised gender oppression from their heads. They were therefore still male-identified, not woman-identified, and therefore were not lesbians.

However in practice, while most lesbian feminists believed heterosexual women could not be feminists, it was rarely said that S/M dykes were not actually lesbians. They were more commonly seen as anti-feminist lesbians than as non-lesbians. This was because for most women in the community, lesbianism was not solely defined by radical or revolutionary feminist notions of it. Lesbianism remained as much of an 'authentic' sexual identity as it was a route towards an authentic gender identity, a point to which I will return.

5. DICHOTOMIES AND PLURALISMS

It has been seen that radical and revolutionary feminisms regard common or dominant assumptions about gender and sexuality as political constructions. 'Political' here means those concepts are socially constructed in the interests of one group (men) against those of another group (women). 'Society' is thus not viewed as an holistically or organically structured system, but the location of two antagonistic interest groups (men versus women). The interaction between them is seen as being based on a power imbalance between them. The source of the 'oppression' therefore lies in the everyday *relations* between men and women, and not in an inequality created by the structure of the system (which was viewed more as the *result* of these relations than the cause of them). This conception of social existence is thus fundamentally grounded in analysing the experience of personal relations rather than analysing the system and its structures. It is one of the reasons that personal practice was more strongly emphasised than, for example, it is within socialist feminism or psychoanalytic feminism.[17]

In community terms, the result was that lesbian feminist political practice was always directed as much towards personal conduct and interrelations within the community as it was in attacking patriarchy outside the community. This was not an easy way to live, and the experience could frequently lead to emotional exhaustion. For many, it was not possible to go from the demonstration, the collective meeting, the preparation of a journal, and hang your feminist coat on the hook when you got back home. It was there, the politics, constantly.

In summary, this approach argues that your gender identity (woman or man) constitutes a political standpoint, in which the two genders have fundamentally opposed interests and perspectives.[18] An antagonistic gender dichotomy was seen as the basis upon which every aspect of social action, thought, belief, speech and text operates in contemporary patriarchal society. Without the assumption of such a dichotomy, there would be no perceived need to develop or maintain a lesbian feminist community, separated completely from men.

In practice however, there were also other identities held by people within the community, forming the basis of other political standpoints which challenged the gender dichotomy model: in particular, ethnic identity (associated with black feminism) and sexual orientation (associated with gay liberation). These defined the identities of antagonistic interest groups within society rather differently, with the result that there were conflicts within the community about which identity was the cause of your oppression. This was known pejoratively as 'identity politics' (what is today referred to as 'political correctness').

While most (Anglo-Saxon) lesbian feminists were keen to endorse the anti-racist movement and readily agreed that lesbian feminist conceptions had in the past been 'white/western-biased', this caused difficulties for the lesbian feminist platform. The implication of the anti-racist movement was that there were some oppressions women experienced which were not based only on gender oppression. Some lesbian feminists saw this as 'diluting' the power of the gender dichotomy analysis and fragmenting the unity of the category 'woman'. Most importantly, if one accepts the pluralistic approach (there are many identities, and many oppressions based on them), the fixity and dichotomous nature of gender *identity* becomes problematic. To put it crudely, if a black woman and a white woman are not the same, then in what sense is their gender the same? Could it be that there are in fact multiple genders, and not just two?[19]

The issue is further complicated by gay liberation, which constructs the antagonistic dichotomy in society along sexual orientation lines (homosexual versus heterosexual), rather than gender lines (men versus women). For lesbian feminists, sexuality was the medium through which gender oppression occurred, and therefore lesbians and gay men would experience entirely different forms of oppression, not the same kind, as asserted within gay liberation. However, although this gender-based approach meant that lesbianism was defined as a political *gender* identity and not the 'gay lib' idea of a *sexual* identity, in practice things were somewhat different. This can be seen most clearly in the frequent hostility directed towards 'political lesbians' within the community. In practice, there was an underlying discomfort about accepting women who had become lesbians on *purely* political grounds into the community: if their politics changed, then presumably they would cease to be lesbians, and that was disturbing to many women. For most lesbian feminists, there was more to being a lesbian than woman-identification. To an important degree, lesbian feminists in practice retained a notion of 'authentic' lesbianism as a sexual orientation, and not only as a gender identity.

Thus competing representations of identity, social existence and claims to legitimacy existed, which at times seriously conflicted with radical and revolutionary feminist ideas. Since theory was explicitly and reflexively related to practice by lesbian feminists, these conflicts were experienced not so much as theoretical contradictions but as divisions between groups of people who shared, for one reason or another, the same physical space in London.

6. 'DIFFERENCE' AND 'COMMUNITY'

Conflicts over the representation of identity between lesbian feminists and gay liberationists were often expressed as conflicts over the public physical spaces in the community, concerning who had the right to define and control them. For both, their feeling of oppression within the wider social world was central to their motivation for carving out a physical space separated from that world (gay space, women-only space, etc). But this is also where a conflict with the concept of community arises. Both theories emphasise that autonomy (women's autonomy, gay autonomy) is the key to freedom from an oppressive heterosexist and/or patriarchal social order. Therefore, the physical spaces were formed partly to give people autonomy, freedom for the individual in the face of society's strictures against them, a place where individuals could be themselves without being condemned or discriminated against for it. Both highlighted the opposition between the person (an individual woman, an individual homosexual) and the social (that which constrains and oppresses the individual); both put a premium on experience (personal identity and interrelations are the source of oppression, but also the potential source of release from that oppression) and therefore on difference (no one has the right to deny others' unique personal experiences – that is tantamount to defining them). There was thus a continual tension between the notion of 'community', seen as representing commonality, sociality and therefore in some senses a suppression of difference (i.e., individuality), and the notion of full autonomy.[20]

The links between this and other notions of difference described above in discussing ethnicity, class, and so on, are obvious: they are part of the same construction of ideas concerning the opposition between the individual (possessed of her/his own 'essence', or authentic, unique identity) and the social, an old idea indeed within Western philosophical constructions of social reality.[21] The phrase 'identity politics' sums it up very well.

On a theoretical level, lesbian feminists both desired a community (as the realisation of a women's non-patriarchal sociality) and resented it (as the imposition of the social upon the individual), and therefore the community continually had an air of illusion about it, that it was not really there, and yet it was. To complicate things further, the strongest sense of community *in practice* was associated with lesbian 'authenticity' rather than woman 'authenticity'. The key behind this was not so much intellectual theory, but personal and social interrelations: what made the community feel like a community for most women was their networks of friends, lovers and ex-lovers. Public demonstrations, political groups and organisations, the production of journals and pamphlets and so on were generally regarded as being made possible by those personal and social networks. Such public events demonstrated the existence and relative strength of the community, and they made the community 'visible' to many women; but the community's existence *per se* was based on personal ties, and these ties were based on lesbian relationships, as is explored in Chapter 3.

This tension between community/public and autonomy/private was most clearly seen in the two uses to which radical and revolutionary feminist ideas were put. On the one hand, they were aimed at the 'external' world, at highlighting and battling against the relations between men and women which placed women in a disadvantageous position. Here, the community was a vantage point from which to attack 'hetero-patriarchy.' On the other hand, they were directed inward, reflexively scrutinising women's behaviour and beliefs within the community itself, and frequently finding them wanting. Those women who made it their business to monitor the activities of the community and publicly speak and write about them brought the battle against hetero-patriarchy into the confines of the community itself, thereby creating a series of prescriptions and proscriptions about how community life and personal relations ought (and ought not) to be conducted. This exposed the tension between a desire for a women's community and the autonomy imperative. The concern was whether this new sociality was allowing the expression of women's 'authentic' selves, or imposing a new set of restrictions upon them.

To withdraw from hetero-patriarchy was therefore not the same as to construct a community. Furthermore, what was constructed was not built in an empty space, but in a space that was already occupied, already informed by other representations, other people with other interests (see Chapter 4). Lesbian feminists were not solely living for their politics, which were in any event not composed of unambiguous versions of lesbian feminism, but also for themselves, and this was implied within the political project itself.

What I want to emphasise again is that any boundaries, physical or conceptual, which existed between the community and what surrounded it were only ever temporary and partial, and they had to be continually recreated. The community was generated and continually regenerated from the conditions of the city and it formed a part of that city.

This approach contrasts with most other studies on lesbian feminist 'communities', which generally views them as being in a state of 'becoming' (see Chapter 4). In this view, a new 'alternative culture' or 'counterculture' or 'subculture' was in the process of development within the confines of a distinct and potentially coherent community, in which conflicts and contradictions indicated 'growing pains', to be resolved eventually. Apart from my disagreement that there was any such cultural separation between the community and the wider context, I shall be arguing that this 'state of becoming' *characterised* the community, it was not a phase of development.

I am arguing that identity – its source(s), its consequences, its nature, its coherence – was always problematic in this community and was being continually reflexively reworked. The period I spent in London involved many changes, some perhaps permanent, others perhaps temporary, and I suggest in Chapter 6 that the basis upon which the concept of identity itself was constructed was beginning to come apart in the community. With a few years having passed since that time, it is clear that the community did not disappear, but reformulated itself, reconstructed itself once again, shifting its conceptual space and location as it did so. New banners and slogans were constructed to publicly represent itself: the Rainbow Alliance, Queer Nation, OutRage, and so on.

For many, the feminism of the previous period has dissipated in amongst this new dominance of the lesbian and gay, as opposed to the feminist/gender oppression aspect of the community. Others regard the feminism as having been absorbed, incorporated into the new conceptual space. To my own mind, there are still 'Amazons' in this community, but the changes reflect, and are reflected in, the wider context in which the community exists. One could hardly expect it to stay in one place.

2 Spaces in Between

1. LOCATION IN THE CITY

Patterns in the location of the community had more to do with the characteristics of London and aspects of its recent history than any deliberate planning on the part of lesbian feminists. Moreover, locations were not static: venues and organisations frequently started up as others closed down, and lesbian feminists themselves often moved homes. Yet there was some physical shape to the public parts of the community, albeit peripatetic.

With the exception of women's centres, most buildings used by lesbian feminists were in central London, concentrated in the southern sections of Camden and Islington (Figure 3). They were often shared with others, usually either feminist or lesbian/gay organisations and groups. This area also contained a number of social meeting places, three 'alternative' book-shops, most of the lesbian and gay venues and organisations, as well as several 'S/M dyke' venues. There was a smaller concentration of places further north, covering central parts of west Islington and east Hackney, around Dalston Junction.

In contrast, households were more scattered. A high proportion of lesbian feminists lived in the more northern regions of inner London (Islington, southern and central areas of Haringey and most areas of Hackney). Those who lived in central London almost always lived in council housing, often on short let, or in housing association properties, whose rents remained relatively low. And although there were few public spaces south of the river, many lesbian feminists also lived in the southern boroughs of Lambeth, Lewisham and Southwark, and some lived in the poorer areas of Wandsworth and Greenwich. A few lived in West London, in the Notting Hill area, mostly due to housing association properties being based there.

Table 1 is an analysis of the addresses of lesbian feminists in London on the mailing list of the Lesbian Archive in 1988, and reflects the pattern described above.

A similar pattern was found in the mailing list for participants of the Lesbian Summer School (about one third of whom were also on the Archive mailing list).

Figure 3 Distribution and Density of Buildings and Venues

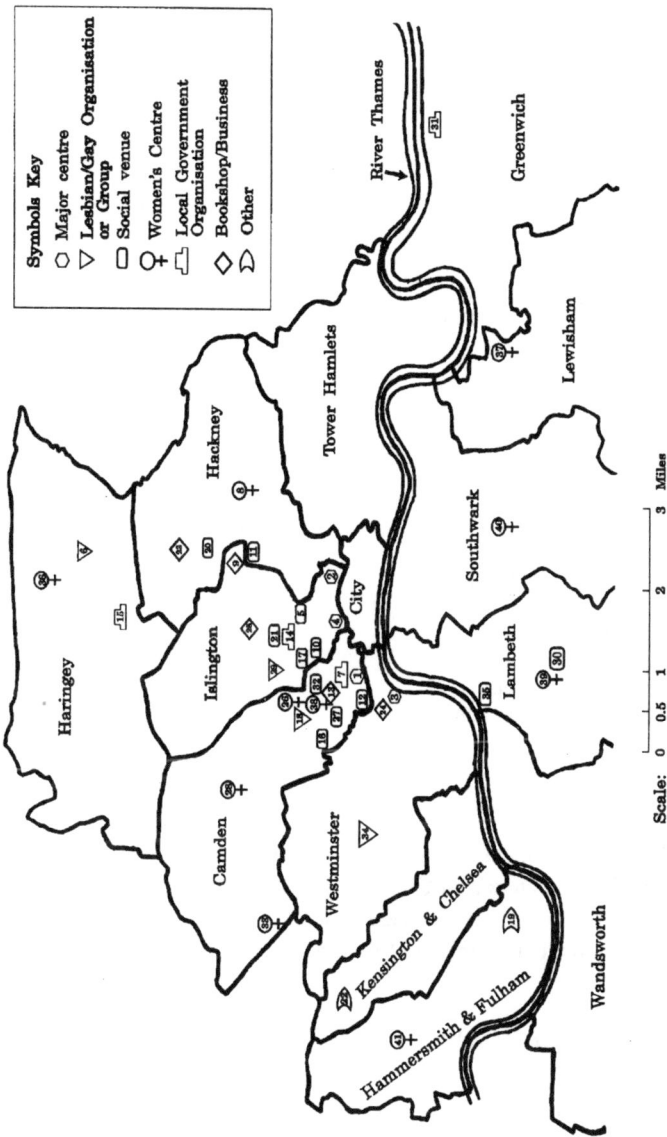

Table 1   Sample Distribution of Lesbian Feminist Residence in London

Area/Borough	Total residing in Area/Borough	Percent of Total
	n	%
NORTH LONDON	223	54.1
Islington	51	12.4
Hackney	64	15.5
Haringey	36	8.7
Camden	42	10.2
Others, Inner London (Westminster, Tower Hamlets, the City)	14	3.4
Others, Outer North London (Enfield, Brent, Newham, Redbridge, Waltham Forest)	16	3.9
SOUTH LONDON	168	40.8
Southwark	51	12.4
Lambeth	65	15.8
Lewisham	20	4.9
Greenwich	8	1.9
Wandsworth	17	4.1
Others (Croydon and Bromley)	7	1.7
WEST LONDON	21	5.1
Kensington & Chelsea	12	2.9
Hammersmith & Fulham	6	1.5
Others (Hounslow and Ealing)	3	0.7
TOTALS	412	100.0

Domestic life, social venues and activities and personal friendship networks will be discussed in Chapter 3. Here, the more public and political spaces are the focus, which were crucial in the construction of a visible lesbian feminist community in London.

2. PUBLIC SPACE

Central London is extremely densely packed, forming the heart of the city's business, shopping and entertainment sectors. There is a continual buzz of activity, and there never seems to be enough room to accommodate everyone. The long history of the city's development can be seen in the architectural styles of the buildings: here an office block built by a trading company during the height of the colonial era, displaying every ounce of grandeur and self-confidence of the period; there a 1930s example of the starkness and insecurity of the Depression; and over there, a enormous concrete and glass construction built during the height of the 1980s boom, displaying the opulence and wealth its owners mistakenly thought would last.

Lesbian feminist spaces were scattered thinly in amongst all of this. Billboards and businesses dominated the environment, and the majority of the throng of people on the streets represented, by the way they were dressed, the way they behaved and the way they spoke, everything lesbian feminists opposed. So lesbian feminists were not isolated from the rest of London – on the contrary. And as Alice, a black American lesbian feminist, put it: 'Life here keeps reminding me I'm outside the mainstream [laughs]. I come face to face with my marginalisation all the time.'

The central location of many buildings used by lesbian feminists was a recent development. The majority, apart from clubs and pubs, were or had been owned by local authorities or by the GLC, and the organisations housed in them were funded with local authority grants (see Chapter 5). Reports from lesbian feminists who lived in London before the 1981–1986 GLC administration suggested a more scattered existence, with fewer venues available and wider use of squatting than was evident during the late 1980s (see Chapter 3).

The majority of buildings used became available between 1982 and 1987. This included the four major centres which housed organisations, provided rooms for meetings, conferences, social events and groups. They were: Wesley House, located near Holborn, also known as the London Women's Centre, which housed between ten and fifteen women's organisations at any one time, including the Archive, and had meeting and conference facilities; A Woman's Place, which began as a women's squat during the late 1970s, but was rehoused in a large build-ing on the Embankment in 1984 (it was permanently closed down in 1988), and contained a number of lesbian/feminist organisations, includ-ing the Feminist Library; Tindlemanor in central east London, housing a number of women's and lesbian organisations; and the London Lesbian and Gay Centre (LLGC) in Farringdon, an enormous four-storey build-ing, which housed many lesbian and gay organisations, and provided social spaces and rooms for meetings and conferences. Amongst the smaller buildings was the Camden Lesbian Centre and Black Lesbian Group (CLC/BLG), opened in 1986. No other organisations were housed here, as it was a small space, but lesbian/feminist groups used it to hold meetings.

Not all the organisations (whether lesbian feminist or not) using the buildings were founded as recently as that. A number existed elsewhere or without premises before moving into one of the buildings. One of the oldest was Women and Manual Trades (WAMT), which helped women find skilled manual work and get training. It was now housed in Tindlemanor, but had been in existence since 1975 as a voluntary group until it was funded by the GLC in 1984.

Dependence on increasingly scarce grant aid to keep these buildings open was one source of a sense of impermanence. Barbara, a worker in a lesbian feminist organisation, summarised the point:

> We have low expectations of anything continuing. I think that's really heartbreaking. And if it doesn't fall apart because you're kicked out of a venue, or a group loses its financial backing or whatever, it'll fall apart because of internal conflict. I think there is a tremendous feeling that all this could disappear.

Impermanence was also a part of women's personal lives. Housing was a chronic problem and almost all the women I met spoke of their difficulties in finding housing in London, and many lived in temporary accommodation (see Chapter 3). Only a fraction of the women I met owned their own homes. Jobs were also frequently insecure, especially for those working within the voluntary sector and therefore dependent on grant-aid.

Thus a lack of stability and security existed in many areas of women's material lives in the community. What *was* seen as depressingly static by many was the world in which it existed – the non-feminist, dominantly heterosexual, conservative world. That world was regarded as the enemy of lesbian feminist space, continually attempting to destroy it, to silence lesbian feminist views and to make lesbian feminists' lives as difficult as possible. There was a constant sense of threat and of having to be on guard to protect what there was. Hostility towards lesbian feminists from the London local press, the Government, sometimes the courts and from some members of the public reinforced this sense. And for revolutionary feminists, whose analysis focused on the sexual violence they felt underpinned the 'hetero-patriarchy' in which they lived, the 'mainstream' world could appear deeply threatening at all times.

Figure 4: Some leaflets produced by lesbian/feminist organisations and groups

Having introduced a broad outline of 'public' space, Wesley House and the Lesbian Archive are described below to look at one space in more detail. The Archive was an example of a specifically lesbian feminist organisation; two others, the Lesbians and Policing Project (LESPOP) and Rights of Women (ROW) will be used to explore the differences between types of organisations in community terms.

Figure 5:   Some leaflets produced by lesbian/gay organisations and groups

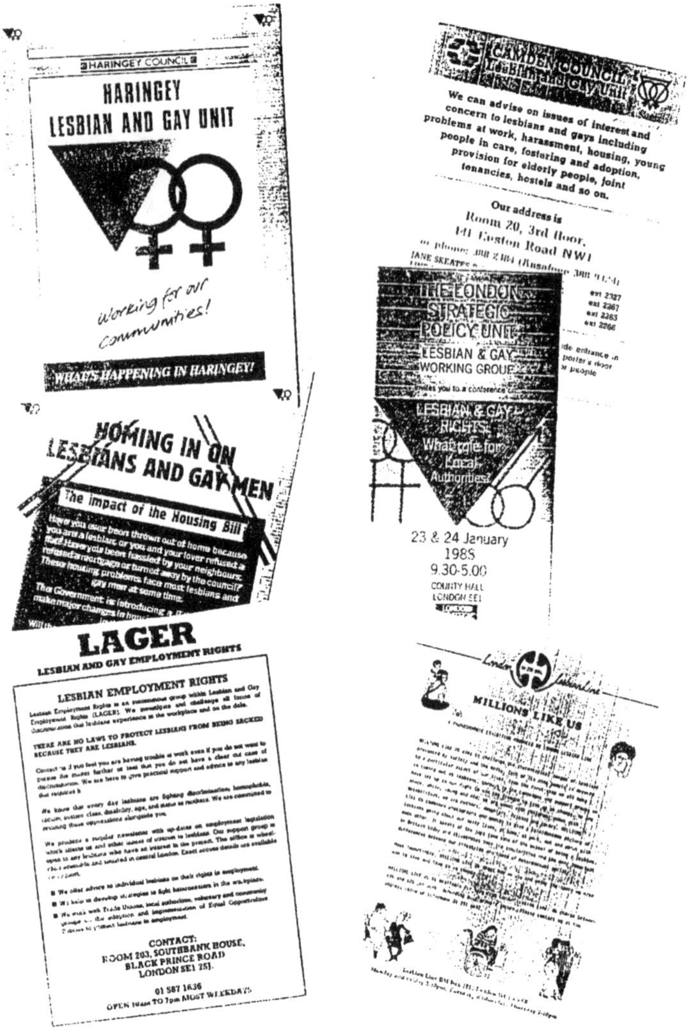

(a) Wesley House and the Lesbian Archive

The Archive office consisted of a room located in Wesley House. The entrance to the building was via a small side street, and its identity was poorly marked. The steps which used to lead to the door had been removed and replaced with a concrete ramp, making it accessible for the disabled.

The door was electronically controlled and a security camera was fixed on it. At the beginning of the study, the guard was a man from a security firm hired by Camden Council, the owners of the building. He was the only man I met working in buildings housing lesbian feminist organisations. Lesbian feminist groups did sometimes use places also used by men, invariably lesbian and gay venues, but these usually provided 'women only' space or times when men were excluded. For example, the London Lesbian and Gay Centre (LLGC), provided a women-only floor and had regular women-only social events, though the building was being boycotted by many lesbian feminists during the late 1980s, as a protest over the decision to allow 'S/M' groups to meet there.[22] The presence of the male security guard at Wesley House therefore rankled with most of the groups housed in the building, and eventually women security guards were used.

Electronic locks on entrance doors was standard practice in buildings housing women-only organisations, and I was frequently told there was a genuine need for it. It was an expression of the sense of lack of safety often present amongst lesbian feminist groups in London. The need for 'safe space', a phrase used frequently, was partly connected with this sense of danger, and will be discussed further below.

The six-storey Wesley House building, bought by the GLC Women's Committee from the West London Methodist Mission[23] had a sense of opulence about it: high ceilings, wide stone painted staircases and four conference rooms with polished wooden floors. These rooms, one of which was equipped for musical or theatrical performances, could be hired by any women's group. On the ground floor there was a fully equipped gymnasium with sauna and whirlpool. It was not used during my time there, as there were no funds for workers and instructors. Apart from the Archive, there were fourteen other organisations using offices in the building, and there was also a children's centre and a nursery there.

The Archive had little to do with the other organisations in Wesley House, though one or two workers in them were passing acquaintances with Anne and Paula, the Lesbian Archive workers. None of the other organisations reflected the lesbian feminist ideas which informed the Archive's formation as an organisation, and only a few women in other organisations had much to do with the lesbian feminist community in general.

However, of all the buildings in central London, Wesley House was most frequently used by lesbian feminists for meetings, conferences and other events, and it was the 'home' of a variety of lesbian feminist groups and activities. While these groups met and events held, the meeting rooms constituted community space, but this was not so at other times.

On most days, there was a variety of women and groups present in the building, though it was never crowded except during the Lesbian Summer School held in July 1988. Women came in to drop off or pick up their children from the nursery (occasionally fathers came as well); some came in for advice from one of the organisations; others came to attend a class or discussion group. And some came to visit the Archive or to attend a lesbian/feminist meeting or group.

The Archive was founded in 1984 by a small group of radical and revolutionary lesbian feminists who formed a collective. After being funded by the GLC in 1986, two workers were hired and the Archive moved into Wesley House. By the time I arrived, only three of the original collective – Paula, Jean and Mary (see below) – were still members. Some had left because they had moved out of London, some because they did not have the time to commit themselves anymore, and others because of internal disagreements. Earlier in 1987, there had been a dispute over the direction in which the Archive was going, and several members left on bad terms.

Officially, the Archive stated that it was set up 'as a means of reclaiming our Lesbian history, celebrating our Lesbian lives and ensuring that our stories are recorded for the future' (*News from the LAIC*, Feb. 1988; no page number). In practice, it was made clear that the Archive was a radical and revolutionary lesbian feminist organisation, which became the source of conflict during a collective dispute in 1988 (see Chapter 5). Before this, the overtly lesbian feminist stance made it a key part of the lesbian feminist community. Yet it was not only physically located in central London, but the building itself was not limited to lesbian feminist groups. It was only the Archive, and in a different way, LESPOP, which were properly seen as community space created and controlled by lesbian feminists.

The difference in the type of spaces LESPOP and the Archive constituted was connected to their formal functions. LESPOP, founded by a mixed-race group, was perceived as being there for the community and was run by lesbian feminists, but its reasons for existence differed from the Archive's. Its job was to help lesbians who became involved with the police, to keep abreast of changes in the law which affected lesbians and to campaign against police discrimination against lesbians. At most marches or demonstrations attended by lesbians in London, LESPOP representatives would hand out 'bust cards', advising women what to do if they were arrested, and LESPOP also provided stewards, in conjunction with the police, to manage crowds.

The Archive did not provide any practical service like this. It was an information resource, a collector of lesbian history, literature and 'culture'. It was one of the places where lesbian feminist existence was given substance and where it was therefore defined. For many women new to London, it also opened the door into the lesbian feminist community.

The Archive's walls were covered with fliers advertising forthcoming lesbian and lesbian feminist events, recent publications, requests for volunteers, housing, information and so on. The office itself consisted of crowded shelves of books, four large work tables in the middle of the room and others along three walls, and a display of lesbian and lesbian feminist badges. There was also a shelf containing a large collection of tapes – recordings of conversations with lesbians and lesbian readings, events and music. Underneath the computer table was a collection of reels of film (part of an incomplete lesbian movie). Above the computer were collections of photographs of lesbians, newspaper clippings about lesbians and various reports, including one about the trial of Radclyffe Hall (who was prosecuted in 1928 under the Obscene Publications Act for the publication of *The Well of Loneliness*, because of its lesbian content).

The lower shelves on the walls contained dozens of boxes of periodicals, both lesbian and feminist in nature. In a filing cabinet were administrative files, and the 'closed' files. These contained 'offensive' lesbian material – for example, lesbian sado-masochistic material from Germany, copies of *On Our Backs* (an American 'S/M dyke' journal) and various similar items. Such material was not solicited by the Archive, but if it was donated it was kept. Visitors could look at the closed files, but had to ask permission to do so, which was rare because few women knew of their existence, and might have been surprised, knowing the Archive was lesbian feminist, to find that they were kept.

Under the table to the left of the door there was a box of 'memorabilia', some of which could be described as 'lesbian kitsch.' Anything which could not be filed in a folder because of its shape went into that box. A piece of stained glass hung on one of the windows. It had been used in the film *Desert Hearts*, known as a classic lesbian movie. On a shelf tucked opposite an alcove were books written by men about lesbianism or homosexuality. On my first visit, Paula pointedly said that these books had not yet been catalogued. Overall, it was a smallish, crowded office, but light and inviting.

Anne and Paula were there more often than anyone else. They both had post-graduate qualifications in women's studies and had been involved in feminist campaigning and groups for some years. Both also saw themselves as revolutionary feminist separatists at the beginning of fieldwork, but this was to change. Anne was in her late thirties and had moved to Britain from Australia several years before. She was continually active, and saw herself as the driving force which had revitalised the Archive since she became its finance worker in May 1987. It was Anne's idea that 'Information Centre' be added to the name of the Archive to improve chances of attracting grants, and it was also she who worked towards increasing the numbers of the Archive collective's membership. Although she was a committed lesbian feminist, she had a strong sense of the practical and felt that in dealing with external agencies, minimising lesbian feminist assertions was legitimate if being explicit about them was likely to prevent getting what was wanted. This earned her the reputation of being an 'operator' or 'entrepreneur', something many women admired in that she was able to 'pull things off', but it also made her a little suspect. Someone who could so easily conceal her political commitments for practical ends and showed such a capacity for getting her own way might not be altogether trustworthy.

This 'practical' approach was one major difference between Anne and Jean, who was also seen as a powerful personality within the Archive, mostly because of her public speaking abilities. Jean, in her early forties, was a strongly committed revolutionary feminist separatist, and never subordinated her political project to anything else. During the Archive collective dispute which developed following the expansion of the collective membership (an expansion which considerably broadened the feminist perspectives represented within the membership), she was willing to see the Archive's grant revoked rather than compromise her revolutionary feminist ideals. Anne, on the other hand, did not see her activities towards external agencies as compromising anything: it was more a manipulation of those agencies. However, there was also a difference between Jean and Anne's feminist perspectives, which meant Anne was less antagonistic towards grant bodies than Jean. This difference would eventually prove to be explosive, as will be described in Chapter 5.

Paula, in her late thirties, had been a collective member since the Archive's inception. She was much quieter and less assertive than Anne. As the archivist, she spent most of her time working with the materials collected and generally avoided becoming embroiled in Anne's latest plan for an event, a benefit or some other kind of fund-raising or publicity drive.

On March 31 1988, both Anne and Paula were made redundant because the Archive's funding was revoked. The collective appealed against this decision and, much to everyone's surprise, won the appeal in June 1988.

Both workers stayed on until after the decision was made, but they also found other jobs in two women's businesses in case the appeal failed.

Visitors and volunteers would appear most days, though never more than two or three a day. Most volunteers were also Archive members and/or newsletter subscribers. There were over 700 women and more than 400 groups, organisations and journals on the mailing list. The majority of members had little practical involvement with the running of the Archive, but they often donated material and would turn up to benefits. Their political views varied greatly, but volunteers at least were all lesbian feminists of various hues: radical feminists, revolutionary feminists, even socialist feminists from time to time, or combinations of these. The boundaries between political positions were frequently much starker as abstract ideas than they were in terms of what particular women actually believed. Often, the only level of co-operation which was needed for practical tasks was that all women were more or less agreed that feminism (of some sort) was a good thing; that lesbianism was important to a woman's life; and that men, on the whole, were suspect. The more profound political divisions emerged when women's reason for being together required an explicit political statement.

Although this kind of 'fuzziness at the edges' might seem surprising for a group usually regarded as unyielding in its political commitments ('urban amazons'), it is understandable in terms of practical daily existence, where considerable leeway for differences of opinion existed, usually unremarked. In any event, as was outlined in Chapter 1, the political rhetoric of radical and revolutionary feminism was only one aspect of the sense of community these women had. As important were their social networks, and their sexual, rather than gendered, identity as lesbians. However, because of the insistence on reflecting on the political implications of practical existence amongst lesbian feminists, periods of this kind of 'fuzziness at the edges' were usually short-lived and frequently broken by the explicit statement of differences, which usually led to conflicts.

In terms of the minimum 'lesbian and feminist' qualification for volunteering at the Archive, the one exception was Kate, a woman in her late fifties who occasionally came in to volunteer at the beginning of fieldwork. She came, she said, because she had no job and got bored sitting at home while her lover was at work. Kate said she had no understanding of why men were excluded at the Archive, even though Paula had explained, Kate said, 'that men are a no-no'. Paula said she found Kate 'a bit of an embarrassment, because she doesn't understand the Archive's politics at all.' But Kate was not excluded, although she was never offered a place on the collective. She was, after all, a lesbian.

The office was supposed to be lesbian-only space, though exceptions were made on two occasions while I was there, once to allow a male window cleaner hired by the building to come in, and another to allow a group of women doing a summer women's studies course to visit. However, 'lesbians' did not include S/M dykes, who were formally banned from entering the office. In practice, this meant women who wore 'S/M gear' – black leather, chains, jack boots, dog collars with steel studs, Nazi badges and so on. This was one area where lesbian feminists would not compromise over who could, and could not, be allowed – even temporarily – into lesbian feminists' part of the community. Heterosexual women and 'straight dykes' (apolitical lesbians), posed little threat to the Archive's space. S/M dykes, however, did directly threaten that space. By being lesbians, they formed a part of the lesbian and gay community with which the lesbian feminist community overlapped. By explicitly advertising themselves as being in favour of dominance and submission forms of sexual practice, however, they challenged the stance lesbian feminists took, and therefore threatened lesbian feminists' definition of their space.

The phone in the Archive rang regularly, and enquiries ranged from how to get to the Archive, whether there were any jobs available or accommodation to let, through to questions about anything to do with lesbians/feminists in London, lesbian history, details of literature, events and so on. Occasionally, 'crank' callers would telephone (for example, a transvestite wanting to know what kind of 'equipment' the Archive held), and once or twice men called 'on behalf of my wife, who is too nervous to phone you.' These calls were politely but firmly rebuffed, as were the occasional calls from transsexuals saying they were lesbians.[24]

One can clearly see here a picture emerging of the kinds of boundaries to 'community space' which were being imposed. It was not those people who were entirely outside the community who were most strongly excluded, but rather those women who were part of an overlapping community, but who directly challenged the lesbian feminist position on what that community should represent – S/M dykes.

I was invited to join the Archive's collective by Anne, and attended the first meeting on April 13, 1988. The invitation was part of Anne's desire, agreed by the collective, to expand and widen the interests of the collective, a policy which would later prove to be contentious. Five other women joined at the same time – Ellen, Gillian, Pat, Emma and Monica – increasing the size of the collective to 11 women, though one resigned as the new members joined. Two more women joined later in the year (Rachel and Vera), making a maximum of 12 women. All were white, none were from ethnic or religious minorities, and three were perceived as working class (all new members).

Collective meetings were held about once a fortnight in the evenings and lasted for about three hours. Anne and Paula almost always attended, as did Monica, Jean and Emma. Of the others, Ellen, Pat, Gillian and Vera frequently attended, and Mary and Rachel less frequently. Most collective members came in from time to time to do voluntary work, involving accessioning new material, typing transcripts of tapes, cutting out newspaper clippings, dealing with correspondence, answering the telephone, updating the mailing list and supervising external volunteers.

Monica was in her mid-thirties and was a committed separatist (tending more towards revolutionary than radical feminism) except for her job, which involved working with men. This was not unusual, though most separatists I spoke to would have preferred to be working in a women-only environment. Like Anne and Paula, Monica had participated in a number of lesbian/feminist organisations, groups and campaigns.

Jean was in her early forties and was a highly active revolutionary feminist separatist, had been involved in founding a number of lesbian feminist groups and organisations, had published widely on lesbian feminist subjects, and had been one of the founding members of the Archive (four other collective members had also published some articles). It was commonly perceived that Jean had been the driving force behind the creation of the Archive, and this is important in terms of her later sense of betrayal when the politics of the Archive started to shift away from her own position.

Emma was a quiet and slight woman in her early forties, and rather unusually for lesbian feminists during fieldwork, was not very assertive, but she too was involved in a variety of lesbian/feminist groups and organisations, and was a separatist tending towards revolutionary feminism.

Ellen worked for a London local authority, and had done research on lesbians at the Archive before joining its collective. She was a lesbian feminist tending towards radical feminism, and although somewhat less politically 'aligned' along separatist lines than others, she was politically committed and spoke her mind confidently.

Pat was an active lesbian feminist separatist in her twenties, but she did not contribute a great deal to collective discussions, probably due to feeling unsure in the company of older and more experienced women, and to her not having entirely decided what her own political position was as yet.

Vera, in her late thirties, had worked in lesbian/feminist organisations before and had been active in various collectives and groups. She had been a separatist tending towards radical feminism, but was now beginning to move away from this position, and due to a variety of disputes in lesbian/feminist organisations she had worked in before, had become somewhat disillusioned and was beginning to question whether she was able to make any clear statement anymore regarding her political position.

Mary, in her mid- to late forties, had been a member of the Archive collective since its inception, and had also been involved in a variety of groups and campaigns. She too had a full time job outside lesbian feminist space, and she saw herself primarily as a revolutionary feminist.

Rachel was a less actively involved lesbian feminist, tending more towards radical than revolutionary feminism. She was particularly interested in recent lesbian history, which was how she began to become involved with the Archive. Although she would often chip in with comments about practical matters, she rarely became involved in debates concerning the political position of the collective.

Finally, Paula and Anne, the two workers have already been described. To recap, both were separatists – at least at the beginning of my time in London – but whereas Anne tended to be more informed by radical feminist politics, Paula had, until recently, been more informed by revolutionary feminist politics. Her stance had already begun to change, mostly due to the challenge against such politics presented by black feminist groups.[25]

Two things can be noted about this composition. First, all founding members of the Archive tended towards revolutionary, rather than radical feminism. The Archive was clearly developed more as a revolutionary, rather than a radical, feminist organisation, though that had begun to change over the years. And secondly, the newer members of the collective were more varied politically and less certain now of their own political positions.

All these women had a number of connections with one another outside the collective, though some less so than others, and most had worked together before on lesbian feminist projects and campaigns. Although the majority had partners at the time of my study, no partners were members of the collective. Five collective members – Jean, Monica, Ellen, Pat and Mary – were also members of a lesbian feminist discussion group which met fortnightly at Wesley House. At the time, this group was more strongly revolutionary feminist than the collective. In the past, Paula had attended the group, but no longer did so.

Anne and Jean were clearly dominant in directing the discussions during collective meetings, though Monica frequently contributed. During the non-dispute period, discussions centred around day-to-day administrative and policy decisions. Anne would usually prepare an agenda and a statement about what had happened since the last collective meeting. She almost always also discussed funding. The following is a summary of one collective meeting held in the spring of 1988, which illustrates how such meetings generally proceeded.

Several collective members had conversations with one another before the meeting began, both about the Archive and social matters. Monica said I had misunderstood a telephone conversation I had had with Brenda, a lesbian feminist worker at the Rights of Women Lesbian Custody Project, concerning the Lesbian Summer School. She was a friend of Brenda's and had talked to her about the conversation.

Eventually, all the members sat around the central tables. Anne began the meeting, and read out a list of items to be discussed. One or two people suggested other issues. Jean particularly wanted to talk about confidentiality within the collective.

Most of the discussion involved routine matters, such as the need to recover office keys from ex-members, and which newspapers should be surveyed for clippings. Anne discussed two planned fund-raising benefits, and decisions were made about who would help organise them. Paula announced that the Stop The Clause campaign had made a collection for the Archive on hearing that its funding had been cut. She also said that a stall was going to be set up at an anti-Clause rally by a women's bookshop which had agreed to sell Archive T-shirts and newsletters, and that Lesbian Line was having a conference soon and needed offers of accommodation for delegates.

Anne then discussed financial matters to do with the appeal against the Archive's funding cut, and said new publicity leaflets needed to be printed. She also suggested that sub-groups of the collective were needed to deal with different administrative jobs. Six were initially agreed upon, covering finance, correspondence, fund raising, organising volunteers, advertising events and dealing with acquisitions to the Archive's collections. This formal approach to organising the Archive's activities was one of the reasons some members of the collective had left the previous year. They thought it had become too 'bureaucratised'. But no objections were made on this occasion.

There was then a long discussion about the planning of the Lesbian Summer School. It was being organised separately by a committee set up through the Archive, though Anne was effectively in charge of it. She announced that Greater London Arts had provided a grant of £1500 for equipment hire. She also spent some time going through names of organisations and women who might teach or assist at the conference, and others joined in with their own suggestions. There was also some debate about providing facilities for the disabled, and how this would be funded. There were further discussions concerning whether or not the people giving workshops should be paid, and how much women would be charged for attending. It was agreed that tutors would not be paid and that a band of charges to women attending would range from £20 for low waged and unwaged to £80 for high waged women (the terms 'unemployed' and 'salaried' were deliberately not used). These were unusually large sums for lesbian feminist conferences. Jean strongly supported the fees by saying that the conference's main aim was to raise money for the Archive, which was not in a position to be either paying tutors (Jean herself was going to be one) or offering tickets to the conference at a loss. Monica made her disagreement known by remaining silent. It was understood that she felt such events should be available to all lesbian feminists to attend irrespective of income.

The issue of the cost of events and whether women should be paid for their work was continually debated during the late 1980s. It was argued that if women were not paid, women's skills were being devalued. The general lack of funds within the community caused numerous dilemmas of this sort. It was also interesting that Jean, who always made certain that no key revolutionary feminist principles were being flouted by the collective, strongly supported the high fees. For her, what was most important politically was that the Archive, as a lesbian feminist, and mostly revolutionary feminist space, should remain open. The Archive's survival as a political organisation was far more important to Jean than making the Summer School accessible to all.

Those with some sympathy for the more socialist feminist stance – that economic discrimination was also a key factor in women's oppression – felt differently. However, Jean always made her strong opposition to any socialist feminist viewpoints crystal clear, and therefore Monica knew that if she wished to openly question Jean, she would have to make a considerable battle of it. It would mean crossing the line beyond the careful balance between the imperative to express one's political views, for the Archive was one of the organisations that carried the banner of lesbian feminism for the community, and the need to temper that with continued co-operation within the collective. Monica was not willing to cross that line on this occasion.

Finally, at Jean's request, the collective discussed the fact that someone from LESPOP had contacted the Archive and complained about an apparently racist (anti-Irish) comment allegedly made by Jean during a recent Archive collective meeting. Jean's concern was that a collective member (now an ex-member, who had left on bad terms) had passed on information about the meeting to someone outside the collective, and had done so 'maliciously.' Jean objected to being 'policed' by the community, and suggested that in future collective meetings should be confidential.[26] This incident had damaged relations between LESPOP and the Archive, which never fully recovered during my stay in London. LESPOP had always emphasised an anti-racist stance, contained a mixture of ethnic minority and white women, and was suspicious of the fact that the Archive lacked any ethnic minority collective members.

This brief outline reveals a great deal about threads within lesbian feminist public community life. The interconnections between different organisations and groups were clearly expressed. The request from Lesbian Line for accommodation, the offer of a collection from Stop The Clause, the offer from the bookshop to sell Archive items at a rally, the intervention of LESPOP on the race issue, and lengthy considerations of who could be called upon for assistance and teaching at the Summer School (without being paid) all highlight active networking around the community and across a number of overlapping boundaries with other parts of the community.

Ways in which the geographical separation between groups, organisations and individuals was dealt was also shown. The use of leaflets and newsletters was pervasive. Advertising in *City Limits*, *Time Out* and the *Pink Paper*, and occasionally in *Village Voice*, a black-run newspaper, and *Capital Gay*, a predominantly male gay newspaper, was also used. By these means, up to date information about new groups and forthcoming events (as well as closures) spread quickly.[27]

The issue of differences between lesbians also arose – race, disability and economic inequality on this occasion. They were contentious issues generally and were the cause of many, if not most, collective disputes. The 'difference' issue could not be avoided, because of the lesbian feminist imperative to apply the dictum of 'the personal is political'; yet at the same time, any kind of 'difference' which implied that the source of oppression was not, or not solely, due to gender difference, could be regarded as an attack against lesbian feminist principles. This ultimately irresolvable difficulty was widely recognised as the cause of the dissolution of many a lesbian feminist collective.

Jean's anger at being 'policed' was a clear expression of these tensions. Women were constantly on guard about their own behaviour and its implications, and were ready to question anyone who behaved in a way which revealed some form of 'ism' – racism, classism, disablism, heterosexism and so on. The knowledge that others would not flinch to criticise was effective in making women think about their behaviour and choice of words before acting or speaking. Jean was expressing a resentment which many other women expressed about this constant monitoring, though she herself often criticised others' behaviour.

However, Jean's criticisms were crucially different from accusations of racism and other '-isms'. Jean would berate women for anti-feminist or patriarchal behaviour; others who attacked women (including Jean) about their attitudes to race, disability, age, and so on were not talking about *patriarchy* – they were talking about racism, disablism and ageism. Where Jean was talking about the conflict of interest between men and women, others were talking about the conflicts which divided some women from other women.

This was a common division in forms of conflict between women within lesbian feminist collectives and the community as a whole during the late 1980s. As the 1990s drew on, women who regularly criticised others for being 'anti-feminist' (as opposed to racist, classist, etc) were increasingly labelled 'the thought police', and Jean was constantly ascribed that label. This marked a trend towards focusing on the differences between women, rather than on their commonalities as an oppressed group within a hetero-patriarchal world, something which will be discussed at length in Chapter 6.

The hurt that could be inflicted by such criticisms should not be underestimated. Lesbian feminists took their politics seriously, and one of its main threads was that one's personal behaviour must strive to be free of oppressive misrepresentations. This required continual reflexive contemplation, a constant vigil over the emergence of previously unrecognised prejudices and assumptions, both in oneself and in others. To attack a woman about her behaviour was therefore appropriate within this perspective, but of their nature, such attacks were very personal. They involved 'rubbishing people', as some women put it.

(i) Safe space
The existence of constant criticism was closely connected to the concept of 'safe space'. The places used by lesbian feminists, dotted around the city, wedged in between others filled with the general London throng, surrounded by things lesbian feminists felt both angered and threatened by, were like pockets of resistance, small folds in which women could feel safe, for a time, from the hostility of the outside world. But electronic doors do not necessarily exclude ideas, beliefs or representations, and what constitutes 'safe' depends on what is perceived as the 'threat'.

For example, the revolutionary feminist desire for a separatist community was not the same as a lesbian's desire for a lesbian community. The revolutionary feminist approach was about creating safe spaces for women – safe literally from male violence, both emotional and physical. However, explicitly lesbian feminist spaces also excluded some women: heterosexual women, non-feminists or anti-feminists, and S/M dykes. It was thus not so much men, but *ideas* which were being excluded; 'men' was a conceptual category, people who not only created, but in themselves represented, maintained and continually reproduced hetero-patriarchal concepts and structures in their own image. Certain kinds of women could be, even if they were not the creators of the 'hetero-patriarchy', its representatives and supporters. They could bring the 'hetero-patriarchy' into lesbian feminist space with them.

Thus 'safe space' hinged on an assertion of *sameness* – the exclusion of difference between women in terms of the source of their oppression. The space was made 'safe' by representations, sets of ideas – just as the world outside it was made 'unsafe' by other kinds of representation (which generated concrete effects that were damaging to women). But the lesbian feminist perspective could not be simply accepted as 'the Word', the unquestionable truth; it had to be continually judged against every woman's experience. This implied two things: the possibility that the representation of women within lesbian feminism would not match women's own sense of themselves as women, and that the presence of competing ideas would render space 'unsafe'.

This is why S/M dykes were the object of particular exclusion: as discussed above, to many lesbian feminists, such women endorsed hetero-patriarchal abuse of women: sexual relations based on violent inequality. The cases of anti-racism and gay liberation were rather different, however: they were competing and cross-cutting representations of what caused the threat, rather than being the embodiment of it.

In short, space could only be 'safe' in places where women were of like minds and experience, which was rare, and tended not to be sustained for long. Attacking other women for their behaviour exposed these tensions and began to make spaces feel distinctly 'unsafe'. Such conflicts also continually reminded lesbian feminists that they shared their space with other people (and certainly more so in the late 1980s than a decade earlier), who had different interests and representations.

The issue of 'safe space' thus highlights the continual challenges which were made against attempts to control the representation of space within the community. This ongoing battle was the result of three main factors. First, lesbian feminist theory, with its emphasis on women's individual experiences in the construction of truth, conflicted with the concept of 'community' defined as an assertion of commonality (someone else's truth would have to become your truth). This conflict could only be resolved by asserting that there was something universal about all women, which was clearly difficult to defend in London in practice in the late 1980s. Second, the range of perspectives within the label 'lesbian feminist' covered a number of different approaches which, although they had common elements, caused conflicts in practice. And third, the community – even the lesbian feminist section of it – was never exclusively lesbian feminist anyway.

There was no possibility in this situation of having a non-reflexive 'doxa' in Bourdieu's terms.[28] The Archive was 'safe space' so long as it continued to represent particular interpretations of radical/revolutionary feminism. But in the end, the attempt to sustain that stance failed, and the dispute which ensued was ultimately a battle for the right to define that particular space, as is described in Chapters 5 and 6. Although the new composition of the Archive collective played a central part in this outcome, a key factor was the historical moment: the wider community, London and even general social, political and economic conditions in Britain had changed since the years when the Archive was first conceived as a revolutionary feminist organisation. As a revolutionary feminist organisation, it was increasingly becoming distant from the community it was supposed to represent.

(b) Rights of Women (ROW) and Tindlemanor

ROW constituted a space in which lesbian feminists interacted continually with people and structures outside the community, and for the most part ROW did not serve the community as such at all. It was a profoundly political organisation, but its activities were directed outwards, not inwards as were the Archive's activities. Only one section of ROW, the Lesbian Custody Project, had any dealings with the community, and even these were fairly minimal.

Unlike LESPOP, which was formed as a lesbian group, ROW was founded as a feminist group in 1975. ROW campaigned for changes in laws which discriminated against women, and for new laws to prevent discrimination in practice, particularly in employment and the family. It was funded by the GLC in 1982, and moved into Tindlemanor with other groups when the building opened with money from the GLC.

ROW's structure was more complex and formal than the Archive's, providing a clearer division of labour. It had various administrative groups in addition to the collective, including a worker's group, a policy decision group and an administration group, and it held annual general meetings (AGMs) at which members elected the new policy decision group. The workers were not members of the policy making group, though they could advise.

There were four projects run by ROW, which had both campaigning and help and advice functions: the Lesbian Custody Project, an employment law project, a social policy project (which dealt mostly with immigration and sexual harassment) and a family law project. There were also four groups associated with ROW which met to discuss feminist issues and work out campaigns about them: the Sexual Violence and the Law Group, the Lesbian Custody Support Group, the Women's Legal Defence Fund and the European Network of Women. The Sexual Violence and the Law Group had in the past been closely associated with Women Against Violence Against Women (WAVAW). WAVAW was a national feminist organisation (in the USA as well as Britain) divided into regional groups. Central London WAVAW had been dominated by revolutionary feminist separatists. In the late 1980s, it had almost ceased to exist in London, though it had been a large and active group from the late 1970s to the mid-1980s.

Two workers shared a job in the Lesbian Custody Project, which dealt mostly with lesbians involved in custody disputes with their ex-husbands. Few of the women they helped were involved with the community. Many had only recently identified themselves as lesbians, and as a result had separated from their husbands, followed by a custody dispute in which the woman's lesbianism was frequently used as a means for the ex-husband to win custody of their children.[29]

Both workers in the Lesbian Custody Project were lesbian mothers and had been married themselves. Brenda, a white woman in her early forties, was a revolutionary feminist and had been involved in many lesbian feminist campaigns, groups and organisations. I had seen her often at meetings and events before visiting ROW, and she was close friends with many women I came to know, including members of the Archive. The other, Carol, a black woman in her thirties, had only recently 'come out' as a lesbian and had been involved in a custody dispute with her husband in the previous year. Unlike Brenda, she felt that lesbian feminists constituted the 'thought police' of the 'lesbian community', and she objected strongly to being told by them how she should behave. This level of difference in political stance was far wider than existed between any of the Archive collective members. Yet Brenda and Carol got on well, working together in a team without conflict most of the time. This was in no small part due to Brenda's restraint in expressing her views while at work.

However, not all the workers at ROW were lesbians, and the majority of their work did not deal with lesbian issues. The women who contacted

ROW were often referred by Citizens Advice Bureaux, law centres and the Law Society. The ROW office did not therefore constitute 'community space' in the sense that the Archive did. The lesbian feminists who worked at ROW directed their activities, while there, at the 'outside world', not at community conflicts over representations of space and so on. Brenda was particularly conscious of this. She regretted the lack of revolutionary feminist ideas in ROW's newsletter, and spoke of the underlying tensions with other ROW workers, where political commitments had to be kept deliberately in check. Both in dealings with the 'outside world' and with the community, compromises had to be made. For example, Brenda advised lesbians involved in custody disputes that when the court-appointed social worker came, they should remove any lesbian feminist posters from the walls and, as she put it, 'find an apron'. The same went for dealings with the courts:

> You can't go into court and say, 'I'm a lesbian mother, I'm out and I'm proud.' That will obviously alienate the court. So you have to work out strategies. And it is a problem for me, yes. [...] Probably the purists on either side of the Archive dispute wouldn't agree with that at all. But I have a responsibility to the lesbian mothers out there who need the Project.

Brenda's reference to the Archive was an acknowledgement that ROW was linked to the community, even though it did not serve it directly. There had been some discussion about the Archive dispute amongst ROW workers, and a letter was sent from ROW to the Archive asking that it be resolved in order to preserve the organisation for the community, but at this point the discussion within ROW ceased. If the issues were taken any further, Brenda explained, there was a risk that ROW would fall into dispute as well, because of the underlying political differences between the women there. Differences within the community were thus intentionally 'papered over' at ROW, for very practical reasons. This was not possible at the Archive, which was essentially a space in which the community was defined: once the differences between collective members were explicitly stated, there was no possibility of such things being 'papered over'. It became a question of what the community should represent, and that inevitably meant one side had to win, and the other had to lose.

Unlike the Archive, ROW continually had dealings with the other organisations at Tindlemanor. Staff from other offices were constantly coming in to use facilities, borrow things and to have chats with ROW workers, and ROW workers (including Brenda and Carol) also visited the other offices. All the organisations campaigned on behalf of women (or particular groups of women) and provided some sort of service for them, and like ROW, they all directed their activities outwards.

It should be clear by now that the term 'community' is becoming increasingly distant from its commonly understood meaning. My reasons for retaining it will be discussed in the next chapter. I will move on now, however, to look at some other aspects of the 'public community'.

3. TEMPORARY SPACE: EVENTS AND COURSES

(a) Conferences

Lesbian feminist conferences were spaces where social and political differences between women were most intensively discussed, and where there was the clearest expression of transitions and conflicts within the community. The Summer School, which involved four days of intensive debate and courses on various lesbian/feminist issues, was a particularly good example of this and will be discussed in detail in Chapter 6.

These kinds of conferences further provided an intellectual link between the community and the wider context in which it existed, whereas organisations such as ROW provided a more practical link. Papers and books were often published out of conference proceedings, and therefore the debates reached wide audiences. Issues which were experienced within the community would be debated at conferences, and later published, and sometimes, the debates would become part of new gender theory in academic literature – separated from their context now, but clearly informed by that context. That literature would then be read by women in the community, and the (re-cycled) ideas would be fed back into community debates. Through feminist literature, there was thus a two-way interaction between community debates based on community experiences, and debates going on elsewhere.

(b) Groups

Most groups consisted of women who came together because they had common interests, to confirm their commonalities and/or to articulate arguments against challenges to them. They were essentially 'safe space', in that they excluded differences, where conferences tended to bring differences together.

Since groups did not have premises or workers, they were not constrained by the restrictions of grant aid and they did not have to provide a service. Groups could therefore be wholly community spaces – or rather, that representation of the community they wished to articulate. Groups met regularly and members often formed close relations with one another, if they did not have such relations before the group was started.

For example, the Lesbian History Group (LHG) was founded by a small group of mostly revolutionary feminists, and for most of the fieldwork period, only they and their friends attended. Later on, it became much larger, having attracted a wider variety of women, and ceased to be the type of group discussed here, taking on more the characteristics of courses, discussed below. LHG Meetings were held fortnightly in 'women-only space', and usually consisted of discussions about lesbian/feminist books (mostly historical, but also some modern texts, both fiction and non-fiction), a pre-prepared discussion topic or a talk given by a recently published author.

During group meetings, there were few challenges made of other women, and when they occurred, they were not taken as personal attacks but disagreements open to amicable discussion. As the group members held substantially the same perspective, it was easy to discuss difficult questions without tension. I rarely saw revolutionary feminists as relaxed while discussing feminist ideas as they were at LHG meetings. For a short time, the continual challenges to their representations present else-where in the community were excluded. It was as close to 'safe space' as existed in a context where political issues were discussed, and it was the most 'private' of lesbian feminist 'public' space, except for collective meetings.

Lesbian 'Support Groups', though they also provided 'safe space', were different again. There were always at least five or six such groups in inner London, and most met in women's centres in residential areas, rather than one of the central London buildings. They were discussion groups for local lesbians and social meeting places outside the context of bars or clubs. Although many women attending were lesbian feminists, many others were relatively uninvolved in the community, had recently 'come out' or were new to London. Women with a large network of friends who were more centrally involved in other groups and organisations did not often attend Support Groups.

Again, the atmosphere in such groups was more relaxed than in organ-isations or at conferences, but this required deliberate effort. Appeals for women to refrain from verbally attacking each other were common. For example, at the first meeting of a new group in North London, one of the organisers announced that she did not want women, 'trashing each other. We should respect each other, okay?' This was yet another method used in attempts to make space 'safe'. In ROW, where women holding different perspectives had to work together, differences between women were suppressed; in groups such as LHG and the London Separatist Group, differences between women were excluded by pre-defining the perspective or identity of the group (a variety of 'black women only', Asian, Jewish, Irish, disabled and working class lesbians' groups and so on worked on the same principle); in support groups, where women were often not known to one another initially, explicit requests to temporarily suppress differences had to be made.

Two support groups in which radical/revolutionary lesbian feminists rarely involved themselves should be mentioned, Sappho and Kenric. They were both founded before radical/revolutionary feminism had any substantial effect on the lesbian community in London. During my time in London, both groups catered mostly for lesbians who were not 'out of the closet'. They allowed lesbians to meet, socialise together and keep in contact between meetings through newsletters. All of this was done in confidence to protect anonymity. Most of their members were therefore not part of the lesbian feminist community, which consisted of women who, as a rule, were pointedly open about their lesbianism.

(c) Courses

There were always at least one or two courses on lesbian/feminist topics under way, each lasting from six to twelve weeks. Three I attended were entitled 'Lesbians As Rebel', held in a room above a popular lesbian and gay pub in Islington, 'Celebrating Lesbian Sexuality', held in a women's centre in Hackney, and 'Lesbian History', held in a college in the evenings. All were run by lesbian feminists, though they were organised and funded through extra-mural education schemes set up by colleges or universities in London, or local authority adult education schemes.

Keeping groups small was desired in meetings of any type. In courses, it was connected to the explicit intention that they should not be 'taught' but 'shared'. Tutors were most often referred to as 'facilitators', women who helped the participants to discuss issues, rather than teaching 'at them'. Facilitators almost invariably sat with the students in a circle, rather than stand at the front of the room. Courses were thus based on the model of the early 1970s radical feminist 'consciousness raising' groups more than university lectures.[30] There was always a great deal of discussion of women's personal experiences, and participants' discussions always formed the major part of meetings. This approach would obviously not succeed with large numbers. Once again, there was a deliberate shaping

Figure 6:   Examples of lesbian/feminist courses, groups and meeting

and control of the use and representation of space, imposed both by facilitators and the participants.

The 'Rebel' course looked at lesbian creative writing and helped participants practice prose. Ruth, the facilitator, was a published writer herself, which was not unusual. A substantial number of lesbian/feminist authors lived in London and most of their publishers were also located there. Publishers also regularly organised readings in women's bookshops or women's centres, occasionally given by authors from abroad. During my time there, Mary Daly, Sheila Jeffreys, Joan Nestle, Anne Cameron, Janice Raymond, Anna Livia, Gillian Hanscombe, Audrey Lorde and Sarah Hoagland, amongst other well-known feminist and lesbian feminist authors, all gave readings in London. Thus for lesbian feminists living there, much of what was published was neither dislocated from the authors nor their publishers. Moreover, differences within the community were reflected in texts.

For example, Sheba was perceived as heading in a strongly 'libertarian' direction, a matter which caused some controversy amongst lesbian feminists. In particular, the publication of Joan Nestle's autobiographical book *A Restricted Country* (1987), and the Sheba collective's edited volume, *Serious Pleasure: Lesbian erotic stories and poetry* (1989), gave radical/revolutionary feminists to believe that Sheba was promoting an anti-feminist stance in attitudes towards gender and sexuality. Joan Nestle, who was head of the New York Lesbian Archives and identified herself as a 'femme' lesbian, was felt to be a leading light in the 'libertarian' movement by many lesbian feminists in London. Nestle herself, as her book explains, felt that she was attempting to reclaim aspects of working class lesbian history (1950s and 60s butch/femme relations in particular) which, she argued, middle class lesbian feminists had rejected and ridiculed. These issues will be discussed further in Chapter 6.

About half the participants in the 'Rebel' course both knew each other and Ruth. The other half had experienced little contact with the community before. There was no tension in the course, the only difficulty being various tussles Ruth had with the pub's staff about allocation of rooms – a problem she blamed on the attitudes of the gay men working there. There was a common sense among lesbians that public so-called lesbian and gay spaces predominantly catered to gay men, and that lesbians were either ignored, tolerated on sufferance, or even excluded altogether. The fact that the pub staff occasionally forgot to book Ruth's room or even double-booked it reconfirmed Ruth's prior assumptions.

The common assumption outside gay communities that lesbians and gay men have a lot in common was frequently belied by these kinds of separations existing between lesbian and gay parts of the community. Such separations obviously had more to do with wider gender divisions than they had to do with community politics or sexuality. Gay men could generally command higher incomes than lesbians, and as a result, gay men were able to go out more often, and had more capital to invest in setting up gay businesses. And in the same way as public space is generally more accessible to men than to women, this was also the case for lesbian and gay public spaces. Furthermore, the overlap which frequently occurred between different groups within the community because of sharing available venues constantly resulted in these kinds of spatial skirmishes. Because gay men were generally dominant numerically in public spaces (except, obviously, in women-only venues), lesbians – whether lesbian feminists or not – were frequently made to feel as if they were temporarily borrowing somebody else's space.

The sexuality course was held in a completely different kind of space, the Hackney Women's centre, and there was nobody else there during the evenings it was held. It was run by two facilitators, Susan and Lisa, who were lesbian feminists I had met occasionally before. Most participants were part of the lesbian feminist community, though again, others were not. After a couple of weeks, several women dropped out because they felt it was not sufficiently 'radical' for them. I had seen most of these women before in lesbian feminist circles.

The course explored issues to do with lesbian sexuality, looking at medical and psychological as well as lesbian feminist texts. One question was whether the recent expansion of explicit descriptions of lesbian sexual practice in lesbian literature was acceptable, and whether such descriptions would be mis-used and misinterpreted, given the nature of wider assumptions about lesbianism. The course also considered the symbolism of the way participants were dressed and discussed the significance of 'spotting' (looking out for lesbians in public places, or guessing which famous women might be lesbians; see Chapter 3).

The last two meetings of the course looked at 'butch-femme' roles, sado-masochism, and asymmetries in lesbian relationships in general. Where most of the meetings had been relaxed, these last two were not, and the facilitators were clearly nervous about raising the issues. They felt these subjects would sorely test participants' willingness to suspend comments likely to cause conflict. The participants, some of whom had recently attended the Lesbian Summer School in which the same issues had caused acrimonious disputes (see Chapter 6), picked up the tension, but said afterwards in a pub that in this context a discussion could have occurred without conflict, had the tutors not been so nervous. In the event, the discussion got no further than 'butch-femme'.

Several attempts were made after the course was over to maintain links between participants, but these did not succeed. On the whole, participants did not move in the same circles outside the course. This again distinguished courses from groups. Courses were set up by tutors who advertised them, attracting participants who enroled, and they had limited duration. Once groups started to advertise in the same way, they too began to take on the characteristics of courses.

The history course was slightly more formal than either 'Rebel' or the sexuality course. The facilitator, Toby – who was more of a socialist than radical/revolutionary feminist – stood at the front of the room and gave a short talk during each session. The class also remained as a large group for a good portion of each session, breaking up into small groups for discussions from time to time. Further, the meetings were held in a college in the evenings, rather than in women-only or lesbian space.

The background to the course is worth mentioning. Frances, who was the adult education organiser for a local education authority, was so incensed by the Clause 28 legislation which prohibited the 'promotion of homosexuality' by local authorities or by schools, that she put the course on the curriculum. It would never have occurred to her, she said, to set the course had it not been for Clause 28. The following year, she organised three lesbian-related courses. She had experienced considerable resistance from her colleagues, some of whom suggested that under Clause 28 it was illegal, but the education authority was never challenged about it.

The history course thus had different roots from either the 'Rebel' or the sexuality course, which were reflected in the women who attended. I had met few of them in other lesbian feminist contexts, and their differing perspectives were often expressed in discussions, which dealt with the questions of what constitutes lesbian identity, how this related to questions of gender, and whether it is a meaningful concept historically.

During discussions, participants were asked what being a lesbian meant. A much wider variety of responses were given than I heard from lesbian feminists. One participant said that she was a 'gay woman' rather than a lesbian, which surprised most of the other participants, and a long conversation ensued about the differing implications of the two terms. No lesbian feminists I met called themselves 'gay', as the term implied a conceptual connection with homosexuality (male and female) rather than with feminist re-interpretations of lesbianism. Within the community, use of the phrase 'gay woman' was taken to mean a disinclination to be politically active in any way, either within gay or feminist politics. Lesbians who were active within the lesbian and gay community, politically or otherwise, tended to call themselves either 'lesbians' or 'dykes' (a term which did not have any derogatory meanings in the community).

Courses thus stood on the conceptual borderline of the lesbian feminist community, and made drawing boundaries a difficult affair, highlighting the continual interaction between different groups and networks. Anyone could join these courses, and a wide range of women did so, both from every section of the community and from those who did not consider themselves part of the community. Furthermore, such courses constituted, as did so many organisations and events, spaces in which representations were reflexively considered and worked through. In the process, any 'taken for grantedness' about the way people behaved and thought was minimised. The wide use of available texts often introduced participants to ideas and beliefs which were new to them, and their discussions provided the means to share different experiences and perspectives. They further provided a 'gateway' into the community, in a context where the harsher personal challenges often experienced elsewhere, such as in conferences or collectives, were deliberately controlled.

(d) Marches and demonstrations

Marches and demonstrations were the most public of the activities in which lesbian feminists engaged, and they contained the same multiplicity of groups and perspectives as existed in organisations and courses.

(i) Strength and Pride

Lesbian Strength and Gay Pride is an annual event in London (as it is in many other major cities around the globe), which during the late 1980s consisted of two weeks of lesbian and gay social events held in gay venues all over the city, and culminating in two separate marches through a central part of the city, one lesbian-only and the other lesbian and gay, followed by a festival and fair at the end of the final march. Since 1989, the Lesbian Strength march was abandoned and the title of the event was changed to Lesbian and Gay Pride, a measure of some of the changes underway within the community – although in 1995, the now single march had the theme of 'Lesbian Visibility'.

A variety of lesbian and gay events were organised in the two weeks surrounding the marches, sponsored mostly by Camden, Islington, Hackney and Haringey local councils – all of which are in north central London, and all of which had consistently strongly socialist administrations during the 1980s. The whole two-week period took on an air of being a lesbian and gay community festival, which is precisely what was intended.

In 1988, both marches started at Speaker's Corner in Hyde Park in central London, and led through the centre of London, passing the Houses of Parliament. The mixed march ended with a large celebration at Jubilee Gardens on the South Bank, whereas Lesbian Strength, held a week before, ended at the London Lesbian and Gay Centre, where a disco was planned. The Lesbian Strength march was much smaller and had less pomp and ceremony surrounding it than the mixed march the following week. Many of the gay men in that march (which had around 15,000 participants) dressed up in drag and designed floats, whereas the women in the Strength march came in their usual clothes.

The more steadfastly separatist lesbian feminists only attended the Lesbian Strength march (about 6,000 participants), whereas numerous others attended both marches. Although gay men did not participate in this first march, many lined the pavements on the route, cheering. There was also a group of S/M dykes standing with a banner on the pavement, wearing S/M gear and waving, but they were mostly studiously ignored. At the end of the march at the LLGC, a group of S/M dykes, in protest at the price of tickets to attend the disco, invaded the building, grabbed the tickets and scattered them amongst the crowd outside. The LLGC staff were forced to negotiate the price down.

At both marches, organisations and groups brought banners, and many people were handing out leaflets to marchers advertising events and groups. The marchers were escorted by lines of police and LESPOP stewards. Occasionally marchers broke into song, the favourite being one which started, 'Two, four, six, eight, is that copper really straight?' Many women at the Strength march were wearing lesbian/feminist badges, as well as badges protesting against Clause 28. Most of these badges had inverted pink or black triangles on them. Both triangles had been sown on prisoners' clothing in Nazi prisons and concentration camps during the Second World War: the pink triangle identified a homosexual prisoner, but was used only for men, as lesbianism had not been explicitly criminalised by the Nazi state; the black triangle was used as a general category of 'anti-social' and political prisoners, and most lesbians who were imprisoned during the period were found guilty of these offenses instead.[31]

At the end of the mixed march, there were hundreds of stalls selling books, journals, crafts, clothes and food and beer. There was a stage for mixed shows, and a large separate tent in which women-only shows were performed. The whole event certainly gave the impression of the existence of a large community. Being visible was the main point – visible not only to onlookers but also, and perhaps more importantly, to the marchers themselves.

However, what was being made visible for the most part was sexual identity, not gender identity, even in the Lesbian Strength march. The Lesbian Strength march did have the effect of highlighting gender, and the absence of an equivalent men-only march highlighted the unequal difference which gender makes, within this community as any other. But this

Figure 7: Strength and Pride Leaflets
Leaflets showing the four inner north London Labour Boroughs' commitment to
Lesbian Strength and Gay Pride, despite Clause 28.

NORTH
LONDON

STRENGTH AND PRIDE

I I JUNE – 30 JUNE

Hackney
LESBIAN
STRENGTH
and
GAY
PRIDE
14th - 26th June
A programme of fun,
entertainment and action

HACKNEY
STRENGTH
AND
PRIDE
1988

LESBIAN STRENGTH & GAY PRIDE FESTIVAL '89

NORTH LONDON
89

The four north London boroughs of Camden, Hackney,
Haringey and Islington come together in '89 to organise
a festival celebrating Lesbian Strength & Gay Pride
incorporating the 20th anniversary of Stonewall's call for
justice for lesbians and gay men.

This year's celebrations will include theatre, films, music
gigs, cabaret, exhibitions, talks and readings; as well as
social and recreation activities.

10 June - 1 July

LOCAL STRENGTH; LOCAL PRIDE; GET INVOLVED; GET IN TOUCH

approach *distinguishes* gender and sexuality as two separate issues, rather than merging them as was the case in lesbian feminism. Thus the event overall was a gay liberation representation of the community, not a lesbian feminist one, even though many of the women participating in the Strength march did so for lesbian feminist, rather than 'gay lib', reasons.

In any event, although intellectual and political standpoints may have starkly differed amongst the marchers, many women in practice held a number of these perspectives simultaneously, expressing one or the other depending on the context, or even being deliberately unclear. But there were limits: the fact that the one S/M dyke group with a banner did not join the march, but stood to one side with the gay men, gives some measure of the limitations of the flexibility. For lesbian feminists S/M dykes were a transgressive and unacceptable part of the lesbian community, and were thus excluded from the lesbian feminist community. The S/M dykes' position on the sidelines (waving their support along with the gay men) spatially represented the limits of the overlap between different groups.

(ii) Lesbians Against the Clause demonstration

Most of the politically-motivated demonstrations about specific issues during my time in London related to protests against Clause 28. Amongst these was a Lesbians Against the Clause demonstration held at Piccadilly Circus on February 1, 1988. The two mixed lesbian and gay campaigning groups, Stop The Clause and the Organisation of Lesbian and Gay Action (OLGA), were against the demonstration because they felt it might cause bad publicity – their view of lesbian feminists being that these 'urban amazons' were the unacceptable face of homosexuality. In the event, around 70 women, all of them lesbian feminists, turned up (see Plates 1–4).

This demonstration was using visibility in a quite different way from Strength and Pride. Although Strength and Pride were also protests, the intention was to put across an image of festive enjoyment, a celebration of lesbian and gay identities, with the deliberate absence of any shame or guilt. It was a way of rendering lesbian and gay people 'visible' – and united, more or less. In contrast, the Piccadilly Circus demonstration was an explicitly lesbian feminist protest against a particular piece of legislation – though it is doubtful that many passers-by understood what the demonstration was about. Few people outside the community understood that there *were* differences between different lesbian, and lesbian and gay constituencies; and not many were even aware of Clause 28. But it was important for these women to stage a public protest against the legislation which was informed by a lesbian feminist, rather than a gay liberation, perspective – and this was at least clearly understood by the mixed lesbian and gay anti-Clause 28 groups which disapproved of the event.

Although the demonstration was informed by lesbian feminism, none of the demonstrations and marches during fieldwork were specifically *about* lesbian feminist issues. All were related to lesbian identity, and almost invariably what was made visible to outside observers when lesbian feminists were present at these events was their lesbian, not their feminist, identity.

This brief overview of the public side of the lesbian feminist community has illustrated the complexity of placing any boundaries within or around the community. It is both accurate and a misrepresentation to call it a 'community', as opposed to 'communities'. The difficulty with the term 'community' is its implied static and homogenous character – in spatial, temporal and symbolic terms. This 'community' was a restless, shifting community – in spatial, temporal and symbolic terms. Venues frequently moved, and even when the same building was used, it often changed what it represented symbolically at different times of the day, week or month; groups, organisations and demonstrations often uneasily balanced the varieties of interpretations of sexual and gender identities which existed amongst the participants and others they may have served or with whom they interacted; and either just under the surface, or in full view, a range of other differences between people – ethnicity, class, age, disability – were always there and had to be dealt with in some way or another. There were fracture lines scattered throughout this community, if such it can be called; but even though these differences were always present, they were not expressed at all times, in all contexts.

The way in which radical/revolutionary lesbian feminists engaged with this multiple, forever altering shape of the community, with forever changing internal and external lines and divisions depending on context, was as complicated as anyone else's engagement with it. On a general level, the abstract political rhetoric of lesbian feminism provided a clear line and a clear position, and one could locate it as representing one sector within the community. Looked at more closely, however, even the abstract rhetoric sub-divided into a variety perspectives and positions, based as it was on an analysis of personal experience, rather than on a system or structure. And looked at from the viewpoint of what particular lesbian feminists believed, the clear line becomes even fuzzier, for most engaged both with a variety of different aspects or sectors of the community at different times, and with a variety of political perspectives. It is this level, the more personal level, of lesbian feminists' lives, which needs to be considered next before discussing further what kind of 'community' this was in the late 1980s.

3 Relations Within: Continuity and Discontinuity

INTRODUCTION

Friendship networks were involved in much of the 'public' activity described in the last chapter, which meant important interrelations existed between lesbian feminists' public and personal lives. However, important separations also existed – both physical distances between public and personal spaces, and tensions between public and personal relations.

The separation between these spheres involved a four-way 'domestic/ public – personal/political' distinction, found in contemporary British society generally: work lives, home lives, political and leisure activities are usually separated, and this was, roughly speaking, true for lesbian feminists as well.

That is worth noting for several reasons. First, the 'community' was not structured as a sect or commune (utopian or otherwise), which breaks down distinctions between public/private and personal/political. Secondly, lesbian feminist theory suggests that the separation between public and private spheres is a central mechanism by which hetero-patriarchy is maintained. So it may appear odd that they remained separated in lesbian feminists' lives. However, the *nature*, not the fact of the separation was seen as the source of women's oppression: in radical/revolutionary feminist theory, representing the personal and domestic as 'private' masked its socially constructed and political character. Privacy in itself is not anti-feminist. The recognition that private space is a deeply political space, and the most important space in which women should change personal relations and behaviour to reflect lesbian feminist perspectives does not *require* the space to be made 'public'. Working towards altering personal relations is in effect putting lesbian feminism into practice, whether this is in public or not.

However, things were more complicated than this in practice, which partly involved the relationship between the 'public political' and the 'private political' aspects of the community. This involved the following paradox: if something is 'private political', then does the 'public political' arena have the right to judge or comment upon it? And that gets back to the conflict between autonomy and sociality. There was also the tension

60

between the idea of 'authentic sexual identity' as opposed to 'authentic gender identity' already discussed in terms of the structure of the community as opposed to the structure of lesbian feminist thought. In practice, ideas which informed the personal and domestic spheres overlapped with, but differed, from those which informed lesbian feminist 'public/political' spheres.

The overall effect of these separations between public and private was a differentiated distribution of activities and people in the community which revealed conceptual tensions in spatial and structural terms. Keeping in mind the discussion in Chapter 2, the more personal aspects of the community and women's lives within it are discussed below. The first section, which concerns public spaces regarded as 'personal', is mostly about the representation of self in a public context, and for this reason I will be focusing on styles and groups.

1. THE 'SCENE', STYLES AND SOCIAL EVENTS: PUBLIC/PERSONAL

Many lesbian feminists socialised in certain pubs, clubs, discos, coffee shops, social events held in women's centres and some theatres (Figure 3). Together with a number of venues they deliberately avoided, these comprised 'the scene'. The 'scene' was distinguished from other social spaces in London by its explicitly lesbian/gay character. The 'scene' provided places where lesbians and gay men were temporarily free from 'heterosexism' – the ubiquitous assumption of heterosexuality (and its superiority to anything else).

The 'scene' was therefore 'gay space', and as such, lesbian feminist concerns, which centred around gender, were not predominantly represented there. Yet although in that sense lesbian feminists were using rather than defining those spaces, many felt as much a part of the 'scene' as any other women there.

In other respects, the 'scene' had similar characteristics to most night life in London: it catered mostly to young interests; different venues attracted different clientele; dress styles were important; people most often went with personal friends and/or their lovers, outside working hours and separate from political activities; and it usually involved music and the consumption of alcohol. Certain parts of the 'scene', especially discos and clubs, were dominated by people in their twenties and early thirties. Groups like the Older Lesbian Network and Pink Wrinkles (as well as

Sappho and Kenric) provided social events for older women specifically because of the lack of older people in 'public' lesbian/gay space.

The 'scene' was personal space and reflected representations of lesbianism which centred on sexual identity as the basis of commonality, rather than gender identity, though the latter was relevant. A brief summary of some parts of the 'scene' provides an outline of this in practice.

(a) Pubs and coffee shops

(i) The Fallen Angel
The Fallen Angel (F.A.) was a lesbian and gay pub which served food and had upstairs rooms for meetings.[32] It was well-furnished and bright, unlike some venues, and it regularly provided live music. Tuesdays and Saturdays had been 'women-only' nights, but Saturdays later became mixed. A variety of lesbian and gay papers were available in the pub, and there were notice boards which could be used to advertise accommodation, forthcoming events and selling/buying items. During the day, it was a quiet meeting place to have lunch. In the evenings, it was usually full and the music was often loud.

Prices were as high as prices anywhere in London. This meant lesbians could not go there as often as gay men, because of the differentials in their respective incomes (see below). Lesbian feminists particularly, who avoided working in male-owned, profit-making businesses, had little disposable income. This partly accounted for the predominance of gay men at the F.A., which was true of most lesbian/gay venues. In fact, gay men were more numerous than lesbians in all sections of the lesbian/gay 'community': there were many more gay men's clubs than lesbian ones; the mixed venues were almost always owned by gay men (or heterosexual men); most gay businesses were owned by gay men; gay newspapers and journals were dominated by gay men and most mixed lesbian and gay groups tended to have twice as many gay members as lesbian ones.

The domination of gay men meant they controlled most representations in the scene. Lesbian feminists were not only 'visitors' in many parts of the 'scene' because they were feminists: it was also because they were women. Women-only times and events, an idea informed by radical feminism, carved out a temporary lesbian space in a predominantly gay men's arena.

Some women, like Nicola, a lesbian feminist in her thirties who lived in Islington, regarded the F.A. as their 'local', and went there regularly to meet friends. Others made a special trip across London. Nicola, like most lesbian feminists, preferred to go on women-only nights. She sometimes went on her own, knowing she would meet someone there she knew. She did not dress specially to go to the F.A., and generally wore stout trousers and shirts, jumpers, DMs or trainers and often a labrys earring (a double-bladed axe which generally signified 'lesbian feminist'). Her hair was cut short, and if it ever grew close to her ear, she regarded it as long and had a haircut. This was typical of many lesbian feminists' styles, and was the most common seen at lesbian feminist events and in collectives. A number of women dressed similarly could be seen at the F.A. on most evenings.

There were a variety of other styles to be seen at the F.A., however. Among younger women, colours ranged widely, though black was dominant. This could have a striking effect with the platinum-blond crew-cut that was popular at the time. DMs or trainers were also dominant with this style. There was a greater use of accessories – scarves, shawls, bangles, rings, earrings, bracelets, necklaces and so on. The overall effect was a young, stylish and confident look with a strong hint of masculinity counterpoised against aspects of femininity. There was often little indication that these young women's styles had been deliberately informed by feminist thought, and if they had been, it was probably not radical/ revolutionary feminist thought. There was more of a sense of play with ideas about gender in these styles – 'gender-bending', as it were – than there was a sense of avoiding 'hetero-patriarchal' images of femininity. Moreover, the 'conformity' they represented was more towards current trends and fashions within the scene than they were towards any explicit political perspective. These styles changed most frequently, and were sometimes called the 'designer dyke' look – meaning the wearer kept up with the changing fashions amongst lesbians on the 'scene'.

A third range of styles seen at the F.A. was known as the 'ethnic' look (when worn by white women). Indian cotton patterned cloth was most dominant, worn either as baggy trousers or (less often) as a long skirt, with cheesecloth or cotton shirts or blouses, frequently with large, colourful jumpers. Shoes tended to be flat-soled soft leather (often earth brown but also other colours – light green, yellow and red were popular) or sandals. Women wearing this style tended to have longer hair than either the lesbian feminist 'look' or the 'designer dyke' look, and I rarely saw the style worn in strictly separatist contexts.

Obviously, the 'ethnic look' is taken from what could be called 'eco-fashion', connected to another kind of 'personal is political' campaign – the environment, which involved issues such as preserving environmental resources, critiquing the sources of global pollution, promoting alternative health, medicine and nutrition, and encouraging alternative personal

philosophies. This movement constituted another overlap in the wider
London context for many lesbian feminists.

The clientele of the F.A. was thus mixed, but generally did not attract
'S/M dykes' nor many 'libertarians'. This made it an acceptable place for
lesbian feminists.

(ii) The Duke of Wellington Pub

The Duke of Wellington was owned by a woman who organised the first
women-only discos in London during the 1970s.[33] The front section
looked much like most pubs in London, but there was also a back room
frequently used for women-only live music and theatre. Many of the
performances were feminist or lesbian feminist in nature.

The 'Duke' was an unusual pub for the 'scene': it attracted more lesbians
than gay men and, more strikingly, the front bar attracted local 'walk-in'
trade. These were mostly local men drinking beer, and they seemed oblivious
to the many posters on the walls advertising lesbian/gay events and the avail-
ability of the *Pink Paper*. These men were ignored by lesbian feminists, and
there was no antagonism between the two groups. In fact, I once conducted a
taped interview with a revolutionary feminist there, on her suggestion. The
manner in which the two groups mingled in the same space but managed
conceptually to exclude each other was a testament to Ulf Hannerz's research
on the urban interactions he referred to as 'traffic' (Hannerz, 1980).

Towards the end of 1989, the Duke started to be frequented by a few
'libertarians' and 'baby dykes'. The hallmark of their dress styles was
occasional use of black leather (though not in the manner of 'S/M gear')
and mixtures of clearly feminine counterpoised with strongly masculine
clothing, with frequent use of make-up. No clothing or hair style was 'out
of bounds' for 'libertarians' or 'baby dykes', seen as a mark of their 'apolitical' stance by lesbian feminists (see Chapter 6). While it was certainly
not informed by radical/revolutionary feminism, this type of dress style
was later, in the 1990s, associated with the development of 'Queer theory'.
Rosemary Hennessy suggests that Queer theory is an, 'in-your-face rejection of the proper response to heteronormativity, a version of acting up'
(Hennessy, 1993, p. 967). The 'baby dyke' dress styles, while not associated with any theory but rather changes in 'trendiness' in the late 1980s,
nevertheless reflected the kinds of shifts going on which also informed the
development of Queer theory (see Chapter 6).

(iii) First Out coffee shop

First Out is located in the centre of London. It provided snacks and coffee
all day, and like the F.A. and the Duke, had varieties of lesbian/gay

posters on the walls and gay newspapers available. It was known to be expensive, its clientele was overwhelmingly gay men, and it had no women-only time or space. Therefore, lesbian feminists rarely used it.

Daytime social venues used by lesbian feminists were scarce, as the 'scene' was overwhelmingly nocturnal. In any event, lesbian feminists who were free during the day were most often unemployed, making daytime women-only social venues virtually unviable; it was difficult enough for women-only evening venues to survive.

(b) Discos and clubs

Most women-only discos involved using a venue which had a different purpose at other times. One of the most regular was held at the LLGC every Saturday, but many lesbian feminists avoided it because the LLGC had agreed to allow 'S/M' groups to meet on its premises.[34]

Other such events were numerous, but they were also the most 'fly-by-night', starting up and closing down again rapidly. Rackets, for example, was a weekly women-only disco held in a normally heterosexual pub; it closed down and opened again four times during fieldwork. Rackets was frequented by some lesbian feminists, but it also attracted 'designer dykes' and some 'baby dykes'.

The Drum was another women-only weekly disco held at a pub, which was more 'dark and dingy' than Rackets, to use one informant's phrase, but it closed down after a few weeks because of a serious attack by some men on two lesbians as they were leaving the venue one evening. The publican decided the event attracted violence and stopped it.

Heds was a weekly disco held in a normally heterosexual club. It was mainly women-only, but men could attend if accompanied by women. Lesbian feminists rarely went there, though some did occasionally if asked by friends. Mostly, it attracted 'designer dykes'.

Venus Rising and Chain Reaction were both predominantly S/M dyke venues, and constituted extremely 'unsafe space' for lesbian feminists. Venus Rising was a women-only disco held once a month at a club in Brixton, south London. It is an enormous venue, and provided laser and video projections, often with explicit sexual content. Though it had been a popular place for many lesbians (feminist or not), it increasingly attracted 'S/M dykes' during my time in London, and was eventually dominated by them.

Unlike other styles described here, 'S/M dyke' clothing was usually entirely gender-divided. The 'butch' look included short back and sides haircut; clothes predominantly black leather (or rubber) jackets and trousers (often incorporating a number of zippers) or shorts with leather ties and white shirts; steel studs and chains; jack boots and leather caps; and occasionally, swastikas. The 'femme' look used the same materials, but included fishnet stockings, mini-skirts, spiked heeled shoes, hair often in a punk style using bright dyes and excessive amounts of make-up. The 'S/M look', which was modelled on a mixture of punk style and gay men's 'S/M look' was intended to be intimidating. Chain Reaction, set up during fieldwork, was an explicitly 'S/M dyke' venue.[35]

Styles in the 'scene' were thus used to define others and self in public places. This is common in cities, where interaction frequently involves making instant assessments of strangers (Hannerz, 1980; Suttles, 1968). Style acts as a quick and easy way of identifying 'types' of people. In the 'community', where a number of overtly antagonistic groups overlapped, it was important to know what people represented. Were they feminists? Were they 'S/M dykes'? Did they emphasise ethnicity more than gender (in, for instance, having 'dreadlocks' rather than a short haircut)?

Style enabled women to emphasise those aspects of their identity they wished to project, and underemphasised others. This is what Goffman (1987) calls 'impression management'. Style provided a common set of symbols to indicate one or a combination of identities. A woman wearing a typical lesbian feminist style was not only projecting that she was a lesbian, but that she had a feminist interpretation of lesbianism and interacted with that sphere of the community. A woman wearing 'S/M gear' was projecting her preferences in sexual practice; but she was also making a deliberate statement against lesbian feminist representations, and she was furthermore wearing a 'uniform' (often literally), identifying herself with the 'S/M' sphere of the 'community' and enabling other 'S/M dykes' to recognise her instantly. The clothing also projected an assertion of her character: that she was strong, 'mean', and possibly violent.

Lesbian feminist style also suggested a character: assertive, serious, likely to be argumentative and, as one 'baby dyke' put it, 'totally lacking in a sense of humour' (in my experience an unjustified assertion, but no matter). In short, styles were used in the representational battles in the 'community', and were a major factor in the representation of different spaces.[36]

In the 'scene', it was assumed that those present were lesbian or gay, and therefore styles distinguished between 'types' of lesbian/gay people. Outside the 'scene', style had another purpose, commonly known as 'spotting'. This involved being in a public place – in the street, on an underground train, in Sainsbury's – and deciding who else was lesbian. Wearing badges was an explicit statement, but there were myriad other indicators.

Although many aspects of the styles described above were worn by heterosexual women as well as lesbians, when a number of 'lesbian markers' were present – for example, a woman with short hair, wearing a lumberjack shirt, Chinos, DMs and no make-up – it warranted a second look. If the look was returned – usually a glance fractionally longer than is usual between strangers, and perhaps a brief smile, the woman could be considered 'spotted'. Most women said they engaged in 'spotting'. Ruth, for example: 'Of course I like spotting. Don't all lesbians? It makes us less invisible to ourselves.'[37]

An important point about this is that styles asserted a fixed sexual orientation: 'spotting' involved looking out for 'authentic' lesbians, and distinguishing them from heterosexuals. Further, many women asserted that they could 'spot' lesbians who were not wearing 'lesbian style', and several women said they could 'spot' women who were not themselves aware they were lesbians. 'It's hard to say exactly how,' Nicola said, 'but you can just tell. Something about the way they look differently at women and men; something about the way they hold themselves, the way they talk about things. I don't know.' Burton's (1978) analysis of the belief in Northern Ireland that Catholics and Protestants could be distinguished, when in fact there were no obvious physical differences between them, was somewhat similar; but in this case, the belief was based partly on interactional and stylistic cues: the way lesbians dressed and behaved towards other women, and towards men, was seen as different from heterosexual women. Styles also of course distinguished between different 'kinds' of lesbians: those who were not likely to be involved in the community and those who were.

(c) Socials, Benefits and shows

(i) Socials
Socials were similar to lesbian support groups and were held either in women's centres or lesbian/gay places. For example, CLC/BLG (Camden Lesbian Centre and Black Lesbian Group) regularly held socials in the early evening, some for black lesbians only. These events mostly attracted women who were new to London or had recently 'come out', but they were also frequented by lesbian feminists on occasion, as an alternative to pubs or clubs. Women often went on their own rather than with friends or lovers. Lesbian discussion groups also acted as socials. For example, there was a regular lesbian discussion group held at Gay's The Word bookshop in the evenings.

Given the young, predominantly male, expensive, late-night and 'trendy' atmosphere of much of the scene, for many women socials provided a much-desired alternative way of meeting new people in an openly lesbian space. Socials of this kind were rarely organised for gay men, being limited mostly to 'coming out' groups or more specialised groups (for example, for young men). The difference was clearly to do with the more general difference in the way men and women relate to, and are represented in, public and private spaces than it is to do with the community, or sexual identity. Lesbian feminists are not the only women who feel unsafe in public spaces, particularly at night; or who feel more comfortable in more personal, female-dominated contexts such as discussion groups. If support groups sound faintly like the stereotypical housewife's coffee morning, this is probably because there are similar reasons why these kinds of social gatherings are often preferred by women as a whole, lesbian feminist or not.

(ii) Benefits
Benefits were arranged by feminist or lesbian/feminist organisations to raise funds. They were usually held in one of the large centres or in a rented hall, rarely in pubs or clubs. Benefits came closest to combining the 'public/political' character of lesbian feminist space with the 'public/personal' character of most of the 'scene'. Women knew they were contributing to the survival of feminist or lesbian/feminist organisations in attending them, and they usually met many friends and acquaintances there. In this sense, benefits were somewhat like party political fundraisers. Moreover, as lesbian/feminist organisations organised these events, they were more strongly controlled by lesbian/feminist representations than other social events. Many women known as 'hard line separatists', who rarely attended other parts of the 'scene', would appear at benefits, often with their lovers.

Almost all organisations associated with the community held a benefit at least once during fieldwork, and some, such as the events staged by Homeless Action and Lesbian Line, were held regularly. Occasionally, benefits had a fancy dress theme. For example, Homeless Action regularly held fancy dress events. Two of these involved a 1960s event, and a jazz/blues event with a 1920s fancy dress competition, where many women turned up dressed as Radclyffe Hall look-a-likes. At the 1920s event, I met many of the women I knew from 'public' lesbian/feminist space, including most of the Archive collective, a number of whom attended with their lovers. The event occurred shortly after the Archive dispute, so it was a somewhat tense affair for the collective members, even though the venue was large and crowded enough to avoid interaction.

The high likelihood of meeting others – friends or foes – at such events continually gave them a sense of intrigue. Women often spoke of meeting ex-lovers at social venues, something regarded as unavoidable, as one woman explained:

> I mean, it is not unusual to go to, say, the '60s bop, and there to be three or four ex-lovers. Or you're with your lover, and you're going to bump into at least one of her ex-lovers. Or one of her lover's ex-lovers.

However, ex-lovers were not always foes – on the contrary, they were often the closest of friends and went to events together. The point here is that interrelationships and networks between lesbian feminists in London had considerable complexity, a fact which was often the subject of jokes between lesbians, and has been noted for lesbian communities elsewhere.[38]

Few lesbian feminists objected to 'dressing up' for benefits, even if they criticised dress styles at other times. This was so even for mixed lesbian/gay fancy dress parties. One such event, called the '1920s Gay Ball', was held a year before fieldwork. Several women reported how they had turned up 'dressed to the nines', complete with ball gowns, evening dresses or tuxedos. One lesbian feminist also recounted how a well-known revolutionary feminist (Jean) appeared at the entrance and 'denounced the event as degrading to women and then turned on her heel. We all heaved a sigh of relief, as we could get on and have fun after that.'

Most lesbian feminists were not beyond poking fun at their own political positions from time to time. Where events were social and the people running and participating in them were seen as relatively 'safe' (that is, lesbian and/or feminist), joking about matters usually taken seriously was acceptable. This not only allowed a space where women could relax for a time and 'let off steam', but it also reinforced the notion of a distinct 'community', which was supportive in a hostile environment, and which had its own private jokes. Where it was understood that participants were consciously aware of the implied gender divisions and hierarchies in donning such styles, it was acceptable to 'break the rules'.

(iii) Shows

Shows involved theatre, films or musical events. Women-only shows or shows with feminist/lesbian content were regularly held in London, and there were several women's theatre companies and music groups. Lesbian feminists often attended, even if they were played to mixed audiences. The Drill Hall, a central London venue which held a women-only night once a week, had a vegetarian restaurant and a relatively cheap bar, and provided regular feminist/lesbian shows in its theatre, was popular among lesbian feminists. Many other 'fringe' theatres, jazz cafés and other venues,

Figure 8:   Some leaflets advertising social events in the 'scene'

particularly in Islington and Hackney, occasionally put on shows which attracted lesbian feminists, and even some of the major arts and theatre centres, such as the ICA and Southbank provided productions of interest to them from time to time.

Many of the venues thus stood outside both the 'scene' and the 'community', but overlapped with them occasionally. Being a separatist did not prevent women from taking advantage of the arts in London. Once again, boundaries existed, both within the 'community' and outside it, but they were continually crossed and informed one another.

This brief outline of the 'scene' and social events shows the variety of groups and aspects of the city with which lesbian feminists overlapped. They were not alone in their 'community'; there were areas they avoided, particularly the 'S/M' venues, but they frequented many others and mixed with many kinds of people – and they did not, at all times and in all places, wear their lesbian feminist politics on their sleeves. All aspects of their lives were influenced by their feminist politics, but its expression was spatially differentiated.[39]

2. HOUSING AND HOUSEHOLDS: PERSONAL/POLITICAL AND PERSONAL/PRIVATE

During the late 1980s, lesbian feminists lived in a wide variety of accommodation, invariably women-only (though occasionally other parts of the building were occupied by men). Most lived in the poorer sections of inner London, which often had high ethnic minority concentrations.[40] There were exceptions, such as two houses in West London, on the edge of a wealthy area. They were bought some years ago by a women's housing association. Other West London homes were in the Notting Hill area, which was far poorer than the areas surrounding it, and had high numbers of Afro-caribbean residents.

Some brief examples: Suki, a young Chinese woman, had recently moved into a flat in a housing association in Islington. Before that, she had been homeless for over two years since being evicted from her parents' house after 'coming out' to them, and stayed on friends' floors, in night shelters and hostels. Vera and Ruth, both considerably older than Suki, had lived in separate flats in a women-only housing association house for the last couple of years. Vera's lover lived elsewhere. Mandy lived in a council flat with her lover, but was having a battle with her council over its plan to 'billet' her home. It was a two-bedroom flat, and Mandy's lover was not officially a tenant; to reduce homelessness in the borough, the council was considering housing 'difficult cases' in flats which had 'spare' bedrooms. Clara lived in a rented house with her daughter, and had moved several times. Sandy lived in a women's mixed-race co-operative household in south London. The house was owned by the council, but it was sub-standard and would eventually be torn down, so Sandy and her friends lived there for little rent on a 'short-life' arrangement. They could have been evicted at any time. Barbara lived in a house in north London with her lover, and was one of the few women I met who had a mortgage, which she had acquired with some difficulty. Beverley had moved to a women-only housing association in the last year. Nadia lived in a Camden council flat set aside as 'lesbian/gay couple' housing. Later, she broke up with her lover and moved out of the flat because of harassment from a man living next door. Penny had moved many times in recent years, once because, she said, 'the woman upstairs was anti-lesbian, and she also stole my post. It got so bad I called the police. They could only do her for interfering with the Royal Mail, they couldn't do anything about her being anti-lesbian.' Debbie had lived in a women-only collective household in north London at the beginning of fieldwork, but the household broke up and she moved to south London to share another house with friends. Table 2 summarises the living arrangements of the 30 interviewees.

Housing was a chronic problem in London for anyone with a limited income. Some chose boroughs they knew contained many lesbians (Hackney in particular had this reputation), and others were against living south of the river, as the majority of lesbian/feminist activities were located in the north, with travel between the two involving a long and tedious journey. As in Penny's case, a number of women had experienced discrimination in homes they had shared with heterosexual women (six interviewees mentioned it), and for that reason they preferred to live in lesbian-only houses if possible.[41]

As shown in Table 2, some women lived in 'short life' accommodation – houses owned by councils which needed considerable maintenance or renovation. It was cheap, but it was also unpredictably temporary. As Kaye put it:

A lot of my housing has been short life and it's been in women's co-ops....It's been a big problem for me, short life, in terms of stability.

Squatting was almost unknown by the late 1980s, though it had been standard practice during the 1970s. This is how Beverley described the 1970s context:

Table 2   Housing and living arrangements

Housing Type	Total n = 30
Council tenant	9
Short-life housing	4
Private Rent	5
Housing Association	8
Squat	0
Mortgage	4
Living Arrangements	
Living alone	10
Share house with friends	13
Living with lover	7
Living with children*	3
Length of residence	
Up to 1 year	6
1–3 years	10
3–5 years	9
5 years and over	5

* Two lived alone and one lived with her lover. Three other interviewees had children, but they were grown and did not live with them.

Lots of women were squatting houses and living together in groups – lesbians, mostly. And we kind of overlapped with the mixed squatting movement. And some of the women became lesbians and moved into the women-only houses, which was quite a new thing at the time. It was very difficult too, on a material level. You know, getting the plumbing and electricity, and dealing with the council and all that sort of stuff.

However, after 1981, and following the new socialist Greater London Council's lead, many Labour-controlled London boroughs gave housing priority to newly-defined 'disadvantaged' groups, including lesbians and gay men, single women and single mothers, which made squatting less of a necessity. And from the other end of the political spectrum, the national Thatcher government led a crack-down against squatting during the 1980s.

Thus an odd combination of political factors virtually eliminated squatting in London: a strongly socialist local government which recognised the needs of many groups for the first time; and a strongly conservative national government, which increasingly supported property-owners' rights by reducing the amount of bureaucracy needed to take action against unwanted residents, and at the same reducing the rights of the homeless.

However, during the 1970s, squatting was common and seen as part of the feminist project. For example, Beverley helped to set up an 'informal women's centre' in one squatted house, and it was used as a base from which to help other women:

> We helped quite a lot of women squat, women who weren't involved in the women's liberation movement, who heard about us and came along and who were desperate and with kids and so on, and we used to break into houses and things for them.

This had been the origin of A Woman's Place (AWP), which relocated several times as the squatters were evicted, until the GLC provided AWP with permanent accommodation (it closed in 1988 after funding was cut).

By the late 1980s, as outlined in Chapter 2, feminist organisations were mostly located in grant-funded buildings, away from women's homes, creating a spatial division between the domestic sphere and the 'public/ political' sphere. For Beverley, the women's centre squat had also been her home. This was never the case for the women I met; I personally knew of three collective households, and none were squats.

Those 1970s collective households were quite different from late 1980s households. Groups of women – perhaps friends from a consciousness-raising group or women who participated in a feminist campaign together – would break into an empty house, and formed a collective. The aim was to live according to lesbian feminist principles and help organise campaigns, produce newsletters and so on, all from one base. Merging the public and private, the domestic and political *in practice* was a central part of the lesbian feminist project at the time. Usually this meant a suppression of the 'private' altogether, both in conceptual terms and in terms of simply not having any private physical space.

The women ran such households together. Decisions over household policies included both political and practical matters: whether men or boys would be allowed to visit, whether the house would be vegan, as well as what time loud music should be switched off at night. Collective decisions were also made about whether a potential new resident was acceptable, which was partly decided by the candidate's political standpoint. Meetings also attempted to resolve any disputes. Household expenses were shared, and there was usually a 'kitty' into which women would put all their money when and if they had any. Rotas were arranged for household chores, and all the household members would eat together in the evenings.

The collective households I visited, although they were lesbian feminist, differed substantially from the 1970s versions. They were not squats and all residents paid equal rent, whatever their income. And although there were discussions about feminism and how it should be practised, there was no collective arrangement of feminist actions outside the home, although co-residents often attended events or demonstrations together. Changes in household policies were agreed collectively, as was the acceptability of new residents. The rotas and the 'kitty' remained (mostly used to cover shared food, and women by no means put most of their money in it). Ideally women ate together, but in practice this was often difficult to arrange.

The 1970s merging of the 'private' with the 'public' was obviously informed by 1960s 'anti-establishment' and new left movements (see Chapter 4), and was not directly connected to radical/revolutionary feminism. Unlike more socialist-informed politics, there was no *necessity* to 'destroy the private' as private space – only a requirement that it should be changed, 'politicised'. Within radical/revolutionary feminism, the ideology informing personal interrelations caused women's oppression, not the structure of society as such, which was seen more as an outcome of this ideology rather than its cause.

This allowed considerable flexibility in how public and private were to be related together within a lesbian feminist community. At times, such as during the 1970s, the subordination of the private to the public was dominant; by the late 1980s, virtually the reverse was the case. As differences between women were increasingly emphasised, the notion of a united, public-private-merged community seemed increasingly anachronistic – or at any rate, unviable.

There were also practical factors which led to the decline of collective households. The relocation of women's organisations into funded local authority buildings was an important factor. Furthermore, many women who lived collectively said they found it 'too stressful', and that collectives frequently had disputes and broke apart. For example, Barbara expressed extreme relief that 'the days when you had to live collectively with your sisters in order to be politically correct are over.' Although lesbian feminists continued to attempt to live their feminism in their personal lives, most now rejected collective living, where they felt they had no privacy and continually had to sustain criticism for their behaviour.

However, the most important factor was the emergence of the 'politics of difference'. The 1960s social and political context of collective living no longer existed: the increased emphasis on differences between women, rather than a unity based on 'sameness', made collective living neither desirable nor viable for many anymore. Women repeatedly said that during the 1970s, the 'community' was more close-knit, 'communal', less diverse and much smaller than in the late 1980s, by which time it had become large, amorphous and in the process of 'fragmentation' – by no means regarded as an *entirely* negative development.

Before looking more closely at activities in the home and their inter-relations with other aspects of the 'community', I will briefly outline the fourth major sphere of lesbian feminists' lives – their paid occupations outside lesbian/feminist organisations.

3. EMPLOYMENT OUTSIDE THE 'COMMUNITY': PERSONAL/POLITICAL – PERSONAL/PRIVATE

For most lesbian feminists, paid work existed outside 'community', and was not often discussed in lesbian feminist contexts. In fact, the lack of discussion about employment was a marked difference between radical/revolutionary feminists and socialist feminists. Many worked primarily to pay the bills, though there were limits to the jobs women were willing to do, and an increasing number were pursuing a professional career – either self-employed or within a business, not necessarily women-only.

Lesbian feminists were relatively poor, even though many had high educational qualifications. Of the 30 interviewees, 17 had a degree or higher qualification, and of the remainder, five had professional vocational qualifications, and a further two were studying for degrees. From my knowledge of other lesbian feminists in London, this was not an unusual sample. Low incomes were partly due to women's incomes being generally lower than men's in Britain, but it was also due to lesbian feminists' rejection of stereotypical 'feminine' jobs – those involving 'servicing' a man, such as secretary and personal assistant, and of employment in 'patriarchal' businesses – businesses owned and run by men, seen as acting to maintain patriarchal institutions, and demanding certain types of dress codes from their female workforce. No lesbian feminists I met had such jobs, though many were employed in typically woman-dominated occupations in the social services. Table 3 overleaf summarises the types of occupations 117 lesbian feminists had (including the 30 interviewees).

I did not collect information on earnings, as women were loathe to discuss their incomes. But judging from newspaper advertisements specifying salaries for these types of occupation, only three women in Table 3

Table 3   Categories of Employment

Type of Occupation	Total
Unemployed/in full-time voluntary work	4
Unemployed/seeking employment	4
Local government/social services/NHS	24
Teaching*	14
Part/full-time student	12
Grant-aided voluntary organisation work	19
Grant-aided arts/media	9
Part-time casual work	8
Self-employed	6
Women-only business**	11
Other business**	6

* Ten taught feminist, lesbian or lesbian feminist-related topics.
** These were mostly women employed in women's, lesbian/gay or radical bookshops, women's publishers, etc. Two were qualified professionals working in male-owned businesses.

were likely to earn more than £14,000 per annum (one was successfully self-employed), and the majority probably earned less than £12,000. In London in the late 1980s, this did not go far. In 1988, for example, the average *main* income of first-time London home buyers paying less than a 5% deposit was £18,900.[42]

In short, lesbian feminists had little disposable income, considering the cost of living. Furthermore, 52 of the 97 women in any kind of employment in Table 3 were being supported by state funds, which gives an indication of their importance, a subject explored further in Chapter 5.

Of the 97 women who were employed, 68 were openly lesbian at work. This is a surprisingly high number: among lesbians and gay men in general, one of the last places that homosexuality is revealed is at work (followed closely by immediate family), and many never reveal it there.[43] It was seen as a major area where direct discrimination was likely. That so many women I spoke to were 'out' at work was due to the political importance they placed on this identity. Twelve interviewees said they had experienced some form of discrimination at work because they were lesbians. This ranged from suspecting they did not get a job because of their sexuality or 'dykey' appearance, as Nicola put it, to being dismissed once their lesbianism was revealed at work.[44]

These sorts of experiences, both in employment and housing, continually reminded women that their sexual identity involved forms of discrimination different from, and often more explicit than, discrimination on
the basis of their gender identity – forms of discrimination which were
more like those experienced by gay men than those experienced by heterosexual women. Being employed as a woman and then being dismissed as a
lesbian could hardly more explicitly demonstrate the different social
implications of each. Thus, although feminist considerations came into
choice of employment and behaviour at work, women's identity as lesbians (as opposed to woman-identified-women) was also centrally
involved.

4. LIVING AS A LESBIAN FEMINIST

All women in the community involved themselves in these different
spheres of public/private to different degrees. Of the majority – i.e., white,
middle class women – those who did not participate a great deal in either
the 'scene' or in lesbian/feminist organisations or groups considered themselves fairly peripheral in the community, though they still felt they were
members. Those who participated a great deal in the 'scene' but not in
lesbian/feminist activities considered themselves more lesbian than feminist. Many of these women were involved in gay liberation activities, and
many also had gay male friends. Those who participated a great deal in
lesbian/feminist activities but not the 'scene' considered themselves as
feminist as they were lesbian, and rarely had gay male friends.

Women of ethnic minorities and working class women could participate in similar ways, but the cross-cutting factors of race and class
affected their experience of the community, and many became additionally
involved in black-women only, Jewish, Irish, working class and so on
groups in addition to mixed groups. In a brief outline of several women's
lives, some of how this was experienced in practice will become clearer.

(a) Coming out stories: becoming a member of the community

Nicola was thirty years old, white and had lived in London most of her
life, being brought up in a working class household in the East End, except
for a period when she went to study for a degree. She 'came out' as a
lesbian before becoming a feminist, and her first contact with the
'community' was the 'scene'. However, many others (18 of the 30 interviewees) did not 'come out' until they became involved with feminism,

and many said they did not think they would have 'come out', or at least not so painlessly, had it not been for feminism.

In fact, one Asian woman, Rashida, said she had thought she might be a lesbian from the age of 12, and she resisted involvement with feminism because of this: 'I had fears at first about becoming too close to women through feminism, because I was fighting my own sexuality. And it's harder to fight being a lesbian if you're very woman-identified [laughs]'. This was also Vera's experience, a white north American woman in her early forties. She had worried that if she read any feminism, she would throw her boyfriend out, which would be, as she put it, 'disruptive'. Table 4 summarises the experiences of 'coming out' by the interviewees (the totals do not add up to 30, as many women had combinations of these experiences).

All women had a 'coming out story' – accounts of the process through which they concluded they were lesbians, accepted it, then revealed it to others. Exchanging such stories was a central part of making friends within the community: it established a bond based on common experiences. The coming out process marked the period when the world began to look very different for these women.

There were different ways in which women remembered the process, but all established lesbianism as an 'authentic' identity. An important part was a feeling of crossing a huge social boundary: by concluding they were lesbian, they moved into a new social status. Many recalled how at first, they felt poorly informed about this new identity and attempted to find out more – often secretly, which made it that much more difficult. Others described how they could not connect what they had heard about lesbianism with themselves, and became confused for quite some time.

The process of learning and deciding what lesbianism meant – both socially and to themselves – was a central part of the 'coming out' process. And for many, one important aspect was a break which had to be made with immediate family, particularly parents. Some, like Suki, a young Chinese woman, had been completely rejected and evicted from their parental homes. This was by no means always the case, but a high level of parental admonishment, resulting in family rifts lasting for years was common – for 16 of the 30 interviewees, for example.

Many said the 'coming out' process took years and was painful. Paula, now in her early forties, described how she had struggled with it for ten years, during which time she had become involved in a variety of both lesbian and feminist groups, in an attempt to replace her own, very negative, attitude towards lesbianism with something more positive. Others said the process was short and very positive, as it had been for Anne and Ruth

Table 4   'Coming Out' Experiences

Type of experience	Total n = 30
Thought about it during childhood	22
'Came out' before involvement with feminist groups	12
'Came out' after involvement with feminist groups/can't separate the two	18
'Came out' before having any relationships with women	5
Became involved with the 'scene' before involvement with feminism	4
Initially attempted to deny lesbianism/saw it as negative	14
Initially saw it as positive	16

(tutor of the 'Rebel' course). For most, it involved a mixture of apprehension and excitement. Nicola recounted how she had been both 'terrified' and deeply intrigued by the idea she might be lesbian. When she first thought about it in her early teens, she 'freaked out' and set about proving to herself and others that it was untrue by going out with as many boys as possible.

This was a familiar experience for many women. Some went through a 'bisexual phase', which they now interpreted as a period when they were unwilling to accept their lesbianism, or at least its social implications. Nicola's period of going out with boys ended after she was 'seduced', she said, by an older woman.

Unlike all the other interviewees, Charlotte did not interpret her past as revealing a 'latent lesbianism', even though she (openly) had sexual encounters with girlfriends at school. She thought these encounters were 'all part of the rich tapestry of life.' She went on: 'I had a tremendous fondness for women...but I think I was as heterosexual as the next woman when I was younger. I'm not now, but I think I was when I was younger.' Charlotte did not call herself a lesbian until she became involved with revolutionary feminism in the early 1980s. A radical/revolutionary feminist conference convinced her that 'men were the enemy' and she became a separatist. She now considered herself an 'authentic' lesbian, but said she had 'developed those sexual feelings quite gradually'.

Other women had adolescent sexual experiences with girls or women, or were attracted to them, but did not 'have the language', as Alice put it, to connect these experiences with the term 'lesbian'. In addition to Alice, this was how both Suki and Brenda described their earlier years. It is notable that none of these three women were white and middle class. Suki was Chinese, Alice was African American and Brenda was white working class British. This kind of variation in knowledge about lesbianism across class and race has also been noted by Faderman (1992) for the USA.

Brenda had a girlfriend from her early teens, and assumed all school girls 'did that sort of thing'. In their late teens, they realised they ought to be 'going out with boys', so together they found two boyfriends, as Brenda put it. They eventually married them and both couples lived together in a flat, with Brenda and her lover carrying on their relationship while having children with their husbands. This arrangement was eventually ended by Brenda's lover's husband, who realised what was going on and moved to another country with his wife.

In sum, women had a variety of 'coming out stories', but all had one thing in common: the stories established their lesbianism as both deeply personal and 'authentic' to them (including Charlotte, eventually); some even 'came out' before they had a relationship with a woman (five of the interviewees). The coming out story represented something different from the strictly 'political' definition of lesbian feminism described in Chapter 1.

(b) Politics and lesbianism: living in the community

Nicola distinguished the period before becoming a separatist lesbian feminist by saying she had been a 'straight dyke'. A similar phrase was used by Alice, who said she had been a 'bar dyke' before becoming a separatist (though she was no longer a separatist by 1989). Nicola made a sudden break with this earlier period, marked by 'dumping' all her male friends, who had been mostly gay men she knew from the 'scene'. This, Nicola explained, was her 'rigid' revolutionary feminist phase. She eventually questioned revolutionary feminism because she felt it did not adequately deal with race, but she was still a separatist, except at work.

Nicola lived alone in a three-bedroom council flat in Islington, though she had previously shared it with a lover. The flat had been occupied by several lesbian feminists before Nicola moved there. This frequently happened: once a lesbian feminist had moved into a place, it tended to be handed on to other lesbian feminists, even if it was council accommodation.

Nicola often went out 'on the scene'. She regularly visited the Fallen Angel on women-only nights, Rackets and the Duke of Wellington, all of which are in Islington. She also attended women-only discos, benefits and occasionally went to places like Heds if she was asked to by friends.

Nicola felt that living as a lesbian feminist was hard, and she recounted how she once tried giving it up, but could not:

I tried to give my politics up once [laughs]. I tried. I had some very interesting conversations with some friends who were also trying to – who were also straight dykes first and became feminists. There was one in particular I remember – it was quite a drunken conversation – and we both decided to become straight dykes again. And then we bumped into each other again, and were comparing notes about how we'd done. And we decided we were tainted with feminism, and it was something we were never going to get rid of [laughs]. So I can understand women who want to give up their politics, cos' it's fucking hard.
Q. What do you think is hard about it?
A. Because you have to keep questioning and challenging yourself and others all the time.

What made lesbian feminism hard for Nicola is also what made it imposs-ible for her to give it up: she had become reflexive about her own exis-tence through feminism, and that is something difficult to reverse.

Nicola worked in a local authority social services department. She enjoyed the work, but separated it from the rest of her life. Although she thought of several of her women colleagues as friends, she did not meet them outside working hours, and she deliberately kept her male colleagues at a distance. She was 'out' at work, which had occasionally caused prob-lems, but she was supported by women colleagues whenever trouble arose. What she did not discuss was her political beliefs, because she felt these would be seen as too extreme:

I'm constantly having to check myself at work. I have this big split between the way I am at work and how I am the rest of the time. Cos' I have to keep what I feel are my politics in check at work.

This attitude was true of most lesbian feminists working outside the 'community'. But even within women-only organisations, lesbian fem-inists had to keep their politics 'in check'. As mentioned when discussing ROW, when people are practising, rather than theorising their political positions, compromises have to be made: the world in which lesbian fem-inists lived was not a lesbian feminist world except in scattered pockets, and even there the potential for conflict often moderated women's behav-iour. The continual question facing lesbian feminists was: where are the limits? How much compromise was too much? Once again, being con-tinually faced with these situations made lesbian feminists' lives frequently hard on an emotional level.

Barbara's life provides another example of a fairly active lesbian fem-inist's experiences in London. Barbara was 41 and had an adult daughter living abroad from a previous marriage. Unlike Nicola, she had 'come out' after involvement with feminism. As a result, she had found coming out an entirely positive experience, but in retrospect thought this was the result of 'naivety'. She knew nothing about lesbianism from the small town where she grew up, and so only had the positive 'woman-identified-woman' image from feminism to go on, which never emphasised the discrimination lesbians experienced:

> I very much appreciated feminism being around, because if I'd become a lesbian without feminism, it would have been a very gruelling sort of process. Whereas I found lesbianism a very positive process, you know. I was innocent. I thought it was wonderful.

Barbara lived in a women's squat when she first moved to London in 1984, but there were frequent disputes within the household's collective. After moving five times in one year, she became tired of squatting, found a basement flat with no bedrooms and took out a mortgage, where she was now living with her lover, Judith. She got the mortgage, she said, from a broker who 'didn't ask too many questions about my income.' A similar phrase was used by Brenda, who had bought a flat in south London. Barbara had been active in feminist and lesbian feminist politics since moving to London, and most of her life was taken up working on lesbian/feminist campaigns. She helped to found a number of feminist projects and worked almost entirely in women-only jobs. In 1988, she worked full time in a lesbian/feminist organisation.

Politically, Barbara 'reluctantly' defined herself as a 'revolutionary radical feminist', though like Nicola she now expressed doubts about the adequacy of the theory to cope with race in particular, and differences between women in general. Most white women I met expressed similar doubts. The continual accusations during the 1980s that revolutionary and radical feminist perspectives ignored ethnic minority women's experiences had been at least partially accepted as valid criticisms by most lesbian feminists by the late 1980s. Barbara strongly accepted these criticisms, and felt that people like herself should actively attempt to address the problem.

It was these kinds of changes in opinion, often made individually (in the context of a community which was much larger and more diverse than it had been in the 1970s) that began to move the emphasis, and even the underlying philosophy, of lesbian feminist thought. By placing a strong emphasis on differences between women, the focus shifted from the relationship between men and women and what to do about it, to a focus on the relationship between different kinds of women and what to do about it. In community terms, that shifted the focus away from patriarchy and men as the culpable and oppressive forces, and instead towards racism, ageism, classism, etc, as the culpable and oppressive forces. Both perspectives were present, but the 'politics of difference' approach was gaining the moral high ground by the late 1980s.

Socially, Barbara was a separatist and did not mix with men at all:

> I mean, I don't even mix with straight lesbians [i.e., non-political lesbians]. And that's because of the divisions within the lesbian community. I do know, I suppose I have, through [Judith], met a couple of women who don't have anything to do with politics per se. But their consciousness is such that they're very intelligent women, and they're critical of everything, so you know, they don't have to be overtly discussing lesbian feminist topics all the time for me to feel comfortable with them.

It is worth noting that Barbara's criterion for the acceptability of Judith's 'non-political' friends was that they were 'critical of everything'.

The divisions in the community to which Barbara referred were those between the 'scene' and public/political lesbian feminist activities. Although she felt she was on one side of the divide (the lesbian feminist side), she also accepted that she had contacts across those divisions.

Furthermore, although Barbara's lover (Judith), had been actively involved in feminist activity in the past, she had become 'burned out' and had now withdrawn from involvement to a great extent:

> [Judith] had been involved in the first lesbian liberation group in London and...she's burned out and sick of it all....If we go out to a party together, I get involved in talking about all the politics again, and she gets pissed off.

'Burn out' describes the combination of physical exhaustion and emotional stress which can result from intensive involvement in lesbian/ feminist activities. It was a phrase I came to understand well following my own experience in the Archive dispute. Beverley, who had been involved in the WLM since the late 1960s, described how she had experienced it:

> I think I got a case of, you know, good old classic 1970s burn-out, really....We worked all the time, but we never called it work and we never got paid for it, you know....It was exhausting. Especially all that personal politics stuff – like every little emotion you had, you analysed and worked on, and changed the way you lived and everything. Plus

you were out there all the time, confronting men, confronting the structures of patriarchy. You know, it was just knackering.

Barbara expressed similar sentiments. Despite her self-placement in the 'public/political' sphere, she deliberately divided her personal life from her 'public' lesbian feminist life, a division which had been virtually absent during the 1970s period. Nowadays, Barbara hated to be called at home by collective co-members, and when she socialised, it was often with Judith or with personal friends who had few connections with her political activities. She also socialised with political colleagues because the majority of her friends were active lesbian feminists, but she made distinctions between 'political socialising' and 'personal socialising'.

Barbara, like all the women I spoke to, believed that she lived in a community, but she had a complex approach to it:

> When I think of community, I do tend to think of the part that I'm aware of. And it's very white. Not totally white, but it is probably white. I mean, if you went to Rackets, while Rackets was still going, the majority there were white lesbians....When we had the Jane Rule event here [a benefit], there were probably 120 women, 80 of whom I knew. You know, it's just like, there it is. So that's not the community, that's just the bit I feel connected to in some way. But there's vast patches, huge areas – what are young lesbians doing, what are social groups doing – I've got no idea about them. I see them as part of the community, but it's a phenomenally difficult task to bring those together. It's not as though people all share this sense of community, of the same community. We don't, I think.

Most women I spoke to agreed with this understanding of the 'community' – that it was something large, complex, amorphous, involving people you know nothing about, but nevertheless somehow feel connected to.

Barbara also said that for her, there could be no 'community' without public events:

> The only way that you know there's a community is that when some big event happens, loads of dykes turn up.... Cos' obviously, when you go to the Lesbian Strength march, you know you've got a community, cos' a lot of them are there. So there's got to be things around which a community can focus. If we lose those, there'll be no sense of community at all.

Thus even though Barbara was one of the most active and committed lesbian feminists I met, she nevertheless associated the 'community' with being lesbian rather than with being lesbian *feminist* per se: the 'community' was made visible by the existence of 'loads of dykes' and a typical 'community' event was the Lesbian Strength march. Barbara did not choose to say that the community was visible because of the existence of collectives or because of feminist campaigns. The rarity of large feminist-inspired demonstrations during the late 1980s probably contributed to Barbara's perception. But as public visibility was important in feeling that a community existed, the fact that the vast majority of events marking public visibility were lesbian and/or gay, rather than specifically lesbian feminist, meant that the community, as a whole, was regarded more in terms of lesbian identity than in terms of feminist identity.

However, there was more to the importance of lesbian, as opposed to lesbian feminist, identity than the issue of public visibility. As the section above on the coming out process illustrated, and as the next section also shows, women's personal interrelations based on their lesbian identity was crucial to the social framework of the community.

(c) Community relationships and networks: lovers, ex-lovers and friends

To illustrate this point, I will return briefly to Nicola's life. Nicola's closest friend was an ex-lover, Jane, who often came round to her flat. They had been in lesbian/feminist collectives together, shared many of the same friends and often went out to pubs and to lesbian feminist meetings and events together. Jane lived in a flat on her own in Hackney, and she worked in a grant-aided social service organisation in Camden. Jane was out at work and generally also outspoken, though she kept her views in check with clients.

Virtually all of Nicola's friends were lesbian feminists, which was true of the overwhelming majority of lesbian feminists I met. She had no close black friends, which she regretted. This was also true of most white lesbian feminists. Other than Jane, Nicola had five or six close friends (some of whom were also ex-lovers) and 'dozens and dozens' of other friends with whom she kept in touch, but saw less frequently:

I have got...a really good friendship network, and I see it as going in sort of concentric circles...if I look at it like a family, there's you're close family, your siblings. And then there's your cousins, and your second cousins, and third cousins, and marriages in between – you know. [Ruth], and people like her, is the next category out. And we very occasionally go out for an evening....But there's, I would say, with people like [Ruth], there's a very strong bond between me and [Ruth]. And there's innumerable ones like that, yeah?

In times of trouble, whether economic, emotional or political, friends were expected to support each other. In collective disputes for example (which most lesbian feminists had experienced at least once), close friends of collective members usually openly supported them. Ruth, for example, strongly supported Anne, who was an ex-lover and close friend, in the Archive dispute. Ruth placed an especially strong emphasis on friendship:

Some women do politics in order to be seen to do politics – at the expense of women, of their lesbian friends. I know a woman who drops her friends of many years because they do something wrong politically....My friends are more important to me ultimately than political theory....I see the betrayal of a friendship as catastrophic, whereas I would have been confident that the Archive would start up again somewhere, even if it had closed down because of the dispute ... . But then often, disputes within collectives become so important because they involve disputes with friends, don't they?

For Nicola, as for Ruth, friendship relations formed a major part of her feeling she was a part of a 'community', and this was true of most women. Nicola expressed an added and common view about the distinction between friends and lovers in this regard:

My friends are the most important thing in my life....I think ultimately for most lesbians, they are. I hope they are, because we need a continuity, and we need to make our own continuity. And I really don't feel lovers can provide that.

So lovers did not provide continuity within the community, whereas close friends (who were often ex-lovers), did. Lovers represented the active sexual, personal and private aspects of lesbian relationships; and they established lesbian 'authenticity' more than any other relationship. In contrast, ex-lovers represented 'authentic' lesbianism without placing it above other, more public and political, aspects of lesbianism, as it was no longer an exclusive relationship. Thus where lovers exposed the ambivalence between radical/revolutionary representations of lesbianism (a public/political gender identity), and lesbian/gay representations of it (a personal/private sexual identity), ex-lovers could bridge the two. None of the Archive collective members' lovers were involved with the Archive, whereas a number of their ex-lovers, though not on the collective, were actively involved.

This situation is worth spending a little time exploring, as it represents a very different situation from descriptions of most communities. There was no formal 'kinship structure' in lesbian feminist personal relations: no marriages or divorces, and so no affines and no blood relatives (except children, who were in a somewhat ambivalent position). And there were no formal economic relations which depended on these social relations: there were no inheritance rules, nor any formal economic rights and obligations between women. Nor did anyone have formal rights over children, except the biological mothers. And the stereotypical western nuclear family model of kinship was explicitly rejected as being entirely oppressive to women.

Yet there were continual suggestions that friends were considered in some senses as 'kin', although kinship metaphors were rarely used. Nicola, who did use kin metaphors during her interview with me, wanted to indicate that her friendships were seen as strong, permanent relations – between lesbians. This is where the different structural positions of lovers and ex-lovers comes in. Ex-lovers who were friends often participated together in all spheres of the 'community', whereas lovers did not, being involved mostly in the 'public/personal' and 'personal/private' spheres. Women tried to keep their involvement with collectives and their lover relationships – in other words, their 'public' and 'private' lives – separate.

The pattern of lover relationships was generally 'serial monogamy', and long-term relationships were regarded as exceptional. Of the 30 interviewees, two were in relationships which had lasted more than four years. This resulted in the existence of numerous ex-lovers in the 'community', and the creation of a kind of 'genealogy' for most women, as networks of friends always included ex-lovers, who were often current lovers of other ex-lovers, whose ex-lovers would also be part of the network. The serial monogamy pattern meant that there was usually a gap between the ending of one relationship and the beginning of another. In this case, friendships with ex-lovers generally survived. If, however, there was a degree of overlap between the two relationships, which was concealed, things were entirely different.

An example of this was the circumstances of the ending of a relationship between Beth and Meg. Sally, who was a close friend of Meg's, secretly began a relationship with Beth, while Beth was still Meg's lover. When Beth and Sally finally told Meg, Meg said she thought Sally did it deliberately to hurt Meg, and never spoke to either of them again during fieldwork.

Although this event ended the friendship with Sally, it did not prevent Meg and Beth from seeing each other (and being seen) as 'related'; the relationship had created a social link between them. Thus when women spoke about Meg, for example, they would often mention that she was an ex-lover of Beth's. There were myriad linkages of this sort between women, which had the effect of establishing their position in, and membership of, the community.

Lesbian feminists often expressed unease about the implications of long-term relationships, frequently called 'marriage', and this was one area where women's politics affected their thoughts about personal relations. 'Straight dykes' did not express any *unease* about long-term relationships, though they may not personally prefer them. For many radical/revolutionary feminists, being personally and privately involved with one woman for a long period of time at the expense of friends and political commitments constituted a retreat into the 'private' sphere, away from the 'public/political' sphere.

In sum, both the (somewhat conflicting) ideals of creating a community of women based on radical/revolutionary feminist principles, and the achievement of individual autonomy (women's subjectivity) through separation from men were being undermined by long-term lover relationships. This is what one lesbian feminist, Madge, had to say about 'married' lesbians:

> being married to me is [...] about the way you live. About whether you continue your politics, or whether you become a sort of quasi-heterosexual, two-up, two-down, 2.2 kid family. [...] if they're married, even if they do politics, they tend to do it together...married means they forget the pronoun 'I', it's always 'we'. It's about losing your individuality.

Ex-lovers and friends, however, did not stand in this relation. They allowed individual autonomy, and thus ex-lovers and friends bridged the divisions between public/personal, public/political and personal/private. The ex-lover in particular was someone who, because of the past relationship, was emotionally close, but had moved into a kind of relative category – a cousin of sorts. She no longer represented the purely personal/private aspect of lesbianism, no longer threatened to remove a woman from its public/political aspects – to de-politicise her, as it were. At the same time, ex-lovers represented 'authentic' lesbianism.

Some examples: as already discussed Nicola and Jane were both in a number of political groups together, and often attended demonstrations, marches and public/political meetings together, which was not seen as 'coupledom' or bringing the private into public/political spheres. Similarly, Ruth supported Anne during the Archive dispute and Anne often called on her to assist in the various projects she was developing. In contrast, the current lovers of Archive collective members did not themselves become involved in the dispute. They emotionally supported their lovers at some meetings, which at times became extremely unpleasant, but they did not join in any of the political activity, and they did not speak out at such meetings. However, ex-lovers and close personal friends did. In fact, Ruth had broken a long-term friendship with Clara (another ex-lover) since the Archive dispute because Clara supported Anne's opponents, and Ruth saw this as a betrayal of friendship. Had Clara simply kept quiet, it would have been alright; but her public opposition to Anne was unforgivable for Ruth. Significantly however, both Ruth and Clara still regarded themselves as 'related', and gathered information about each other through intermediate friends (such as Nicola). Clara had simply moved into the category of 'relatives' Ruth disliked.

This was a similar situation to recent break-ups of lover relationships. One of Charlotte's ex-lovers, Karen, was still in touch with Charlotte, but they had shifted in differing 'public/political' directions within the 'community' (Charlotte had moved in a 'libertarian' direction, whereas Karen had not), and so they usually only met for social occasions. Thus although ex-lover relationships could combine 'public/political' and 'personal/private', the relationship did not end if the two women started to alter their political perspectives. This was rarely the case for colleague/friendship relations based on the 'public/political' sphere. Once the Archive collective broke down for example, the two sides did not socially interact at all, and were not interested in what the other (ex-)members were doing.

This occasional divergence of political perspective between ex-lovers (and friends) was also true of lover relationships. Anne and Jean's lovers did not share their partners' enthusiasm for lesbian feminism, and this was true of a number of partnerships involving one politically active partner and one 'disinterested' one. Moreover, there were several examples I came across where both lovers were politically active but had opposing political perspectives. For example, Margaret, a socialist feminist, was having a relationship with Sadie, a revolutionary feminist. Margaret said she and her lover did not talk about politics much, and that was how they managed to 'avoid coming to blows'. So the separation between the 'public/political' and 'personal/private' spheres allowed close personal relations with public/political opponents.

The opposition between socialist and radical/revolutionary feminists was somewhat complex. Many radical feminists (and to a lesser extent revolutionary feminists) personally accepted much of the socialist feminist analysis of women's disadvantaged economic position. Similarly, many socialist feminists' analysis of patriarchy had borrowed from radical feminist analyses. What they disagreed about was the causes of women's oppression, which generated a serious 'public/political' split. However, what personally bothered many lesbian feminists was socialist feminists' alliance with 'a male-dominated movement', and the fact that socialist feminists placed little importance on the political role of lesbianism. And what bothered many socialist feminists about lesbian feminists was the insistence that one cannot be a feminist without being a lesbian. The *social* antagonism between them, however, was probably connected with the fact that many socialist feminists were heterosexual women, and thus not a part of the community. Where socialist feminists *were* lesbians, they did not occupy the same 'public/political' space as radical/revolutionary feminists, but they did share the same 'public/personal' space, and could (and did) have relationships with their 'public/political' opponents.

This network of personal lesbian friendships between women, often based on ex-lover friendships, created an interrelatedness, and it is what made women feel members of a community. Lesbianism was the criterion for membership, and it was through lesbianism – in 'coming out' stories, in relations with lovers and ex-lovers, in experiences of discrimination – that a 'we' was distinguished from a 'they'.

One further point needs to be made. Relations between community members were always seen in terms of equality, never asymmetry. This was partly because these relations were built upon the idea of friendship as it is commonly conceived, which is characterised, in an idealised way at least, as a relation of equals. And this criterion was one of the sources of ambivalence over children, to which I now turn.

(d) Children: on the margins

At least once a week Tina, the teenage daughter of one of Nicola's closest friends, Sara, came to stay with Nicola. Sara was also a lesbian feminist and Tina was fully aware of both Sara's and Nicola's political views, but did not commit herself to sharing them.

Nicola described herself as Tina's 'co-parent', and she took the responsibility seriously, both on a political and personal level, though the arrangement had been made with Sara, and did not involve the community. Nicola emphasised that she was guided by her feminist beliefs and the desire to construct 'non-nuclear' family structures in the domestic sphere; but the 'public community' did not include children within its conceptual boundaries, and nor were children physically included in either the scene or lesbian feminist groups or organisations.

For this reason, a number of lesbian mothers' groups existed to provide places where lesbian mothers could meet others, share their experiences and arrange baby-sitting and many other practical arrangements involved in childcare. This was in part because of problems many had experienced with heterosexual parents. For example, several lesbian mothers I spoke to told of heterosexual parents in the neighbourhood who did not allow their children to play with lesbians' children.

The probability that children would experience discrimination because of their mothers' lesbianism concerned all lesbian mothers I met, and was the reason many did not reveal their lesbianism to institutions with which the child was involved. Sometimes, they did not reveal it even to their children for many years, but this was not the case amongst lesbian feminist mothers. One woman, Carol, put it this way:

> Some women don't want to say anything to their kids or the schools and all this sort of business because somehow or other the kids will suffer....The kid's going to suffer anyway, you know, irrespective of whether you tell them what's going on or not. I think it gives you and the kids more resistance, to be able to deal with the issue, if they know what it's about.

Clearly, children brought their lesbian mothers into a great deal of contact with institutions outside the community. Carol, who had a young daughter and son (she had won custody of the daughter, but not the son, a court decision which perhaps does not bear careful scrutiny), described some of her own experiences:

> As a lesbian mother, you're coming up against the system all the time....I'm a school governor at my daughter's school, and some people in the school have started to harass me. There's a whole set of women who have totally isolated me in my daughter's school because they know I'm a lesbian....It takes a lot of grit, you know. You've got to be really clear about who you are and why you're entering the school playground. And if you suddenly have this feeling of isolation and loneliness, well then you can hang it up....The point is, you can't rely on that sort of close community of mothers type of thing that some heterosexual mothers do because they fit into the right stereotype.

Thus from the community's perspective, children stood in a 'personal/private' position, whereas from an extra-community perspective, they stood in a 'public/personal' and 'personal/private' position.

The lesbian/feminist community's lack of support in childcare was occasionally noted and complained about by lesbian mothers,[45] but most others agreed that children were the mother's own responsibility. For example, at a separatist meeting held to discuss lesbian motherhood in 1989, a prominent lesbian feminist argued that the provision of crèches at lesbian feminist events was to allow mothers to attend the event, not because the community had any responsibility towards children. Again, the public/private divide was clear, and this highlights another split with socialist feminism. Within socialist feminism, motherhood and child-care shared centre stage with the issue of labour (which of course includes motherhood and childcare). These are precisely the issues which radical/revolutionary feminists underemphasised, focusing instead on the structure of sexual relations. For radical/revolutionary feminists, it was not women's status as mothers and childcarers (nor as employees) *per se* which was at the root of the problem for women: it was women's sexual objectification within patriarchal ideology and the resulting oppression in all areas of women's lives by men that was the problem. Women's relations with their children, if they had any chil-dren, and any difficulties in raising them, was not the main issue. In lesbian feminist terms, this meant children were conceptually outside the community's boundaries.

For example, I only once met a lesbian feminist's daughter in the Archive offices. This was because her mother had come in to help prepare leaflets for the Lesbian Summer School and had not found a babysitter, for which she apologised. Of course, in lesbian/gay community terms, chil-dren were outside its boundaries anyway, as the community was based on an adult sexual identity.

In practice, children emerged as an issue mostly in decisions about whether to provide a crêche for lesbian feminist events, and if so, whether boys would be allowed and up until what age. Apart from the separatist meeting to discuss the issue mentioned above, this was the limit of lesbian feminist discussions on children in my experience. Even at that meeting (which did not provide a crêche and attracted 21 participants, whereas others in the series of meetings attracted well over 100), the general view was that children were a mother's own responsibility and were 'not on the agenda of lesbian feminist politics', as one speaker put it.

In the context of asking what lesbian mothers wanted their children to become, one speaker suggested the possibility of developing lesbian mothers' centres and schools for lesbian children, but these ideas were strongly rejected as 'handicapping' the children. One participant commented that,

> sending a child to a lesbians' school would be like sending a disabled kid to a handicapped school. That's not fair on the kids to separate them like that. I want my kids to have the chances they can get out of life and not handicap them from the start. If you have kids, you have to mix with the rest of the world, there's no choice.

Many women also made it clear that children should be free to choose their own politics, and mothers did not expect daughters to become members of the 'community'. One comment from the meeting:

> I don't see why we should want children to be like us, and you can't make them be like us anyway. I certainly didn't turn out like my parents. You have to accept that children are their own people and will do what they want to do.

This brings out another issue: many lesbian feminists had experienced serious disagreements with their own families, both about their sexual orientation and their political beliefs. This had a strong effect on many lesbian mothers' determination that they would not treat *their* children like that. In any event, this approach tallied with the trend of emphasising personal autonomy within late 1980s radical/revolutionary feminism – women should not be 'told'.

This approach was also a clear indication that there was nothing 'utopian' or 'sect-like' about lesbian feminists' attitudes towards their community. The descriptions of communes and utopian groups (e.g., Kanter, 1972; Abrams and McCulloch, 1976; and Hardy, 1979) indicate that communal and utopian groups were centred on a withdrawal to the domestic sphere; that their members lived and worked together; that, at least for utopian communes, they attempted to construct an entirely autonomous and self-reproducing alternative existence, socially, economically and politically; and that, for more modern communes, living in the commune was the end in itself. Although earlier lesbian feminist collective households had some hankering towards communal life, the situation in London was quite different during the late 1980s. Within lesbian feminist theory, there was certainly nothing approaching a utopian vision of the future, except, perhaps, for its 'matriarchalist' strand, which was not widely adhered to in London.[46]

In practice, lesbian feminists did not break their links with the 'world out there' (though they may have redefined them somewhat), and more importantly they did not locate their community solely in the domestic sphere. On the contrary, as the domestic sphere came closer to its stereotypical character – the presence of children and the inclusion of a permanent partner for example – there was considerable ambivalence about it. Within lesbian feminism, the domestic sphere represented the major location of women's oppression, in terms of women being both restricted to it, and of the sexual and emotional abuses they experienced within it. A retreat to the domestic sphere – even if it was a women-only and feminist-informed domestic sphere – undermined the lesbian feminist project if women did not also participate in the public/political sphere. It was here that children and lovers came into direct conflict both structurally and intellectually with other aspects of the community.

For children, there was a question of asymmetry. Mothers were in an undeniably asymmetrical relationship with their children, which refuted the ideal of equality between autonomous persons. Children not only represented asymmetry, however: they also highlighted the issue of reproduction, and added a reminder that any women's community could never be entirely autonomous. The emphasis on analysing sexuality and patriarchal heterosexual relations in terms of the objectifying and denigrating way it defined femininity tended to lose sight of the issue which socialist feminists emphasised much more – the exploitation of women's *reproductive* labour as a means of domination. Woman as 'mother' is not the autonomous woman envisioned in radical/revolutionary feminism; she is not alone and defining herself only through herself, but is also responsible to a dependent other. The discomfort many lesbian feminists felt in discussing the status of motherhood and children involved a feeling that within hetero-patriarchy, it would be difficult to avoid doing patriarchy's work for it by being a mother. Radical/revolutionary feminism focused on the 'whore' side of the madonna/whore dichotomy most of the time, attacking patriarchy's view of the female sexual being, not the madonna side of woman as mother.

It is thus not surprising that the 'public/political' sphere did not offer guidelines on raising children. And as the 'public/personal' sphere was defined as 'lesbian/gay' space – that is, sexually adult space, children were not represented in either public sphere.

(e) Summary of spatial/conceptual distributions

Figures 9 and 10 outline the different spatial/conceptual distributions discussed so far. The figures illustrate the interactions and separations between different spheres from the perspective of being within the community (figure 9), and from outside the community (figure 10). For the sake of simplicity, only some categories have been included.

Spatially differentiated spheres are marked in ordinary type (the scene, employment outside the community; women-only social events; home life; conferences and collectives); political perspectives and personal practices are marked in italics (gay liberation, feminism, choice of job, lifestyle); types of relationship with people are underlined in bold (lovers, ex-lovers, children).

Figure 9:   Spatial/Conceptual Distribution I: Intra-community perspective

	Public		Private
Personal	The scene		Employment outside 'community'
	Gay Liberation Women-only social events	**Lovers**	**Children** Home life
		Ex-lovers *Choice of job*	
Political	*Feminism* Conferences	Collectives	*Lifestyle*

Figure 10:   Spatial/Conceptual Distribution II: Extra-community perspective

	Public		Private
Personal			The scene
	Employment outside 'community'	**Children**	**Lovers** **Ex-lovers**
			Home life
Political	*Choice of job* *Feminism* *Gay liberation*	*Lifestyle*	Women-only venues Collectives Conferences

To take some examples: from the community perspective, the 'scene' is considered part of personal life, but also quite public, though not entirely so; from the extra-community perspective, while the scene is regarded as personal, it is also quite private. For example, many people who have no contact with the community have no idea where the scene is in geographical terms.

A second example: from the internal community perspective, ex-lovers stand virtually in the middle between all four variables – public, private, personal and political, as described earlier. From the extra-community perspective, they are personal and private relationships.

The position of children in the two diagrams represents the above discussion. From inside the community, children stand in a personal/private position; from the external perspective, while children are regarded as personal, they are located somewhat between public and private, partly due to the numerous public institutions involving children – schools, welfare organisations, health care and so on.

Beyond these kinds of divisions, however, there were further crosscutting overlaps between the community and its wider context. One of the most important of these, as already indicated, was ethnic differences, which was one of the axes along which the community was beginning to change.

(f) Difference and change: transformations within the community

Alice's life and perspective provides a brief illustration of the kinds of transformations under way within the community in the late 1980s.

Alice was 31, a black American, and had moved to London in 1982 after spending a short time in Paris. In 1989, she lived in South London with her lover, Joan, a white woman, in a housing association flat, but was going to move soon into a women's housing co-op without Joan, though she and Joan had not broken up. Most of Alice's housing while she was in London was in short-life women's households and the majority of the time she was the only black woman in them.

Mixed race relationships were unusual among lesbian feminists, and although generally approved of, they were also seen as problematic for the couple, and Alice and Joan were no exception. Alice explained that all her 'major, long-term' relationships – she had had six, five with white women, had,

> kept me very much in a kind of limbo world, because of fears and contradictions, both on my part and on the part of my lover, of not having the means to deal with some of the stuff that came up in being an interracial couple. That's changing, thank God. A lot of it also has to do with me, with me learning about racism and how it works, how it actually affects me, and how I'm silenced by it, and how racism is something out there, but it shapes me.
>
> Q. Is that quite a recent change?
>
> A. Yes, because, like with feminism, although I had black politics, I didn't have a rigorous analysis, or I didn't have an analysis that addressed important things in my experience, in the explaining of my experience....Seeing the way things are constructed, for me, makes a very big difference. And now I can practice the theory and the politics

in my own life. So now I know more, I can bring that…into my negotiations with white feminists in the wider community.

Alice's approach thus did not see a contradiction in the *forms* of knowledge which feminism and black politics provided: both, she said, allowed her to see 'the way things are constructed' – in one case with regard to gender, in the other with regard to race. For Alice, the problem with (radical/revolutionary) feminism had been the lack of acknowledgement of the issue of race which she saw after 'learning about racism and how it works'.

Moreover, Alice's comment that the analysis allowed her to see the way things are *constructed* indicates a change in attitude towards identity and its authenticity that was increasingly being expressed by many lesbian feminists. The phrase Alice used implied that all identities are constructions – they are about what a person comes to believe about themselves and others. Identity in this view is a state of knowledge, rather than a state of being. This makes identity look more prone to change and variation between groups than the notion of 'woman-identified-woman' (see Chapter 1). The idea of a 'woman-identified-woman', as it was used during the 1970s and early 1980s, suggested that a removal of patriarchal constructions of femininity would allow women to unearth their 'authentic' selves.

This distinction is explored further in Chapter 6, but its significance here is this: if the formation of the community in the past had been based on notions of 'authentic' identity – whether as a 'woman' or as a 'lesbian' – this new 'politics of difference' was beginning to challenge the reasons for having a community at all. Radical feminist theory did not preclude this new approach, for it had always focused on the socially constructed (and therefore inauthentic) nature of women's identity within patriarchy; but in the past, there had been a strong assertion that beneath the construction, there was something else, something authentic, waiting to emerge when the cloak of patriarchal constructions of femininity (male-identification) was removed. And it was that something authentic which meant all women had something in common, which could serve as the basis for forming a community. The 'politics of difference' cast considerable doubt on that assumption: all identities are constructions.

Once again, changes underway within the community were in practice often expressed in small ways, by women who thought about what different political approaches meant for them personally. Alice discussed what she had gone through in mixed-race relationships, and she said elsewhere that her shift in opinion about feminism (she had been a separatist previously) reflected a continual process of reflexive change in her opinions.

Another black woman, Jo, who worked in a mixed race lesbian organisation, recalled her own difficulty with 'the overwhelmingly white' character of the visible community when she was 'coming out' as a lesbian:

> I didn't see any black lesbians. Lesbians were people I could support – there weren't any I could identify with....I felt very isolated as a black woman when I did come out, as I had nowhere to go. That has changed a lot in the last four years.

Jo had a less forgiving attitude towards white lesbian feminists' than Alice:

> At the end of the day, the real problem for us – for feminism – is how women can have a free sexuality which is free from exploitation on the basis of gender or race or class or for economic reasons. And that is the real problem which revolutionary feminism didn't address at all....My relations with lesbian feminists when I first came out were very antagonistic, because I had this sense of something being missing, and of this arrogance and contempt....I still can't get it out of my head that lesbian feminism is a white term. So at the moment I just see it as something I struggle against, something that is deliberately trying to white out my truth, you know?[47]

Rashida, an Asian lesbian, felt similarly about radical feminism, and said that she hoped

> it isn't being unfair to radical feminists to say radical feminism stresses gender as the basic unit of oppression in society. I feel that different forms of oppression – race, class, gender, disability – are interconnected, and I wouldn't want to prioritise gender in the way radical feminists do.

These kinds of statements illustrate how ethnic minority women frequently felt they were not represented in lesbian feminist space, and as a result they were somewhat suspicious of white lesbian feminists' activities and perspectives. The radical/revolutionary feminist approach of emphasising the 'community of women' and placing a premium on gender identity as *the* cause of oppression made no sense to such women. Their 'personal' did not appear to them to be 'politicised' in lesbian/feminist contexts, but ignored. For that reason, they did not often attend lesbian/feminist events nor join their collectives.

There was also a social aspect to the separation, however. Organising events and groups relied on social 'networking', and since the majority of white lesbian feminists had few if any ethnic minority friends, it was unlikely that ethnic minority women would participate in these activities. Where organisations were wholly or partly run by ethnic minority women – such as LESPOP – there was invariably a greater participation by them than when white women alone organised them. A benefit organised by LESPOP following its loss of funding attracted as many ethnic minority women as white women, whereas the Lesbian Summer School, organised by white women and despite considerable efforts on Anne's part to attract ethnic minority women, was attended by seven, out of 247 participants.

Alice had abandoned lesbian feminist separatism because of its inability to 'deal with differences between women'. She had recently become involved in what revolutionary feminists termed 'libertarianism' – that area of the 'politics of difference' which focused on representations and constructions of sexuality and sexual desire – and was seen as 'anti-feminist' by many lesbian feminists. Alice disagreed, saying she was still a lesbian feminist, but a 'non-aligned' one. Her interest in the 'libertarian' approach (not a term she would use) was an analysis of the construction of difference in sexual relationships between women, and this had motivated a number of ethnic minority women to become involved in the same way. Neither Rashida nor Jo, however, were interested in 'libertarianism' and saw it as a somewhat retrograde development in the community because of its emphasis on sexual practice. They were much more involved in anti-racist activities and black lesbian groups and organisations. All three were interested in 'difference', but where Rashida and Jo concentrated on combating the inequalities generated by differences between women, Alice was more interested in analysing the nature of difference itself.

Alice had had a number of jobs, mostly in offices and libraries doing clerical work, and saw them as a means to earn money while she developed her career in film making. She was also a member of various feminist groups, all of which concentrated on aspects of women in the media and representation of women in film. Her feminist activism, she said, was expressed more on an individual level than in involvement with collectives or groups:

> The most effective way I am an activist, I think, is in the work I produce, or will produce, I hope. My film work. And with that, the screening contexts – my preference is to have discussion and debate

within a screening situation. So, directly or indirectly, film-making is an activist activity. But also, I suppose, in small ways in my everyday life.

Alice's emphasis on the positive use of visual imagery, particularly sexual imagery, in her feminist 'activism' was something common to many women interested in the 'politics of difference', and it contrasted markedly with radical/revolutionary feminist approaches. If visual sexual imagery of women was used at all by radical/revolutionary feminists, it tended to focus on 'hetero-patriarchal', exploitative, violent or denigrating images of women, most especially pornography. Positive sexual images of women were much more frequently described in words, and the use of film and photography by 'libertarians' was a source of considerable tension between radical/revolutionary feminists and 'libertarians' during the late 1980s and early 1990s (see Chapters 5 and 6).

In the 'libertarian' perspective, it is legitimate to explore ways in which different kinds of women's sexed bodies are constructed, and even attempt to re-construct them differently through the use of film and photography. In contrast, in most lesbian feminist approaches, women's sexual bodies, as visible physical entities, were often absent from the feminist frame, being kept in the anti-feminist frame of women's bodies used as exploitation, oppression, abuse, sexual violence. Definitions of women as nothing *but* bodies, and particularly sexual bodies, was regarded as a key hetero-patriarchal construction of femininity. It was thus difficult for many lesbian feminists to imagine how to visually represent women's sexual bodies without reproducing, intentionally or not, hetero-patriarchal constructions about women and femininity. Thus text and speech were, in practice, the key mediums of communication used by separatists to describe positive images of women's sexuality. The constant focus on visual imagery of the sexual female body by 'libertarians' was a key indicator of back-sliding into patriarchy as far as many revolutionary feminists were concerned.

(g) The shape of the community: overlaps, cross-cuts and change

No two women had exactly the same kind of relationship with different parts of the community. Alice did not move in strongly lesbian feminist networks, whereas Nicola and Barbara did. Nicola and Barbara also had overlapping friendship networks. For instance, Ruth was a close friend of Nicola's and was also an ex-lover (and close friend) of Barbara's. Further, Barbara worked with Mandy, who was also a close friend of Nicola's. Alice, though she had connections with Nicola and Barbara's friendship network, especially through Joan, rarely attended the kinds of events they did. Although Alice mixed socially almost exclusively with lesbians, it was in different spheres of the community – media and film groups, 'libertarian' discussion groups, the 'scene' and occasionally a black lesbian group. She had also recently started attending a mixed gender mountaineering group, and a mixed gender 'psychodrama' group. This was a conscious decision, intended to work out new ways to forge coalitions between diverse groups. Nevertheless, she felt her 'community' was located amongst her lesbian friends:

> I do feel I'm a member of a community because I know quite a number of lesbians now. I think it's because of that. And because I participate in certain events...and I feel it's in those discussions, debates and so on that we bring the community into existence – as well as in the bars. So I do feel I'm part of the community.

Again, it was lesbianism that made the community a community for Alice. Even Paula, who 'came out' at the same time as she became a feminist, said that, 'safe space is *lesbian-only* space, not women-only space'. She needed such spaces, she said, because they provided 'a kind of haven from the constant barrage of heterosexuality.'

In summary, the 'space' of the community consisted of several overlapping spheres – symbolically, socially and politically, and there was an uneasy co-existence between them. Sometimes they were physically separated – as in the location of lesbian/gay activity in the 'scene' and the location of lesbian/feminist activity in groups and organisations which met in grant-funded buildings. But many of the pubs also provided places for lesbian/feminist groups to meet and women-only times for social events; and many of the women who used the 'scene' were also members of lesbian feminist collectives. In practice, boundaries were continually being crossed.

Even conceptually, there were overlaps. For most women, there was no absolute division between lesbianism as represented in lesbian/gay space and as represented by lesbian feminism. Neither Nicola nor Alice had completely replaced their previous existence with a new one, intellectually or socially – they added their (continually changing) feminist perspective to their previous 'straight dyke' lifestyles, and somewhat altered their location in the 'community'. But not completely: Nicola did not stop going to the 'scene', she just preferred to go on women-only nights. Their conceptions of themselves as lesbians and as feminists and where they located themselves within the community therefore had multiple layers, and were continually subject to change. Alice was moving into a different part of the community, rethinking her political and personal approach, and her views reflected the trends leading towards the 'coalition politics' familiar today.

There were continual overlaps between women's personal experiences, their interests and their histories, which informed their personal practices and their relations within the community. Women's experiences prior to involvement with the lesbian feminist community obviously had an impact in how women positioned themselves within it. For example, the 'coming out' process gave women a strong sense of the 'authenticity' of lesbianism as a personal identity – it could never be simply a political standpoint, it was also an expression of themselves. Moreover, lesbians' experiences of discrimination in their everyday lives meant that even if they had a lesbian feminist interpretation of lesbianism, which insisted that it was a political gender identity rather than an apolitical personal sexual identity, the 'world out there' did not share that notion. This imposed a concrete division between 'women' and 'lesbians', which constantly affected lesbian feminists in their personal/political and personal/private lives.

Other identities women brought to the community also affected its structure and women's position within it. Alice attended a number of Black women-only groups, Nicola kept in touch with working class friends, Jane attended Jewish lesbian groups, the 'scene' was dominated by gay men; lesbian feminist groups were seen as white, middle class enclaves; I saw working class lesbian feminists more often in 'the scene' than I did in lesbian feminist groups or collectives, and this was true also of ethnic minority women.

Obviously, women's experiences and identities were not only gleaned from the community, the community did not have a single identity to provide, and it was not isolated from wider cultural and socio-economic conditions but was informed by them, and the community was thus a part of them. This point is being emphasised because other studies of lesbian/feminist communities frequently either passed over the issue or suggested a complete break between intra- and extra-community conditions (see Chapter 4).

However, the community itself was also changing – expanding, diversifying, existing in different economic, political and social conditions than it had done in the 1970s – which was reflected in the changes amongst the women interviewed. They were as much a part of these wider changes as anyone else in London. Barbara, amongst the most active of lesbian feminists was becoming a different kind of lesbian feminist than she had been before, was consciously shifting her location within the community, as the community itself was shifting its location. Perceptions and practices were always in a state of becoming, incomplete, and this is how most described their experience of the community.

Having outlined the community in practice, it now remains to take a look at what all this means in terms of various definitions of lesbianism, which have emerged as so central to community life.

5. POLITICAL LESBIANISM

I have suggested that relations between women as *lesbians* was the basis of continuity and of 'belonging' to the 'community', and that the definition of 'lesbian' in different spheres overlapped but were not the same. There was an unclear distinction between the representation of 'lesbian' as the realisation of women's freedom from and/or rebellion against hetero-patriarchy, and the concept of 'lesbian' as a personal sexual identity. Most lesbian feminists in the late 1980s saw it as both.

The 'fuzziness' is partly due to the way lesbianism is discussed in radical/revolutionary feminism: lesbians, whether feminists or not, were often seen as 'political rebels' against society because they rejected sexual relations with men.[48] There did not have to be a conscious feminist motivation in order for lesbians to be acting politically: their actions were feminist, or indicated an underlying disaffection with patriarchal heterosexual relations, which comes to the same thing.

However, there was an uneasy alliance between the notion of 'sexual identity' and 'political standpoint' in this approach. Lesbian feminist theory implied that lesbians were, or became as a result of living as lesbians, more insightful than heterosexual women about the way the 'hetero-patriarchy' oppressed women. This was a form of 'enlightenment versus false consciousness' concept. But in practice, not all lesbians were perceived as being 'enlightened', as in the case of 'S/M dykes', though that did not prevent them from being accepted as 'authentic' lesbians.

Lesbian 'authenticity' was thus experienced as something different from shedding one's false consciousness as a woman. Many women said that although when they first became lesbian *feminists* they believed there was something fundamentally 'political' about being a lesbian, their practical experiences had taught them otherwise. Alice again:

> woman-identified is what I used to think it was, to be lesbian or feminist.... Now I don't think that's necessarily true, because I recently met a lesbian who is very, very lesbian and yet quite male-identified, which I find freaky. I mean, an incredible contradiction....I think I found it

shocking because I know some women who are heterosexual – well, they call themselves bisexual – that I think are more woman-identified than she is. That's something I've had to sort of juggle around in my head over the past few years.

More significantly, lesbian feminist practice as well as experience contradicted theory at times. The suspicion with which 'political lesbians' were regarded was the clearest illustration of this. Lesbian feminist theory suggests that 'political lesbianism' is the main goal: 'political lesbians' are women who regarded themselves as heterosexual, but decided on feminist grounds that this was politically unacceptable within heteropatriarchy, and therefore became lesbians. Yet many lesbian feminists I met expressed their deep suspicion of 'political lesbians', including Nicola:

> To me, 'political lesbian' is a term that is used for a heterosexual woman who thinks she ought to be a lesbian because she's a feminist, but *doesn't feel it*. It has to happen on two levels: it has to happen on a head level *and* a heart level. And I don't want to know [political lesbians].... Until they can say honestly that they feel it in the heart, then they're not lesbians as far as I'm concerned....The bloodiest workshop I ever went to – I think it was in 1980 – was a workshop called 'political lesbianism', and the room divided into gut lesbians and head lesbians.

Charlotte and Jean were the closest I came to meeting any 'political lesbians'. In fact, Jean's political opponents sometimes suggested that Jean was still a 'political lesbian', despite years of living as a lesbian and having had a number of woman lovers. The implication was that Jean had no right to comment on other lesbians' behaviour.

It was here that the differences between lesbian feminist theory and the social construction of the community came most clearly into conflict. Lesbian 'authenticity' excluded 'political lesbians', who presumably would stop being 'lesbians' if their politics changed. In practice, lesbian 'authenticity' was not established through 'public/political' activities, but individually through the 'coming out' process and socially through personal relations with other lesbian feminists. 'Political lesbians' neither went through the 'coming out' process nor had those personal relations because they became lesbians entirely through the 'public/political' sphere. Any attempt to enter the 'personal/private' sphere on political grounds alone was often regarded as insulting. In other words, there was not a complete match between lesbian feminist representations of lesbianism and its meaning to most lesbian feminists in practice, and this was reflected in the separation of the 'public/political' and the 'public/personal' aspects of the 'community'.

In sum, I am arguing it was personal relations based on lesbian 'authenticity' that kept the 'public/political' sphere going between campaigns, which acted as an information network between groups and organisations, and which was the source of the tremendous amount of labour and energy required to carry out political activity with few resources. And yet at the same time feminism informed many personal aspects of the 'community' – the 'personal/political' aspects of domestic life, women-only events and spaces, lack of social contact with men and so on. The two combined factors gave the community its 'shape' for lesbian feminists, which created an underlying uneasy balance between 'authentic' lesbianism and 'public/political' lesbianism.

4 Comparative and Historical Review

I have argued thus far that within the community, there was no single or homogenous 'ideology'. Instead, there were competing and overlapping, sometimes contradictory beliefs, particularly concerning sexual identity and gender identity. Moreover, both the reflexive approach to theory for lesbian feminists and the plural and complex context of the community, full of separations and overlaps – made it difficult to assert that any single conception of gender or sexuality was true – at all times, for all people, in all places. Furthermore, many of these separations and overlaps reflected those existent in the city as a whole.[49]

Having described the general characteristics of the lesbian feminist community in London during the late 1980s, this chapter makes some comparisons across time and space, which highlights what was distinctive about late 1980s London, as well as what was common to other lesbian/feminist communities elsewhere and at other times, exploring the transformation of such communities.

1. COMPARATIVE RESEARCH ON LESBIAN/FEMINIST COMMUNITIES

The six studies of lesbian/feminist 'communities' summarised below are all based in English-speaking cities. In addition, Barnhart's (1975) paper on relationships in a 'lesbian counterculture community' in Portland, Oregon in the early 1970s, Ross's paper (1990) on the experience of the Lesbian Organization of Toronto (LOOT) between 1976 and 1980, and McCoy and Hicks' paper on lesbian feminism in Los Angeles (1979) provide some useful data.[50] Two general overviews, Faderman's (1992) wide-ranging historical study of the development of lesbian communities in the USA during the twentieth century, and Martin and Lyon's (1983) account of their own experience of lesbian/feminism during the 1970s and 1980s in California, also provide useful comparative material.

To my knowledge, there are no lesbian feminist communities of the kind described here outside the Euro-American, Australian and New Zealand contexts, and what little wider anthropological literature exists on homosexuality concentrates on ritualised homosexuality and on men.[51] There is substantial literature on gay men's 'communities',[52] and there have also been some studies on the significance of the urban context for both lesbian and gay communities (e.g. Ettore, 1978 and Castells, 1983, Chapter 14).

(a) Separatism and women's organisations in Christchurch, New Zealand: Michelle Dominy

Dominy's research was conducted between 1979 and 1980 in Christchurch, a small town compared to London (Dominy, 1986, p. 275). Her study focused on gender identities, and she only peripherally referred to the significance of lesbianism as a sexual identity for lesbian feminists. For her, the lesbian feminist community was informed solely by lesbian feminism, which was interchangeable with separatism (*ibid.*, p. 97). In contrast, London lesbian feminists distinguished between separatism, seen as a practice, and lesbian feminism, seen as an ever-changing theory based on experience, which may or may not lead to being separatist in practice.[53]

Dominy's overall research compared three contrasting types of women's groups and networks: 'traditionalist', 'reformist' and 'separatist'. Her aim was to 'study women's gender conceptions as reflected in political behaviour and ideology' (1983, p. 224). The distinction between separatists and reformists for Dominy was that separatists had a 'biological' view of the male-female gender dichotomy (as did 'traditionalists'), whereas 'reformists' had a social constructionist view (pp. 31–33). This contrasts with my own findings and those of Ponse (see below). An *essential* difference between men and women was asserted by London lesbian feminists, but this is not the same as asserting that the difference is biological.

Dominy only used the term 'community' with reference to separatists, which is worth noting, as they were the only all-lesbian group she studied. Her description of separatist practice was located almost wholly in the household, and she divided separatists into 'visionaries' and 'activists'. 'Visionaries' were interested in feminist spirituality, myths of matriarchies, white witchcraft, and so on – 'those who "drop out" and attempt to achieve freedom from oppression by creating an alternative women's culture' (1983, p. 92). 'Activists' were interested in disruption – 'those who "stir up"....An activist stance demands that women politicize not just themselves but others' (*ibid*).

This again contrasts with London, where 'visionaries' (generally known as 'matriarchalists' or 'witches' in London) were not evident in lesbian feminist collectives or groups. Although some women were 'witches', they were neither separatists nor 'matriarchalist' witches and they separated being witches from their involvement in the community. I was only peripherally aware of the existence of feminist covens. Most radical/ revolutionary feminists I met were dismissive of witchcraft and 'matriarchalism', seeing it as escapist.

In further contrast to Dominy's findings, lesbian feminists' intra-community and extra-community activities in London did not divide into different categories of *people* so much as different spheres of activity. For example, ROW was an organisation which was, for the most part, outward-directed; the Archive was, for the most part, inward-directed. Both contained committed lesbian feminists who involved themselves in both spheres in different contexts, and neither organisation was spiritualist or matriarchalist.

(b) Lesbian feminists in a southwest USA city – Denyse Lockard

Lockard's research concentrated more on lesbian 'space' than feminist 'space', though she suggested that 'the shared values and norms of the lesbian subculture' were 'synonymous with feminist values' (1985, p. 86). She studied a lesbian community during the early 1980s in a small southwest USA city. The women were white, college-educated and mostly in their 20s or 30s.

Whereas Dominy concentrated on gender conceptions, Lockard's interest was the community and its structure. She defined it as having four features:

> It consists of the interacting social networks of lesbians, who share a group identity or consciousness based on their sexual preference along with certain basic values, and who gather together to create and maintain institutions that support their social interaction, and which also serve to support the group identity and shared values. (Lockard, 1985, p. 89)

Lockard suggests that these women were not particularly politically active, which was, 'due in part to the conservative atmosphere of the city and state' (p. 90). This clearly contrasts with London – which, while being fairly conservative in the late 1980s, also had a recent history of socialist local government, and anyway was quite big enough to incorporate a whole variety of political perspectives. Additionally, Lockard's concentration on the lesbian sphere as a whole, which appeared to include a large number of 'straight dykes', rather than lesbian feminists specifically may have given a less 'political' impression to her findings than my own study.

(c) Lesbian feminists in San Francisco – Deborah Goleman Wolf

Wolf's study was conducted earlier than Dominy's or Lockard's – 1972 to 1974 – in San Francisco, which had (and still has) a reputation for containing one of the largest lesbian/gay communities in the world. As a city, Wolf's context was thus closer to that of London, and the early date of the study provides useful comparisons with London lesbian feminists' reports of their own experience of that period.

Although Wolf studied what she termed the 'lesbian feminist community' (1979, p. 11), she described lesbianism as an 'affectional orientation', and did not distinguish this from the redefinition of the term in lesbian feminist theory. This is not altogether surprising, as lesbian feminist theory had hardly developed by then, and was certainly not yet widely known.

Wolf reports that during the early 1970s, separatists were a small minority of lesbian feminists in San Francisco, and unfortunately, she does not discuss them in detail. She argues, rather confusingly, that separatism developed *because* lesbians wished to disassociate themselves from 'political lesbians' (*ibid*, p. 67). This interpretation of separatism – a separation of 'authentic' lesbians from 'political lesbians', rather than a separation from men – is not one I have seen elsewhere.

Wolf presents an image of a cohesive and ideologically unified community which was developing an alternative culture of women, and whose ultimate goal was a 'socialist matriarchy' (*ibid*, p. 170). This again starkly contrasts with London in the late 1980s, where the community did not have any generally agreed goals for the future of society, and where both socialism and matriarchalism were rejected by most lesbian feminists. However, her description does sound a little more like my interviewees' descriptions of the 1970s period – communal living, a lack of clear distinction between socialism and radicalism, a desire for cohesion and so on.

Wolf further refers to the lesbian feminism of the period as a 'world view' consisting of 'a system of classification of people and relationships that makes a shared social reality possible' (*ibid*, p. 169). This once again contrasts with the late 1980s in London, but had some resemblances to descriptions of the earlier period. In the late 1980s, lesbian feminism was seen less as the source of a 'shared social reality' and more as a means to gain individual autonomy through political action, both in the private and public spheres. The shifts in attitude across the years – particularly regarding the relationship between the individual and the social within lesbian feminist thought – becomes very clear when comparing it to Wolf's material.

(d) Lesbians and lesbian feminists in London – E. M. Ettore

Ettore's research also provides some historical comparisons from the 1970s, but unlike Wolf, Ettore takes a socialist perspective. Her study was conducted between 1973 and 1977 in London, but unlike my own study, she concentrated on the 'scene' aspect of the community, and not the more specifically lesbian feminist aspects.

Ettore argues that lesbians, by demonstrating an existence independent of men, and by confusing the categories of men as producers and women as reproducers, would, once they gained a 'political consciousness', mark the beginning of revolutionary change in society (Ettore, 1980, pp. 30–31). Lesbianism, Ettore suggests, 'challenges the total structure of society and exposes all types of oppression within the whole gamut of possible social relationships'.[54]

Ettore focused on women she termed 'social lesbians' or 'pre-political lesbians' – women who had some feminist perspectives, but were not strongly politically committed. She made no reference to their involvement in lesbian/feminist collectives. These kinds of women were termed 'straight dykes' by lesbian feminists during the late 1980s.

Ettore's concentration on the (socialist) revolutionary potential of 'social lesbians' makes comparison difficult. Although some radical feminist lesbians were mentioned, she discussed radical feminism very briefly (pp. 145 and 161) and suggested their approach was unrealistic. She defined a radical feminist as a 'feminist who sees women's oppression as a result of the biological divisions between men and women' (p. 191), a definition which has more affinity with the perspective of those against lesbian feminism than those in favour of it, reflecting perhaps Ettore's own disaffection with radical feminism or separatism. She suggests that separatists are 'anti-feminist' because they deny class as an essential aspect of women's oppression (p. 150), and 'chauvinists' because they separate themselves from women as a whole and deny an historical perspective (pp. 128–129). Ettore saw the community as being in a 'state of becoming', but separatists were not 'becoming' in the correct direction.

Although Ettore, unlike most socialist feminists, placed primary importance on lesbianism as a political force, her argument has many of the elements which caused conflicts between lesbian feminists and socialist feminists discussed in Chapter 3 – particularly concerning the causes of women's oppression and Ettore's suggestion that in the end, the 'revolution' had to include men. In this respect, Ettore's study can be seen as part of the 'public/political' debate existent within the 'community' in London, in addition to providing comparative information.

(e) Lesbian feminists in a northwestern USA city – Barbara Ponse

Ponse's study was conducted in the early to mid-1970s in an unspecified city in northwestern USA. She concentrated on lesbianism rather than feminism, though she did discuss both feminism and gay liberation.

Ponse had a social interactionist approach and was interested in 'the construction and maintenance of lesbian identity' (Ponse, 1978, p. 9). For her, different representations of sexuality existent within the community all acted as a means for lesbians to cope with the stigma attached to lesbianism: either by arguing lesbianism is no different from heterosexuality (the homophile argument), that it is better than heterosexuality (the gay liberation argument), or that it is an escape from patriarchy (the feminist argument). Ponse suggested that lesbian feminists,

> in asserting the primacy of gay identity...develop and emphasize the rhetorics of oppression as an explanation for the difficulty in accepting the gay self. (*ibid*, p. 108)

Unlike either Dominy or Ettore, Ponse argues that lesbian feminist approaches to gender, based on her study, were social constructionist rather than biologically determinist (*ibid.*, p. 100). And also unlike Ettore, Ponse concentrated on the significance of lesbianism for the individual. She argues that individuals define themselves, rather than being defined, and that lesbianism is an actor's social construction which uses information available to her (be it from friends, relatives, the media, religion, law, the community, political ideologies, books or prejudice), and changes over time.

Ponse thus concentrates on lesbian 'authenticity', arguing that both wider society and the 'lesbian world' defines lesbianism in terms of a 'moral essence – a quality that pervades and defines the whole person' (p. 39). However, Ponse argues that this is a fabrication: 'In reality, the self, sexuality, and identity change over the course of time' (p. 172).

In this respect, Ponse differed from the other studies, which suggested a constant meaning to the term 'lesbian'. Her approach draws attention to different representations of sexuality, associating them with different groups:

The lesbian world is composed of many different kinds of groups, some bonded together for reasons of sociability and others grouped together by a shared interest in various political philosophies, such as gay activism, feminism, radicalism and separatism. (Ponse, 1978, p. 18)

Despite this, Ponse concluded that the 'lesbian world' had a particular 'paradigm' (p. 17) and possessed a cohesive 'group identity' resulting in 'a complex and distinctive lesbian subculture' (p. 89).

(f) Lesbian feminists in a small midwestern USA town – Susan Krieger

Krieger's study, conducted in the late 1970s, concentrated on a group of about 60 lesbian feminists known as a community in a small suburban town in mid-western USA. She described the community as, 'a loose-knit social group composed primarily of lesbians' (1983, p. ix). Krieger noted that all the women were white, middle-class and well-educated, most being involved with the local university.

Krieger's interest concerned the conflict between autonomy and community. She saw it as a conflict involving personal identity, summarising her position in her introduction:

The community...presented a basic identity conflict to members and potential members. On the one hand, it promised them that, within it, they would be affirmed for who they *truly and fully* were. Here they might find haven from the outside world, acceptance not available elsewhere, and confirmation of crucial feelings they had about themselves, feelings related to their lesbianism, their feminism and their identification as women. On the other hand, in this community, they could often feel that their differences from others were not valued, their own unique identities given little recognition or room. The community, in other words, would often seem to threaten their selfhood. (Krieger, 1983, p. xii, emphasis added)

Krieger thus argues that conflict occurred because of *similarity*, not difference, in direct contrast to my own findings. The women were so alike that their individuality was threatened: 'the basic struggle with likeness...lies at the heart of the community's reality' (p. xvi). This was not only because all the women had similar socio-economic backgrounds, but also because they shared the same lesbian feminist perspective, concentrating on that aspect which denied difference.

Krieger's study echoes descriptions of London lesbian feminists' involvement in particular groups or organisations, rather than the 'community' as a whole. It also sounds more akin to London women's experiences in the late 1970s and early 1980s, when the community was smaller and less diverse, than the late 1980s. Women in London involved with central London WAVAW during the early to mid-1980s especially reflected this view. For example, Charlotte:

> In Central London WAVAW there was an incredible revolutionary feminist stranglehold...in the world in which I moved, as opposed to the world in which I'd occasionally put my oar in – the socialist feminist world – I felt in the heart of it. WAVAW was my life, really. I was completely absorbed in it. A couple of meetings a week, a picket at the weekend. I socialised with those women who lived and ate male violence, really. My lover at the time, it used to drive her potty.

However, even in these earlier descriptions, there were constant references to relations with other groups, as Charlotte's comments indicates: she occasionally put her 'oar in' the 'socialist feminist world', and her lover was a socialist feminist. And although Krieger describes interrelations between the 'community' and the lesbian 'scene', she suggests that they constituted distinct and separate 'communities', rather than different spheres of one 'community'.

This is not merely a semantic point: the basis of my argument that lesbian feminists in London in the late 1980s did *not* constitute a 'subculture' rests on it. Most lesbian feminists felt that diverse parts of the community were still sections of 'their' community, even though they did not interact with all sections, and were even hostile towards some. The most general boundary of the community was a line between lesbian and non-lesbian spheres of London. This line was not created by lesbian feminists alone, but had been continuously negotiated over the years: partly by dominant understandings of both sexuality and gender, partly by a variety of gay rights campaigns, partly by wider 'anti-establishment' and 'alternative/transgressive' political movements of various types from the 1960s onwards, and partly by lesbian feminism of various hues. It was not a single line marking a homogenous community. This is the point I have been making throughout: the women within the London lesbian/feminist community were as much Londoners as they were lesbian feminists; were as much members of the lesbian and gay community as they were members of the lesbian feminist community; lines and boundaries were being crossed continually, and thus different spheres informed others in an on-going negotiation.

2. SIMILARITIES BETWEEN COMMUNITIES

A summary of the comparison between the communities reveals some interesting points about the different aspects of community life.

(a) Spaces and places

Where spatial location was mentioned in the studies, communities were scattered within an urban area and were not intentionally territorial.[55] As in London, lesbian feminists elsewhere tended to live where they could afford to live, and this meant poorer areas of the city, often containing high proportions of ethnic minorities.[56]

Castells suggests this contrasts with gay men in San Francisco, due to three factors: lesbians establish 'social and interpersonal networks' rather than territories, lesbians are poorer than gay men and 'their politics is less directed towards the established political system' (Castells, 1983, p. 140).

This is an interesting point: it could be that lesbians feminists' political perspective, as well as their wider economic and structural positions as women, tended to dictate against centralised, organised, residential areas.

The use of squats was only mentioned by Ettore, and this may have been a specifically London (or British) phenomenon, though collective households were frequently mentioned.[57] The relatively low levels of income for lesbians was a general finding, contrasting with conditions for gay men, whose levels of income were often high.[58]

Collectives were the major form of 'public/political' organisation in all studies considering lesbian feminists, and the existence of women's and lesbian discussion groups, political groups, conferences, study groups, bookshops, gay bars, clubs, women's centres and so on were also commonly noted.[59]

The impermanence of venues and organisations was commonly mentioned, and overlaps with other groups or 'communities' were noted by Ettore, Dominy, Ponse, Lockard and Krieger. Lockard (p. 93) and Wolf (p. 90) further referred to 'burn-out' experienced by women who had been centrally involved in lesbian feminist organisations for some time.

(b) Social relations

All the studies described social relations as overlapping networks of friends, and most suggested that friendships were particularly important. Some specifically referred to friendship networks and relationships as forms of fictive kinship or alternatives to the 'traditional' heterosexual family.[60] All noted that lover relationships were relatively short-lived and most discussed an ambivalence about lover relationships.[61] Maintaining friendships with ex-lovers was also noted, but this was not related by the researchers to the structure of the 'community'.[62] This could be due to the fact that women lived in collective households much more often than lesbian feminists in my own study, which gave the appearance of no separate spheres in women's lives, especially as the studies paid little attention to employment (with the exceptions of Ettore and Krieger) or childcare (with the exceptions of Wolf and Krieger).

(c) Representational battles and conflicts

Despite all of the studies' assertions of (at least potential) social and intellectual unity, there were frequent references to conflicts, which often formed a central part of lesbian feminist's lives.[63]

Lockard suggests that impermanence of venues and organisations was partly the result of political conflicts, describing how the survival of one club was threatened 'by conflicts among women of varying lifestyles it attracted as members, and differences of opinion about the way it was run' (p. 90). Wolf briefly mentioned two collective disputes, one involving power imbalances between collective members and volunteers, and the other a dispute over race – confirming that the issue of differences between women which cross-cut gender goes back a long way within such communities.

Ettore discussed conflicts between a whole range of groups – separatists and non-separatists, gay liberationists and lesbian feminists, and socialist lesbians and lesbian feminists (1980, Chapter 6). However, in contrast my argument, Ettore suggests this was a passing phase, and expected that over time, the contradictions would be dialectically resolved, producing a cohesive perception of the links between feminism and lesbianism (1980, p. 146). This synthesis had not occurred by the late 1980s, and is highly unlikely, for several reasons. Firstly, the importance of lesbianism as a personal/private identity, whatever else it politically represented, did not decline; secondly, the experience-based rather than analytical approach to theory encouraged an emphasis on difference, not unity; thirdly, the existence of several definitions of lesbianism within different spheres of the 'community' dictated against any one gaining dominance; and fourthly, the lack of isolation of the 'community', the constant interaction with the rest of London, and the continual appearance of new women, many of whom were not familiar with lesbian feminist arguments, discouraged any one perspective from being accepted as the only 'truth'. In fact, the trend

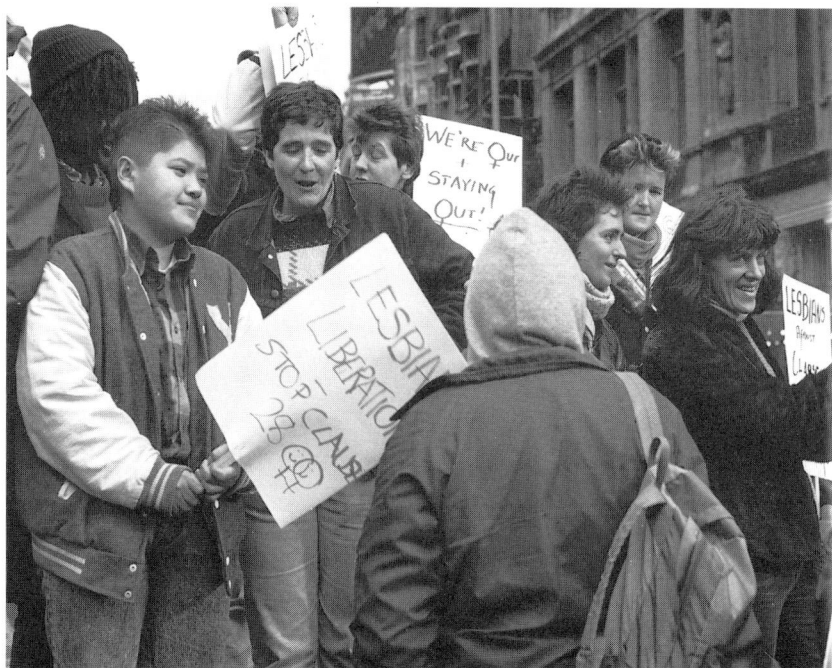

Plates 1. and 2.

Demonstration organised by Lesbians against the Clause held at Piccadilly Circus on 1 February 1988, a day before the abseiling incident. These two photographs show some of the slogans used during the campaign. Note the use of the labyrs (bottom right, plate 2) and the interlinked Venus symbol.

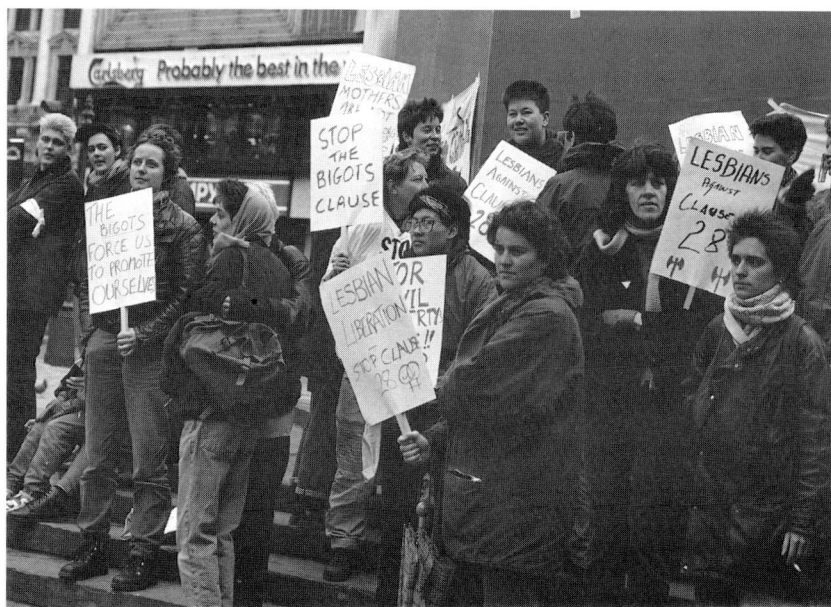

3. (right) A bemused police officer happens on the demonstration while on his beat. He has just been handed a leaflet by one of the demonstrators. There was no formal police attendance at the demonstration, as the police were not notified of the event in advance.

4. (below) The placard in the centre is making a reference to the 'pretended family relationship' section of the clause. The placard reads 'Lesbian (non-nuclear) Family Relationships: We're not Pretending.'

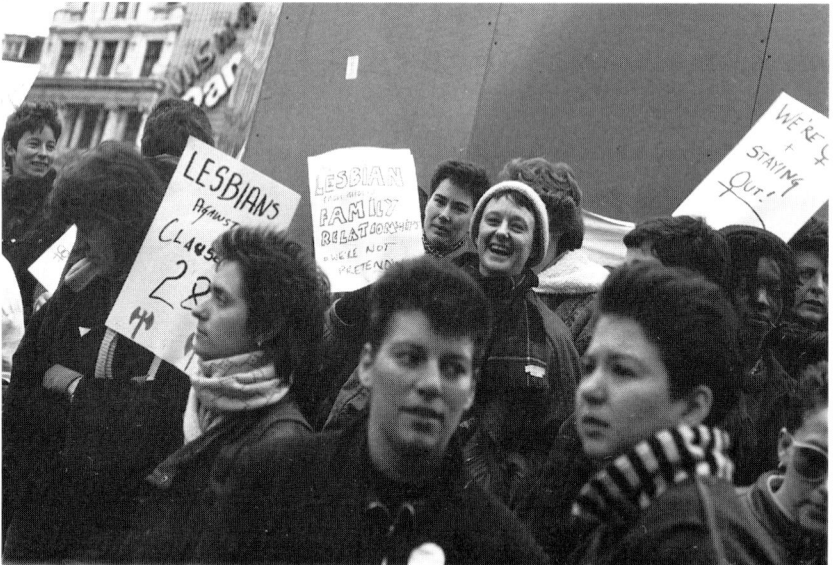

Aspects of Style: Lesbian Strength March, Summer 1988

Plates 5. and 6.   Examples of the styles worn by lesbian feminists: trousers, casual tops and short haircuts.

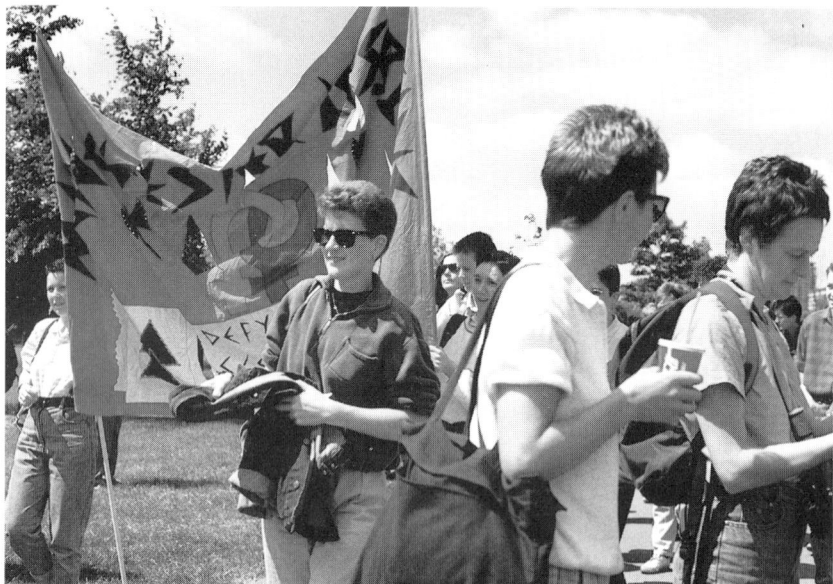

7. (above) Variations on a common theme of hairstyle worn by lesbian/feminists. Compare with Plate 8 (below) examples of some younger women's hairstyles, frequently much more varied than the ones above. Note the woman in the background with plaits and pink hairdye on a portion of her hair. Such styles are often associated with 'libertarians' and 'baby dykes' (cf. Chapter 6).

9. A woman wearing one version of 'S/M gear' at the beginning of the march. Note the zippers and knuckledusters with studs. There are two women looking at her: the one on the far left (partially concealed) is also wearing 'S/M gear'; her shirt has studs, leather straps and a chain attached to it. The woman on the right of her is looking on with some measure of disapproval.

10. A group of 'S/M dykes' with their banner (note the chain links on it), standing by the marchers, as they were banned from participating. As this was a hot day, many had left their leather 'S/M gear' at home. Note the LESPOP steward in the front, who is ensuring that no conflicts occur between the marchers and the S/M group.

11. A mixed anti-Clause 28 march. Note the predominance of men and the presence of a number of women with longer hairstyles than usually seen at marches attended by lesbian feminists.

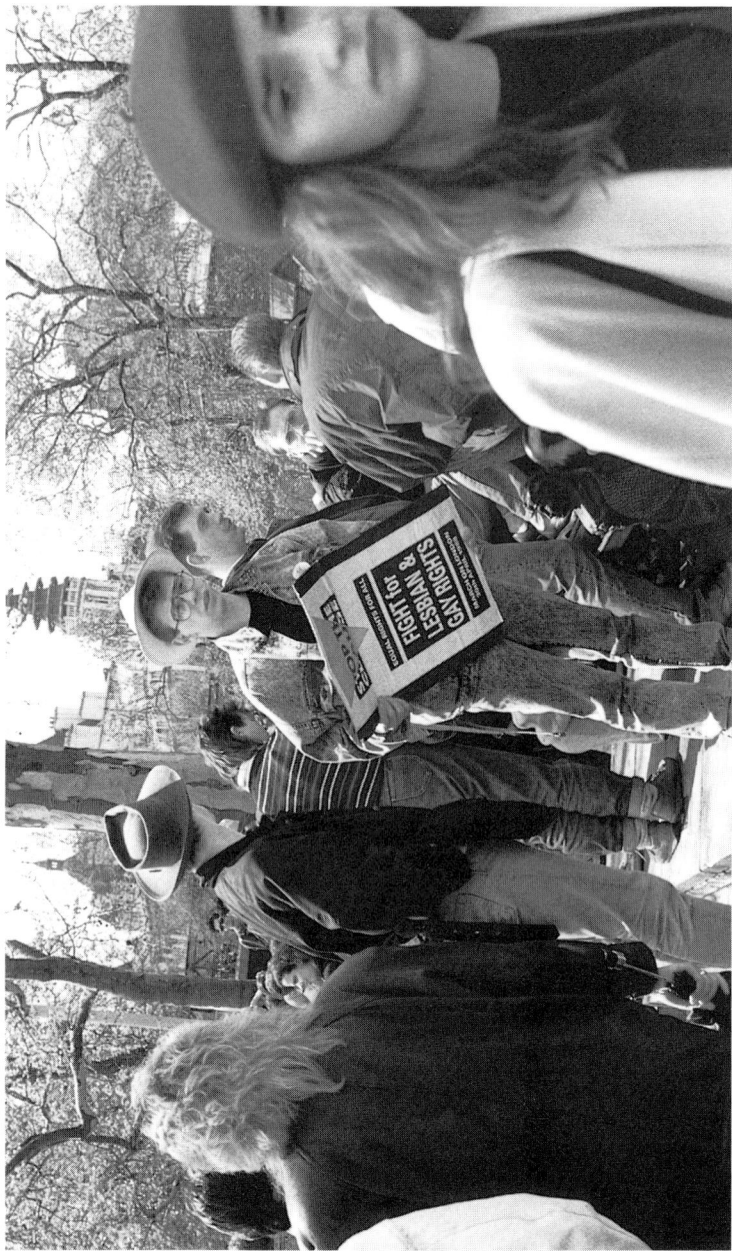

12. A mixed anti-Clause 28 march.

has been in the opposite direction: no unitary politics, no cohesive ideology, but instead fragmentation followed by temporary coalitions and a 'radical doubt' about the 'truth' of any paradigm.

Conflicts were also discussed in Ponse's account of different meanings of homosexuality. The term 'lesbian', for example, was seen by lesbian feminists as 'a total life-style and solidarity with the women's community' (p. 111), whereas for 'traditionalists' ('straight dykes') it constituted an 'ontological status' (p. 110). However, the term 'gay' referred to both an ontological status and described 'the subculture, persons, life-styles, communities, relationships, places and situations' (p. 113). It is clear that a conflict between lesbian feminist and gay liberationist representations were being expressed here.

Krieger also discussed conflicts, this time between 'bar women' and lesbian feminists involving lesbian feminists' rejection of 'butch-femme' role play. For example, Krieger quoted one informant's experience:

> Mike [a woman] would come up to Lisa and put her arm around her and say, "You're my woman." Political women didn't do that. Also, bar women had this way of showing affection: 'Don't be touching my woman or I'm going to whip your ass', a bar woman would say. You wouldn't find a political woman doing that. (p. 135)

However, Krieger saw 'bar dykes' and lesbian feminists as entirely distinct groups, as did Barnhart, who suggested that 'counterculture lesbians' (apparently a mixture of lesbian feminist and gay liberationist lesbians) 'disparagingly saw the "butch/femme" or noncounterculture lesbians as people who "play roles."' (Barnhart, 1975, p. 94).

Ross, discussing a conference organised by a coalition of feminist groups in Toronto, described how it 'degenerated into a bitter shouting match. An eventual stalemate arose largely between socialist feminists...and radical lesbian feminists' (Ross, 1990, p. 84).

Ross also described how a radical lesbian feminist perspective developed at LOOT, which led to numerous battles:

> Against a narrow standard of politically allowable behaviour, butch/femme role playing and lesbian bar culture more generally were spurned....Prostitution, bisexuality, and gay male sexuality (particularly its 'public' and 'anonymous' forms) were all subject to harsh criticism. Mothers, especially those with boy children, were either overtly scorned or simply made to feel unwelcome. [p. 80]...the socialists and the gay liberationists were amongst the first to leave. (p. 83)

'Narrowness' of perspective is often mentioned when lesbian feminists or separatists are discussed. McCoy and Hicks, in a paper on the lesbian feminist 'community' in Los Angeles, noted the frequent conflicts amongst lesbian feminists themselves:

> Those who came to narrowly define a lesbian-feminist mode in terms of 'acceptable' lifestyle, dress, thought and behaviour, or those who drew sharp political lines in their world view, came to be known as 'radicals' those who drew softer, less sharply defined lines in shaping and defining lesbian-feminist politics were identified with labels of denigration such as 'liberal' or 'bourgeois.' An atmosphere of fear began to permeate the community, a fear of being 'trashed' for not being 'politically correct.' Being outcast by the community was a very high price to pay...(McCoy and Hicks, 1979, p. 66)

This description matched those of London lesbian feminists for the late 1970s/early 1980s. In retrospect, the repeated complaints about the 'narrowness' of lesbian feminism indicated the direction of the debate: 'narrowness' meant a denial of personal autonomy and differences between women, an over-emphasis on sameness as the basis for the political project.

This is crucially different from the argument that separatism did not take adequate account (for example) of race. That criticism was based on the argument that some women's experiences were *excluded* from the analysis, which is different from saying that separatism prevents women (all women) from being able to express their own individuality. Faderman succinctly described this shift in opinion in the USA:

> ...separatism had failed to speak to all of the lesbian's complexity. Separatism came to be identified with bigotry by some lesbians because it 'judged people by gender...rather than as *individuals.*' (1992, p. 193, emphasis added)

The way in which things changed now comes out in clear relief. In the early 1970s, there was a belief in the possibility, and more importantly, the *desirability* of unity, but there was never a period without conflicts. This was partly because of the inherent tensions within lesbian feminism of balancing between the individual and the social (autonomy and difference versus community and sameness), but also because lesbian feminists shared their community with 'straight dykes' and gay liberationists (and many had themselves been either or both before), and because that community was socio-economically and ethnically heterogenous. Both theory and practice dictated against there being any extensive commonality amongst these women.

(d) Intellectual ambivalences

The explicit conflict between autonomy and community emerged in several of the studies, and I have already discussed Krieger. Dominy also stated that, 'the ideology provides an explicit contradiction between its anti-individualistic stance and simultaneous rejection of defining the self relative to others', (p. 108). Dominy suggests the aim was to develop an alternative women's culture, but that the contradictions made it difficult. For example, she describes separatists' art as 'part of an *emerging* shared culture and shared body of knowledge' (p. 106, my emphasis), but added that

> Lodged within an alternative community is the meaning of self, and yet that community is ephemeral, constantly shifting its ideology and providing ideological contradictions...while offering no clear vision of the future for its adherents. (p. 108)

This suggests that, as in London, Christchurch separatists did not *unambiguously* desire an alternative 'culture' or 'community', did not live within one, and did not in fact have an 'emerging' cohesive ideology. Moreover, I have suggested that in London, 'the meaning of self' was not 'lodged within an alternative community', but that both community and the 'self' were part of the culture in which they exist. I agree here with Faderman that Euro-American cultures during this century provided 'the wherewithal to create communities and lifestyles such as never before existed' (1992, p. 307).

Several studies also mentioned hostility between 'political lesbians' and 'authentic' lesbians, but did not relate this to a conflict between the lesbian feminist definition of lesbianism (a gender identity) and the notion of 'authentic lesbianism' (a sexual identity). Ettore, as already discussed, saw all such tensions as a passing phase, but nevertheless noted that,

> Real lesbians were lesbians prior to the time when lesbianism became a political choice or 'fashionable' within the women's movement. Political lesbianism, as an alternative, threatened their position as real lesbians. (pp. 145–146)

Ponse also noted a hostility towards 'political lesbians', quoting one interviewee that she 'felt used by those kinds of women because they weren't *really* gay women' (p. 123, my emphasis).

It is easy to draw parallels here with the communist movements of the 1970s: similar complaints were made about middle class communists emulating working class accents and lifestyles in order to experience class

oppression. But giving up privilege voluntarily can be difficult to stomach
for those feeling they had no choice in the matter.

3. SUMMARY OF COMPARISONS

A picture emerges from these studies, spanning the period from 1972 to
1984, of lesbian feminists as a group in a state of 'becoming', women
working towards an alternative culture, yet they were also unhappy about
the 'community' imposing new 'rules' upon them. There was a strong
emphasis on egalitarianism, yet there were difficulties with the negation of
differences between women this implied. There was an overwhelming
concern, especially in the American studies, with personal identity – its
discovery, meaning, construction, alteration, de-stigmatisation.

There was an impermanence about lesbian/feminist venues and organisations. The 'community' meant many things, but lesbian identity was
always a condition of membership. Uniformly, there was a suspicion of
'political lesbians' and an assertion of 'authentic' lesbianism. Life outside
the community (most often at work or in heterosexual company) was seen
as less 'authentic' than life inside the community.[64]

Friends were important, and were often seen as alternative to kin. But
there was also a tension over lover relationships, which were explicitly
seen as negating independence and 'aping' heterosexual marriage, and
anti-community. Ex-lovers frequently stayed friends, and it was often
asserted that they should do.

None of the studies suggested *why* long-term relationships were seen as
'anti-community'. A reason is needed, as marriage in most communities is
not regarded as anti-community – on the contrary. I suggest it was because
the lesbian feminist part of the community was a community of *women*
informed by feminism. Even though lover relationships did not involve
men, the 'personal/private' character of long-term relationships threatened
to remove the couple from the 'public/political' sphere, to put them back
in the 'home'. This tension may not have been as clear in the other studies,
where the division between 'domestic' and 'public' was not as obvious as
it was in late 1980s London.

Several things present in late 1980s London were missing from the
other studies. From Martin and Lyon's account of changes between 1972
and 1982 in San Francisco, many were historical changes also occurring in
the USA (1983, Chapter 11). There was, first, lack of concern over ethnicity in the earlier period, which accords with London lesbian feminists'
reports that race became a major issue in feminist circles after the 1980s.

Second, there was no discussion of external funding for organisations. The GLC and London Labour boroughs' financial support for lesbian/feminist organisations seems to have been unique.

Third, an absence of conflicts between radical/revolutionary feminists and 'libertarians' on issues of lesbian sexual practice and pornography. Although 'libertarians' were relatively new to London during the late 1980s, they had appeared, under various labels, in the USA at least since 1982, the date of the Barnard Conference.[65] And Faderman identifies the conflict between lesbian feminists and 'sex radicals', as she calls them, as being at the centre of disputes which existed in American lesbian/feminist communities during the 1980s (Faderman 1992, Chapter 10).

Fourth, and connected with the last point, an absence of 'S/M dykes' or any debate about their existence in lesbian/feminist communities. In fact, Ponse suggested that one of the distinctions between lesbians and gay men was the absence of 'S/M' in the lesbian 'community' (p. 103). In London, informants suggested that lesbian 'S/M' did not arise as an issue until the early 1980s. Again, Martin and Lyon noted a parallel development in San Francisco (*op. cit.*, p. 299).[66] This does not necessarily mean that 'S/M dykes' did not exist before, but it does suggest that they were not as visible and did not pose a public threat for lesbian feminists in earlier years.[67]

Finally, an absence of lesbian feminists who had fundamentally altered their perspective. In late 1980s London, women were continually reassessing their perspective, and explicitly said this was central to their feminist approach.

In sum, the communities described in earlier studies were smaller and less diverse than in London, and experienced fewer antagonisms. By the late 1980s, earlier lesbian feminist perspectives had been challenged, most particularly over the issue of 'difference'. This development was also paralleled in Toronto, according to Ross:

[T]he 1980s have heralded the subdivision of activist lesbians into specialized groupings: lesbians of colour, Jewish lesbians, working-class lesbians, leather dykes, lesbians against SM, older lesbians, lesbian youth, disabled lesbians and so on. All of these groups sport their own particular brand of identity politics...(Ross, 1990, p. 88)

The belief in 'sisterhood' (the universal 'woman') had not only gone in such communities by the late 1980s, it was increasingly seen as a flawed notion.

However, even in the earlier periods there were ambivalences, and this is where my disagreement with other interpretations of lesbian feminist communities lies. The conflicts in London, rather than representing 'growing pains', *characterised* existence within the 'community'. The community was permanently incomplete, involving continual negotiations between different constituencies. Once again, Faderman concurs with this view, saying that there has been:

> ...constant metamorphoses in the conception of lesbianism and the nature of lesbian communities and lifestyles. Circumstances and events that once seemed inextricably a part of lesbian culture and even of the definition of lesbianism itself have constantly come and gone throughout this century. (Faderman 1992, p. 307)

This continual flux was not only the result, as Faderman suggests, of wider social and economic changes affecting lesbian/feminist communities, but also involved a deeper conceptual problem: the conflict between the desire for a 'community' and a desire for autonomy, and the continued importance of *both* gender identity and sexual identity in different spheres of women's lives. The studies reviewed here tended to reify the 'community' as a 'thing', which exerted pressure on women. I would suggest it was not a 'thing' but an idea.[68] The 'community' could only reflect lesbian feminists' motivations, which were complex and changed over time, they were occasionally contradictory and not always informed by lesbian feminism.

Furthermore, there was no clear break between wider cultural conditions and those in the 'community' – they each informed one another. The conflicts involving autonomy versus community have long been recognised as central dichotomies within Euro-American culture and philosophy in general. These conflicts were therefore not 'counter-cultural' at all. The existence of lesbian feminists is one aspect of the wider 'culture', an expression and reflection of concepts and perceptions generated by it, rather than something separate from it. The 'community' was not producing an *alternative* culture so much as a 'space', both physical and intellectual, in which the taken-for-grantedness of existence was removed.[69]

The result, by the late 1980s in London, was a continual questioning of ideas. The difference between the earlier period and the late 1980s was that in the earlier period, it was still accepted that *some* essential truth must be unearthed. There was later serious doubt about this, which, when combined with ethnic and socio-economic differences between women, created a situation in which no single 'alternative culture' could emerge.

The implication of this argument is that lesbian feminists in London did not live in a 'community' as the word is commonly understood. Sometimes, lesbian feminists themselves denied its existence, as Barbara suggested:

I don't think there is a community, really. It's too anonymous, scattered and fragmented for it to be a community.

These doubts were not restricted to London. For example, for San Francisco, Martin and Lyon asked (without answering) why lesbians 'have been unable to develop a sense of unity' (1983, p. 296). Furthermore, Diana Fuss noted that intellectual changes in both gay liberation theory and feminist theory were tending towards a postmodernist 'deconstruction' of the basis upon which the 'community' had been built.[70]

What kind of 'community' was this, then? What kind of community is it where members sometimes deny its existence and have an ambivalent attitude towards it; that has no fixed or bounded spatial location, no taken-for-granted assumptions about itself, no single ethnic identity, no permanent kinship links, no nationalism, no religion, no undisputed history or myths, no spatial, material or intellectual permanence, a high degree of fragmentation, and which appeared to be based on antagonistic conflict about representations of community space and the meanings of concepts – most especially the meaning of identity, apparently the very reason for there being a community in the first place?

I have argued that this confused expression of community was an outcome of the occasionally contradictory variety of representations within it, combined with the inability and disinclination to be isolated from the wider cultural context. Repeatedly, I have drawn attention to the separations and overlaps between gender identity and sexual identity. I will briefly consider the historical emergence of these two key concepts and how they came to co-exist in the same community 'space', before concluding with some discussion of the concepts of 'community' used in other studies.

4. A BRIEF HISTORY

The connection between feminism and lesbianism current in the 1980s did not exist in early twentieth century feminism.[71] This is not to say that no earlier feminists were lesbians, but that 'first wave' feminism was not connected, either theoretically or socially, with the lesbian and gay 'subcultures' of the day.[72] Furthermore, the representations of lesbianism within these early gay 'subcultures' did not inform lesbian feminism, but have been strongly repudiated.

This separation is reflected in historical research on the different spheres. The emergence of gay 'subcultures' and homosexual 'identity' has been studied by gay activists and gay liberation historians,[73] whereas first wave feminist campaigns concerning male (hetero)sexuality and the historical existence of women's 'communities' have been studied by feminist and lesbian feminist historians.[74] The asserted historical roots of modern day lesbian/gay rather than lesbian feminist 'communities' are thus different. Gay liberationists researched the emergence of sexual orientation as the basis of identity. Lesbian feminist historians focused on emotional bonds between women, labelled 'lesbian' in the early twentieth century, they argued, by the 'heteropatriarchy' in order to undermine women's increasing independence. In other words, the former concentrated on *sexual* identity; the latter on *gender* identity.

(a) The emergence of a homosexual 'identity' and lesbian and gay 'subcultures'

There has been an overwhelming emphasis on male homosexuality in discussions on the emergence of homosexual identity in the West.[75] Gay liberationist historians have drawn on Foucault's work in particular to argue that homosexuality as an *identity* emerged somewhere between the seventeenth century and the nineteenth century in Western cultures.[76] The date suggested depends on the perceived cause of its emergence. Foucault himself argued that medical discourse 'created' a variety of sexual categories, including homosexuality, which would place its emergence somewhere in the late eighteenth century (Foucault, 1987).[77] Adam (1985), D'Emilio (1984) and Ross and Rapp (1984) argued that it emerged with capitalism, which would place it in the seventeenth century.

Foucault (1987) argued that new medical 'disciplines' geared to investigate and categorise every aspect of human bodies and existence developed, which 'invented' sexual categories and identities. The effect was at once totalising and individualising, in that every-body was now considered a unique (objectified) subject, only being aggregated with others through statistics (which would provide the knowledge to reveal the 'truth' about them). Distinctive sexual identities, then, are to be seen as the product of these new disciplines.

Ross and Rapp's and Adam's rather different argument, also endorsed to some extent by Caplan (1987b), was that the development of capitalism led to structural and socio-economic changes which made sexuality an individual matter. The emergence of large cities, dissolution of 'traditional' kinship ties, the separation of consumption from production, of leisure from labour and so on, reorganised the way Euro-American people experienced sexuality, and permitted the possibility of its autonomy – free of its reproductive 'functions' within kinship and related economic and political systems.

There is no space here to discuss these issues in detail. My own view is that 'medicalization' did have an impact on the construction of a homosexual identity, though 'naming' it may not have been the 'cause' of the identity itself.[78] Weeks, for example, argued that homosexual 'subcultures' were emerging in cities anyway and were noted and catalogued by sexologists (1987, pp. 40–41). Certainly, the development of large cities combined with the rise of the state and market economics provided the *possibility* of homosexual 'subcultures' in urban areas. The question of why they actually developed is more difficult to answer. Nevertheless, by the beginning of the twentieth century, definable gay 'subcultures' were in existence.

There are records of lesbian bar 'subcultures' in major cities in Europe and the USA from the 1920s onwards.[79] Most of the data, however, comes from the 1940s–1960s. Uniformly, these 'subcultures' were dominated by 'butch-femme' role play.[80] There was a strong belief, informed partly by sexological opinion at the time,[81] that sexual attraction involved opposite genders. One of a lesbian pair had to be a 'man', in physical appearance, emotionally and socially. This was important for lesbians because of the popular assumption that women were the passive objects of (male) sexual desire.[82] The dominant ideas at the time implied that a 'sexual act' could not occur without an active – that is, a male – partner. Thus in order for two women to have sexual contact in practice, and for this to be *regarded* as a sexual act, rather than a 'passionate friendship' or some such, one of them had to be a 'man' in her sexual 'instincts'. The 'butch-femme' roles in lesbian bars in London strongly reflected this perspective, judging by descriptions from lesbians who lived in London during the 1920s–1950s.[83]

For gay liberation historians, the emergence of a homosexual 'identity' was positive (even if sexologists gave it a negative image). It offered the possibility, which was taken up, of uniting behind an identity to fight legal, social, religious and economic discrimination.[84] In contrast, most lesbian feminist historians' perspective on the emergence of the lesbian label is regarded as negative. Sexology, it is argued, not only confirmed male domination over women, but provided biological justifications for it and accused feminists of the day of going against 'nature' (Jackson, 1987). Even worse, sexologists advised that women should learn to 'enjoy' their sexual domination, which has been called, particularly by revolutionary feminists, the 'eroticization of women's subordination' (Jackson 1987, Jeffreys, 1985).

There is little emphasis on the emergence of male homosexuality in this literature, but lengthy political analyses of the appearance of the 'lesbian' label, reflecting the concern about gender identity rather than sexual identity. Caplan succinctly describes this difference:

> men have involved themselves in (homo) sexual politics because they wished to resist victimization. For many women, however, identification as a lesbian may have been less to do with sexual orientation than it does with identification with female oppressions...(Caplan, 1987b, p. 6)

The emergence of the label 'lesbian' is linked to the period when women were becoming more economically independent, and is viewed as a direct attack on women's emerging autonomy from men. Jeffreys (1985) notes that sexology's ideas about a lesbian 'identity' emerged at the same time as first wave feminism, and that sexologists had an overtly negative view of feminism.[85] Faderman also makes this analysis in her earlier work (1985, Part IIB). Relationships between women, previously regarded as 'passionate friendships', and tolerated because they did not threaten patriarchy (as women were economically dependent on men), became 'evil or morbid', Faderman suggests (1985, p. 411)

However, close relationships between *feminists* were not depicted as 'sexual' by sexologists or by first wave feminists. Lesbianism was not applied as a derogatory label for *feminists* until 1970s feminism. The critics accused the earlier 'spinster' feminists of being 'unnatural' because they were against marriage (or simply because they were not married) and because they were against the 'natural' sexual appetites of men. This is not the same as accusing them of being lesbians – or 'inverts' as the common phrase had it at the time. 'Inverts' were seen as biologically distinguishable people who were not 'women', but a 'third sex'. Neither first wave feminists nor the sexologists saw the emerging lesbian 'butch-femme' 'subcultures' as the location of feminism – and indeed they were not. Both Faderman and Jeffreys see 'butch-femme' as a sexological creation inspired by anti-feminist sentiments, and which some women had internalised.[86]

This approach contrasts with the views of another lesbian historian, Joan Nestle (1987), who describes 'butch-femme' as a unique lesbian cultural creation. Nestle suggests that:

> Butch-femme was an erotic partnership serving both as a conspicuous [*sic*] flag of rebellion and as an intimate exploration of women's sexuality. It was not an accident that butch-femme couples suffered the most street abuse and provoked more assimilated or closeted lesbians to plead with them not to be so obvious. (Nestle, 1987, p. 101)

Nestle further suggests that there is a class element in the feminist hostility towards 'butch-femme', arguing that butch-femme was working class, and middle-class feminists discriminated against it for that reason (*ibid*, p. 108).[87] She concludes that butch-femme lesbians of the 1950s had allowed their 'lives to be trivialised and reinterpreted by feminists who did not share our culture.' (*ibid*, p. 105).

Thus where Jeffreys repudiates the butch-femme 'sub-culture', Nestle embraces it. These debates related to the conflicts within the late 1980s 'community': differing interpretations of the 'community's' history constituted different representations of its current existence.[88]

(b) The emergence of lesbian feminism

It was during second wave feminism that lesbians, who for most of the twentieth century had been depicted as quasi-men, were 'reclaimed' not only as women, but as the only women free of hetero-patriarchal control.[89] Thus the notion of lesbianism as a *political choice*, and the idea that lesbian 'communities' were the obvious location for feminist 'communities' was also recent. And it was only after this that 'butch-femme' role play and other 'anti-feminist' lesbian behaviour became the focus of feminist attention and criticism. When radical feminism redefined lesbianism as 'the same as' woman-identification, the overlap between 'women-only' and 'lesbian' spaces emerged, resulting in the tensions and conflicts already discussed.

Moreover, the popularisation of the idea that *women* possessed an autonomous sexuality (unless they were biologically 'male' in their proclivities) appears to have developed after the first wave feminist movement and the widespread popularisation of Freud's ideas. Without both this and the possibility of socio-economic independence for women, perceiving lesbianism as a political gender identity was a highly unlikely development. However, the details of the emergence of lesbian feminism explains the continued importance of lesbianism as an 'authentic' *sexual*, as opposed to gendered, identity.

The development of radical feminism, which started in the USA, has been comprehensively traced by Echols (1989), who describes how it was first developed by women involved in the new left student movements and the civil rights movements, (Echols, 1989, Introduction and Chapter 1). Echols declares that 'In a sense the individual became the site of political activity in the '60s.' (p. 17).[90] From involvement in the civil rights movement, concern about racism was always present, but rather than depicting ethnic identity as dividing women, it was used as a model for oppressive gender divisions: women are to men as blacks are to whites. There was an explicit denial of difference between women, as opposed to differences between *men* and women, in these early formulations, setting up the conflict that eventually emerged:

> [R]adical feminists' emphasis upon women's commonality masked a fear of difference, one which had serious consequences for the movement. Differences – either those rooted in class, race and sexual preference, or those of skill and expertise – were seen as undermining the movement. (Echols, 1989, p. 11)

An analysis of the social construction of sexuality was a central aspect of the radical feminist critique of patriarchy, as discussed in Chapter 1. In the earlier period, the right of a woman to define and enjoy sexual practice equally with men was strongly asserted, resulting in such classic papers as Anne Koedt's 'The Myth of the Vaginal Orgasm' (1973). Unlike the first wave feminist movement, which depicted sexual practice as something men did to women and which was unhealthy for women, early radical feminism asserted that sexual practice was something women should have a right to enjoy. Sexual practice had by now been fairly securely separated from its reproductive 'functions'.

Radical feminism developed (1968–1975) during the same period as gay liberation (1969–1975), and many lesbians initially joined the Gay Liberation Front rather than the WLM.[91] However, after a relatively short period, many left the GLF, finding it dominated by gay men who apparently had little interest in lesbians or the emerging 'woman question'.[92] A substantial number then joined the WLM, and they were not prepared to have their sexuality ignored, let alone discriminated against. According to all reports, this is exactly what happened.[93] Eventually, both the American and British women's movements were persuaded to add a clause about lesbianism to their official demands, but both were expressed in terms of the right to choose one's own sexuality, not in terms of the political significance of lesbianism.[94]

Thus lesbians found themselves in a position of being marginalised both by the GLF (over gender issues) and by the WLM (over sexuality issues), even though sexuality was a central concern in both organisations. In America and in Britain, many lesbians reacted by developing a separate lesbian feminist movement. And it was out of this movement, developing from the early to mid-1970s, that ideas arose concerning the *political* significance of lesbianism.[95] The discrimination against lesbians was no longer represented, as it had been in the late 1960s and early 1970s, as the result of 'prejudice' based on ignorance: it was the result of the threat it posed to the hetero-patriarchy.

The historical trajectory shows that lesbian feminists initially emphasised both their 'authentic' sexual identity and their feminist stance. Many
1970s lesbian feminists were already involved with lesbian 'communities'.
Feminism may have led them to reassess 'butch-femme' practices, and to
redefine themselves as 'women' rather than 'quasi-men', but the importance of lesbian 'authenticity' was not thereby erased. From lesbian feminism's inception, then, there always had been a connection between both
lesbianism as a sexual identity and as a feminist political choice.

Much lesbian feminist writing of the 1980s, particularly that concentrating on sexual violence and pornography, skipped over this history
and looked back to first-wave feminism, thus masking the more recent
connections between the politicisation of 'authentic' lesbianism and the
emergence of lesbian feminism.

In short, the way lesbian 'communities' developed – and lesbian feminism's eventual involvement in them – informed the conflicts still present
during the late 1980s. These developments brought together conflicting
motivations and interests into one political and social 'space', and placed a
premium on identity as the cause of discrimination – or rather, a variety of
identities, most particularly 'woman', 'lesbian', various classes and, later,
ethnicity or race. These roots further reveal that many women had an
interest in several of these identities and had strong commitments to divergent parts of the 'community'.

Thus different kinds of people with different motivations were thrown
together in this community. And it was perhaps inevitable that the diversity within the community would eventually become a focus of attention
and conflict: lesbian feminists did not feel they had much in common with
gay men; black women did not feel they had much in common with white
women; older women did not feel they had much in common with younger
women; butch-femme lesbians did not feel they had much in common
with lesbian feminists, and so on. The problem emerged of *which* of these
various identities was the source of commonalities between people and/or
the source of discrimination. That problem tended to rattle people's own
previously unquestioned assumptions as much as challenging others',
which eventually made the whole idea of 'authentic' and single identities
somewhat suspect.

So this community was unusual, as communities go, partly due to the
continual poking around in the details of the contents of the identities
which formed boundaries of the community. As a result, those boundaries
were under continual (re)construction during most of this century – from
both 'inside' and 'outside' the community. The renegotiation of gender
identity (the 'woman question') and sexual identity (both in terms of

sexual freedom and 'gay rights question') were frequently debated in the media, in parliament, in academic and medical circles, in the pulpit and in people's living rooms as much as they were within the community. So before going on to look at how this process developed and was experienced in London during the late 1980s among lesbian feminists, I will briefly look at the nature of communities and their relation to identities, making a little clearer what kind of community this was.

5. A QUESTION OF BOUNDARIES

Studies on communities and ethnicity tend to emphasize either the community's or ethnic group's role in the construction of boundaries, with little consideration of external influences.[96] The lesbian feminist community, unlike many ethnic groups studied, was generated out of historically specific conditions of the city, rather than migrating to it from somewhere else.[97] It was and is a peculiarly urban phenomenon, and a peculiarly Euro-American phenomenon: both the city and its cultural conditions were crucial to any boundaries which existed, as already discussed.[98]

Despite a range of interpretations, the literature also agrees that ascription rather than achievement is central to the creation of community or ethnic boundaries (cf. Keyes, 1981). In order to 'imagine', 'symbolize', 'use' or 'assert' these boundaries, an unquestioned acceptance of an 'authentic' common identity is needed, a 'closed box' containing constructed commonalities out of a lump of heterogenous reality. I have argued that in the lesbian feminist community, the contents of this 'closed box' were continually being investigated. At the same time as 'identity politics' was producing a proliferation of 'closed boxes' (the assertion of 'authentic identity'), 'identity politics' itself was being analysed and criticised.

This is slightly complicated. 'The personal is political' demanded that personal experience could not be questioned, and made it illegitimate to proclaim the 'truth' of the experience of the 'other', thereby keeping boxes 'closed' – and more and more 'others' were emerging as time went on. But in the process, concepts of what previously had been considered 'self' were being deconstructed, thereby opening 'boxes'. The category 'woman', for example, was being deconstructed into the categories 'lesbian', 'black', 'white', 'working class', and so on.

A. P. Cohen's (1985) notion of symbolized, rather than objectively existing, boundaries of communities is helpful in escaping a reified notion of 'community';[99] but for him, people symbolising communities are unconscious of the constructed rather than 'authentic' nature of the boundaries, which is what makes them effective. Quoting Geertz speaking about the use of myths and history in this process (1985, p. 80), Cohen suggests that if people fail to 'plug the dikes of their most needed beliefs with whatever mud they can find...then we are in trouble' (Cohen, 1985, p. 100).

This is what lesbian feminists failed to do. They continually discussed the meanings of their own symbols – not to legitimate them, but to question them – and they also lived in a context where many of their 'most needed beliefs' were being challenged by others, *within* their own 'community'. The discussion above on disagreements about the history of homosexual identity and community is a case in point. This did not (often) prevent lesbian feminists from believing in 'community', but it did make them aware of the constructed and contested nature of claims made.

A further difficulty is that Cohen over-emphasises the group's self-definition. The word 'community' he suggests, is only occasioned by the need to express a distinction between one group and another (*op. cit.*, p. 12). In the case of lesbians, the distinction between 'heterosexual' and 'lesbian' existed independently of the 'community' (just as the assertion of differences between ethnic minorities were not initially defined by the minorities). The nature of the distinction was redefined by lesbian feminism, but the distinction itself was not created by the theory.

This is recognised by Cohen to an extent in his use of the idea of 'symbolic reversal'. Cohen uses Goffman (1968) to discuss how people stigmatised by dominant groups sometimes assert the superiority of the characteristics which 'spoil' their identity. Cohen calls this (after Schwimmer, 1972) 'symbolic competition' and uses both the 'Black is Beautiful' movement and the women's movement to illustrate his point (*op. cit.*, p. 60). Quoting Schwimmer, he suggests that a stigmatised group 'uses the stigma as a symbolic means of asserting and embellishing its own boundaries – indeed, as a means of constructing its own boundaries' (p. 62).[100]

However, in terms of relations *within* the 'community' in my material, many instances of 'symbolic competition' were not constructing 'community' boundaries. Rather than try and reverse the 'stigma', many asserted their difference in terms of the *level* of stigma experienced – as in the idea of a 'hierarchy of oppressions'. Thus, a white gay man was less 'oppressed' than a white lesbian, who was less oppressed than an Asian lesbian, and so on. This was an assertion of difference, but it did not establish boundaries between the community and the world around it. It was an assertion that the divisions within the community were the *same* as those outside it. If anything, this removed community boundaries, rather than constructed them, by asserting that the community was in many respects no different from what surrounded it.

Cohen's suggestion that when minority groups have the *appearance* of similarity, there will be intensification of efforts to establish distinctions between them (and in so doing, boundaries are being symbolised; *op. cit.*, p. 40) is more useful in looking at conflicts within the 'community'. For example, one could see the asserted distinction between gay men and lesbians along gender lines as a resistance to the idea that 'homosexuals' form one group. However, there are difficulties with this: although different boundaries were being drawn, they all essentially covered the *same* 'space', but were differing representations of it. It was one community and many, or none, simultaneously. Furthermore, many distinctions were the result of wider socio-economic conditions and perceptions of identity which cross-cut the community, and over which community members had little control. For example, gender does indeed separate gay men from lesbians; they are not a homogenous group at all. Finally, lesbian feminists had interests in a variety of spheres, so they might assert a particular distinction in one context and not in another.[101] Again, boundaries did not enclose people or their beliefs; they enclosed representations, ideas. People held a number of representations, even conflicting ones, either simultaneously or separated by the contexts in which they found themselves at a given moment.

The difficulty with Cohen's analysis is that although he asserts communities are 'symbolised' and do not necessarily have any ongoing visible existence, it is difficult to apply this approach without assuming a coherent pre-existing group and the necessity of territoriality as conditions for a community. Neither of these conditions applied in the late 1980s lesbian feminist community.

All of this leaves open the question of *why* people symbolically construct 'communities', 'ethnicities' or 'identities' at all, and the literature produces a variety of answers.[102] A. P. Cohen argues that 'people assert community, whether in the form of ethnicity or of locality, when they recognise in it the most adequate medium for the expression of their whole selves' (*op.cit.*, p. 107). This is similar to Epstein's argument, who suggests that the assertion of ethnicity arises where individuals' identity is alienated by dominant groups (Epstein, 1978). Pahl (1970, Chapter 7) similarly argues that sometimes, communities come together as a result of threat from without, which creates a solidarity within, and Burton's study (1978) is one example of this. Abner Cohen (1974) argues that ethnicity is asserted for political and economic interests, and that ethnic groups use their ethnic status as a 'weapon' against other groups to gain an advantage.

Glazer and Moynihan (1978) also suggest that personal interest is involved: ethnicity is useful for moving up the social stratification ladder, while at the same time defining individual identity and providing the means to mobilize as an interest group.

These last two suggestions are not entirely helpful for groups who do not stand to gain any political or material rewards by asserting their identities (for example, lesbians or black groups). Again, the question arises about *which* group is constructing the boundary. Minorities may attempt to make the best of their situation and redefine the boundaries, but it cannot be argued that they chose to have the boundary in the first place.

Again, the difficulty with these studies is the emphasis on single identities. Even if, as much of this literature suggests, the unity does not actually exist, it has to be asserted.[103] This was not the basis on which the lesbian feminist community existed. Lesbian feminists frequently crossed, mixed and matched boundaries and identities, as did the variety of other people involved in different aspects of the community. The boundary of the community was the negotiated work of many different groups and ideas, and was continually under reconstruction. Moreover, no 'identity' was a 'closed box' for long and most women within the community did not possess only one 'identity' but several. The community was not therefore composed of people who had a single 'habitus', to borrow Bourdieu's term.[104] Lesbian feminism actually encouraged women to attempt to get out of their 'habitus' as often as possible, and the community, by its nature, was continually presenting lesbian feminists with alternative ways of thinking about things. The one enduring 'us' versus 'them' belief involved the 'authenticity' of lesbianism, but its definition and significance and therefore its ability to 'unify' was continually disputed and debated.

What anthropological accounts lack is an historical analysis. This chapter has considered the conceptual historical conditions which contributed towards the development of the lesbian feminist community in London. Equally important, however, are the historical influences of institutions and state processes in shaping the context in which communities negotiate their boundaries and develop their identities. So I now return to London to consider this aspect.

5 From the Outside In:
A Political Economy

London continually affected the lives of lesbian feminists living there: its size, density, ethnic diversity, social, economic and spatial divisions and opportunities – even the design of the public transport system. And one recent episode in the city's political history, the 1981–1986 Greater London Council (GLC), under the leadership of Ken Livingstone, had a particular impact on the community. That period's influence was still felt in the 'public/political' sphere during the late 1980s, and the Archive dispute of 1988 was in part an expression of the effects of the GLC's policies.

1. LONDON AND THE GLC: AN UNEASY ALLIANCE

The GLC had a curious relationship with the city it was founded to serve. Although it was the largest metropolitan council in Western Europe, it was also one of the weakest. The 32 London Boroughs, the City of Westminster and the national government hold many of the powers over London which metropolitan authorities usually possess, leaving the GLC with an enormous constituency, but not sufficiently empowered to act effectively. The GLC became an extremely large organisation representing the country's capital, but had few formally permitted functions. And this provided the time and resources to develop new activities not previously regarded as local government concerns, much to the persistent annoyance of central government, which was then under the strongly right-wing control of Margaret Thatcher's Conservative Party (cf. Flynn et al., 1985; Forrester et al., 1985, Ch. 4; Carvel, 1987).

The source of the GLC's weakness was that London developed from a collection of separate and independent towns and villages, and over the centuries they have been successful at maintaining a measure of self-determination as London Boroughs (Young, 1984; Forrester et al., 1985, Ch. 2; Sharpe, 1984, pp. 11–12; Rasmussen, 1960). So although the need for central organisation in the city (particularly for long-term area-wide planning, sanitation, transport and housing) has been obvious since London's massive expansion in the mid-nineteenth century, the question of a government for London has always been contentious (Young, 1984, p. 3). The two attempts to produce a single London authority – the London County Council (LCC) created in 1889, and the GLC, created in 1963 – were weakened by both the London boroughs, which did not want to lose their independence, and central government, which wanted a control over the capital. As a result, both the LCC's and the GLC's efforts to implement London-wide plans were hampered by both. This situation of being sandwiched between two political powers thus has a long history, and the GLC's eventual abolition, though clearly motivated by Conservative irritation at the GLC's socialism, was not simply an 'aberration of Thatcherism'.[105] But I return now to the beginning of the last GLC administration, led by Ken Livingstone.

2. 1981: HISTORICAL CONTEXT

In May 1981, the new Labour-controlled GLC took office from the Conservatives after a landslide election. This was a period of strongly socialist politics in local government generally in Britain, at least in the metropolitan areas. The new administrations which gained power after Labour's overwhelming success in the 1981 local government elections (Forrester et al., 1985 p. 59) expressed a more potent brand of socialism than had existed before. A collision course between the Government, which was veering strongly to the right, and the metropolitan areas was set.

The period was also intense for lesbian feminism, during which 'identity politics' emerged as a dominant feature in the community, and deep conflicts within the Women's Liberation Movement (WLM), most especially over the issues of lesbianism, race and class, led to fragmentation so serious that 1978 marked the last WLM conference held in Britain. However, this did not lead to a decline in feminist activity. On the contrary, the now separate camps were particularly vociferous. The Black feminist movement was becoming more insistently critical of 'white' feminism;[106] socialist feminists and lesbian feminists became more hostile towards one another; in 1977, revolutionary feminism emerged, and by 1981 revolutionary feminists were articulating forceful campaigns about sexual violence and pornography, especially through WAVAW (Women Against Violence Against Women); Reclaim The Night marches were held regularly, and cells of Angry Women Brigades were active around London and other cities in Britain, most notably Leeds (where Peter Sutcliffe, the 'Yorkshire Ripper', was still terrorising Leeds' female population). Lesbian feminists were still living in collective households and squatting was widespread; feminist consciousness-raising (CR) groups had appeared all over the city; women's newsletters were being produced; women's bookshops and publishers were being established; arguments were raging over whether lesbian feminists should have children, and whether boy children were acceptable under any circumstances. And so on.

It was into this heady atmosphere that Ken Livingstone and his colleagues entered the arena. Two things particularly concerned Livingstone: countering discrimination against minority and disadvantaged groups, and bringing down the Thatcher government (Carvel, 1987, pp. 86 and 207). That Livingstone and his colleagues saw the wooing of 'disadvantaged groups' as advantageous in Labour's struggle against Thatcherism at both local and national levels is clear (cf. Carvel, 1987, p. 86; *Socialist Organiser*, October 1978). The aim was to encourage such groups to recognise that the oppression they experienced had a common cause: Thatcherite capitalism. Livingstone was clearly genuinely motivated by his desire to improve the lot of the underprivileged, believing that the best way to begin was to remove Margaret Thatcher's government, which was not a particularly extreme belief at the time for anyone with left-of-centre perspectives.

The limited powers of the GLC enabled it at least to fund local groups for some kind of self-help service. The result was a grant-aid 'explosion' in London, where a large variety of groups, either never funded before or minimally funded, suddenly became the recipients of money, facilities, buildings and publicity. The emphasis on grant-aid was due to the lack of GLC powers to incur expenditure on its 'radical' policies in any other way.[107]

Amongst the beneficiaries were lesbian feminists. Before 1981, lesbian/feminist groups had managed without funding by squatting buildings and utilising the commitment of mostly young, white and unemployed radical/revolutionary feminists. Beverley's description of the 'informal women's centre' squat discussed in Chapter 3, where she became involved in the Women's Liberation Workshop (amongst other things), confirmed the reports from many other women:

> This was pre-grants and paid workers, before the possibility of being in a funded organisation. So a lot of us were involved in volunteering...a lot of us were on the dole at the time. What I did mostly was help put out the newsletter and meet women who came in – cos' there were always women coming into the centre. And also, I set up and ran a

crèche there for a while....And there were also groups doing writing, theatre and film work and stuff. And we were all kind of involved with each other, one way or another [laughs].

The Women's Liberation Workshop was later funded by the GLC and rehoused in Hungerford House on the Embankment, a building paid for by the GLC, and the newsletter was later funded by the GLC Women's Committee. The same happened to hundreds of groups around the city; but more than that, hundreds of groups which had not existed before were founded and received GLC backing.

3. THE GRANT AID BOOM

The GLC's total grant budget rose from £6m in 1980 to over £50m in 1984 (Forrester, *op. cit.*, p. 49) – which, although it represented unprecedented quantities for groups receiving funds, was still only a fraction of the GLC's total budget. Eventually, each GLC committee became responsible for grants in its own field. In May 1982, the GLC Women's Committee was formed, chaired by Valerie Wise, whose feminism had its roots in socialism (Livingstone, 1987). The Women's Committee administered women's group grant applications and promoted the interests of women in London.

A number of GLC Working Groups were also formed to advise committees on certain types of grant application. For example, the Lesbian and Gay Working Party advised on applications from lesbian/gay groups received by any committee, and generally promoted the interests of the lesbian/gay community of London. All these committees employed, on principle, at least some members of the community or 'identity' they represented.

The grants programme mushroomed, and along with it an unprecedented publicity campaign about the rights of and wrongs against minority and disadvantaged groups within London and Britain. Knight and Hayes (1984, p. 3) calculated that £47m was spent on over 2000 voluntary organisations in the financial year 1984–5; in 1983, the GLC expanded the Women's Committee budget sevenfold from £1m per annum to £7m per annum (Carvel 1987, p. 204).

Tables 5 and 6 summarises the Women's Committee budgets. Child care was clearly the biggest expenditure, but the contribution to feminist groups was also substantial. Notably, the figures do not include the majority of explicitly lesbian groups funded by the GLC. Lesbianism was treated more as an issue of 'homophobia'[108] than feminism (cf. Tobin, 1990). There was no clear distinction in the Women's Committee between

Table 5   The GLC Women's Committee Budgets 1982–1986[110]

Date	Total Budget	Allocation to Grants
1982–1983	£950,000	£412,622
1983–1984	£7,094,000	£5,689,000
1984–1985	£8,749,000	£6,389,000
1985–1986	£10,801,000	£7,425,000
Totals:	£26,794,000	£18,905,622

Table 6   Groups Funded By the GLC Women's Committee June
1982–September 1985[111]

Type of Group	Totals	Ethnic Groups
Women's Centres	40	16
Resources and Information	31	9
Printing and publications	7	4
Health	11	5
Counselling and support	41	10
Welfare, legal and other	54	18
Arts, media, recreation	15	1
Campaigns and research	35	11
Child care	301	23
Festivals and conferences	5	–
Transport	6	–
Total:	548	97

prejudice against lesbians *and* gay men (i.e. homophobia) as an issue, and prejudice against lesbians *and* heterosexual women (i.e. sexism).[109] The difference between radical and socialist feminist views on lesbianism caused regular disputes in the Women's Committee (Tobin, 1990, and Forrester *et al.*, 1985, p. 45).

The GLC's approach towards grants was adopted in a number of Labour-controlled boroughs around London. Even though these boroughs – particularly in inner London – were experiencing financial difficulties, they maintained, and in some cases greatly raised, their level of grant aid. Table 7 illustrates the change in levels of grants for those boroughs particularly noted for their 'radical' policies.

Table 7   Grants to voluntary organisations in selected
London Boroughs 1980–1983[112]

Borough	1980–1981 £	1982–1983 £
Brent	558,060	1,346,271
Camden	2,321,200	3,271,440
Greenwich	380,520	2,151,220
Hackney	812,230	820,570
Haringey	523,150	1,320,000
Islington	883,780	1,258,466
Lambeth	1,420,166	1,447,670
Lewisham	990,530	1,249,298
Southwark	408,240	1,097,404

Grant aid therefore increased by a substantial amount over a short period. By 1984, the 'public/political' sphere of the lesbian feminist community was largely dependent upon grant aid. Before looking at the effects, something needs to be said about the political package which came with the money: the GLC's approach towards 'identity politics' and its Equal Opportunities Policy ('equal ops').

4. IDENTITY POLITICS AND EQUAL OPPORTUNITIES

(a) The emergence of 'identity politics'

There is no doubt the GLC was justified in its concern about the problems of racism, sexism, disablism, homophobia and so on in London. As in any major city today, these problems are deep-rooted and result in a great deal of hardship. However, the concern here is to consider in retrospect what happened in practice. Some outcomes of the grant-aid boom era were neither what Livingstone intended nor could have predicted. And a key area where the problems arose was in the issue of 'identity politics' (today called 'political correctness').

There were two drives towards 'identity politics' in London: the demands of various minority and disadvantaged groups during the 1980s, and Livingstone's belief that these groups should be promoted (Livingstone, 1987 and Carvel, 1987, p. 234 ff.). That was done largely through grant aid, though lack of planning in the GLC's 'empowering' of disadvantaged groups through funding meant its precise intentions were never clearly established before the event. As Ann Tobin, who worked in the GLC Women's Committee Support Unit, remarked: 'New Left politicians who started to adopt the equalities strategies often had not the slightest idea of what they had let themselves in for.' (1990, p. 58).

The GLC saw such groups as having different experiences of discrimination, but their oppression ultimately derived from the same source (capitalism). Inequality was the same however it was expressed. That minority and disadvantaged groups were viewed more in terms of their 'inequality' rather than their 'differences' from one another is important. Their inequality is what made them different within this perspective: if you removed the inequality, they would be equal to ('the same as') everyone else, at least in terms of rights and powers. That approach supported the development of a 'hierarchy of oppressions', which defined and compared minority and disadvantaged groups according to their inequalities: their position in the hierarchy depended on the amount of 'equality deficit' suffered. Thus black women were higher up the hierarchy than black men, because they were both black (race oppression) and women (gender oppression).

(b) The equal opportunities policy

The GLC's approach to 'identity politics' was implemented through its Equal Opportunities Policy ('equal ops'). Adherence to 'equal ops' was made a condition of all grants, and the intention was to empower minorities and encourage community self-help.[113] Unintentionally, this had the effect of giving the 'hierarchy of oppressions' a formal structure, which contributed to the conflicts occurring anyway within the community over 'identity politics'.

The funded groups felt the impact of 'equal ops' most strongly. Venues had to be made accessible to all, publicity had to contain images of minority groups, constitutions had to be anti-racist, anti-ableist and anti-ageist.

The Women's Committee took up this stance with enthusiasm. Its midterm report on its first year stated that:

> two principles were agreed as a framework to guide future action. These were that the Committee would take particular account of the needs of black and ethnic minority women and of the needs of women with disabilities. (GLC Internal Report W224, p. 12)

In pursuit of this aim, the *Women's Committee Bulletin* often published 'special issues' to describe each minority group's experiences, including issues on racism (No. 13), lesbianism (No. 17) older women (No. 20) and disability (No. 26).

In short, the GLC explicitly intended to influence the activities, behaviour and ideology of the white able-bodied majority towards minorities, especially by encouraging them to give away their power, or at the very least, to share it.[114] In addition to requiring reports demonstrating that this was being done, the GLC funded enough minority-interest groups and organisations within the 'community' to ensure that it was to a large extent self-regulating.

The effects of these changes for the lesbian/feminist community were substantial: they not only altered the physical appearance of the 'public/political' sphere, they introduced a swathe of new people, structures and ideas with which lesbian feminists either had to negotiate or compete.

5. THE EFFECTS

(a) Expansion, expectations, 'femocrats' and diversity

Lesbian feminists were aware of the possible effects of the GLC's intervention. For example, Beverley remembered her mixed feelings about accepting grant aid:

> ...in some ways, it was wonderful. You know, to be able to walk around the South Bank and to see posters saying 'lesbian this' and 'lesbian that', and to actually have local government recognising and making a commitment to all sections of the community....In a sense, it was so ironic, because all my dreams in the sixties and everything – this might be the closest I ever got to a decent society or something being made actually explicit and official, you know...
>
> But also, I think a lot of people sort of felt, and made warning noises about – once you get involved with being funded by the state, even if it's, you know, that bit of the state – you are in danger of...you can become dependent on it, and it can really affect you....Do you lose your radicalism? Does it get diffused by being – is it co-opted by being part of that structure? Does it mean that there will be a stratum of waged people who are workers for the revolution or whatever – and will that kind of divide the movement?

Nevertheless, by the late 1980s, most lesbian/feminist organisations, events, conferences, marches (other than *ad hoc* demonstrations) and buildings (other than clubs and pubs) were funded by a local authority. Unfunded groups met in buildings bought or leased by a local authority to provide women-only or lesbian/gay space. Furthermore, grants were frequently given to publicise organisations and events, to carry out research and publish results for wide dissemination (and money was also often provided to translate such documents into different languages, as well as producing them in braille and on tape), and to publish newspapers and journals.

There was also a selection of businesses either started or assisted through grants. For example, Sheba Feminist Publishers was given a £13,000 grant, *City Limits* was begun as a grant-funded worker's co-operative, and Silver Moon Women's Bookshop was assisted in opening in 1984 with Women's Committee funds.

Grant aid thus vastly expanded the number of lesbian/feminist organisations in existence in London, their visibility, accessibility, and the number of buildings available for their use. It also 'legitimised' much lesbian feminist space: being provided with a legally occupied building like Wesley House altered the conceptual status of the space. For welfare and service-based organisations it was ideal; but for campaigning groups, it marked a significant change – it was one step closer to acceptable legitimacy. As one separatist, Julie Bindel put it, 'what has funding ever done for us except force us into the mainstream?' (1988, p. 50).

There were also greater opportunities for jobs within women-only organisations. It was no longer a choice between being unemployed or working in a 'politically incorrect' job. Many new posts were filled by lesbian feminists, partly because they had been involved in campaigning on women's issues before funding, and so were in place and qualified for the jobs.

The new job market thus created a tier of lesbian feminists who were variously labelled 'femocrats' (feminist bureaucrats) or 'professional lesbians' – salaried 'identity politics'. The GLC was praised for supporting such work; but there was also a feeling that something which had been a political commitment against the 'establishment' was now being given a job description by a section of that 'establishment'.

Furthermore, the majority of the new organisations were service agencies, rather than purely political campaigning groups. They were frequently staffed by lesbian feminists, but the function of the organisations had become service-oriented. The campaigning organisations did not disappear, but they now shared their space with many others, which attracted staff whose perspectives were different from that of radical/revolutionary feminists. The public space of the community had indeed vastly expanded; but it was also now populated by many new groups and interests.

The effects of the GLC approach to 'identity politics' were also numerous. First, groups most likely to be funded were 'double-disadvantaged' groups, which considerably increased the number of 'double-disadvantaged' organisations and led to much greater visibility of a plethora of identities. Second, through its publicity and training projects, the GLC made far more people aware of and informed about the issues than they had been. Third, by introducing a formal set of conditions about 'equal ops', the GLC had a great impact on how these issues were to be approached.

Moreover, the GLC's equal ops new standards, while highly desirable, providing signers and induction loops for the deaf, braille for the blind, making buildings fully accessible, printing information in six or seven different languages and so on, did not come cheaply. During the late 1980s funds to pay for them were rapidly disappearing, but the precedent set meant it was no longer acceptable to hold conferences without these facilities. The days when the lesbian feminist community was small, composed mostly of young, childless, able-bodied, unemployed, middle class white women – practically the only kind of women who could be involved before the assistance of the GLC – were gone, but after the GLC was abolished, so was most of the money.

Lesbian feminists also came to expect events to charge an entrance fee women could afford, which again depended upon grant aid, and the necessity to charge higher fees as grants dwindled continually caused conflicts. The Lesbian Summer School, which provided teaching, screenings and events from ten in the morning until past ten at night for four consecutive days, involving 47 tutors and organisers, 122 hours of organised events and 247 participants, charged a £20 minimum fee for unwaged women (£80 was the maximum fee; six women paid this). There was uproar at the price throughout the four days.

The organisations which emerged through GLC funding, and made the most visible thereby, substantially changed the image of 'public/political' space, its economic base and the people involved in it. In effect the GLC became one (fairly powerful) player in the community's political structure and conflicts, and its influence between 1981 and 1986 continued to reverberate in the late 1980s.

(b) Different perspectives

As already discussed, lesbian feminists were generally hostile towards socialism. The GLC's habit of depicting lesbianism as a 'double disadvantage' was particularly irritating to radical/revolutionary feminists, for in their analysis, lesbianism is a positive political choice for women. Their oppression was seen as hetero-patriarchy trying to defend itself against the threat that lesbianism posed, not as capitalism making sure that the underdogs remained underdogs.

That difference in perspective indicated the GLC did not reflect lesbian feminist views, but this did not have as much effect as the rest of the 'equal ops' package, particularly concerning race. The GLC's intervention in the 'identity politics' conflict made the issue infinitely more urgent, and many (white, able-bodied) radical/revolutionary feminists began to reassess their feminism during this period as a result of being continually challenged by minority groups in general and ethnic minority women's groups in particular. As Nicola described the atmosphere in women-only space during the early 1980's:

> there was a strong tendency that if you put one foot wrong, you were damned for the rest of your life. And of course that's very frightening. It always was like that, there always was an element of that. But when we're talking about 'hey, you white fucking racist', that's an awful lot heavier, being called that, than another white feminist saying, 'gee, I think you're anti-feminist.' There's a huge difference.

Thus one effect of GLC funding was that it guided the terms of debate within the 'community'. It was not that the GLC created 'identity politics', but it provided the means and the space to greatly enlarge and elaborate 'identity politics', and it influenced the direction of the debate. The emphasis on stamping out discrimination rather than, or in addition to, exploring and analysing differences between different groups gave 'equal ops' a strongly prescriptive/proscriptive character. This approach clashed with an equally prescriptive/proscriptive approach from revolutionary feminists and exacerbated the embattled atmosphere in the 'community'.

The GLC's impact was felt most strongly through collectives. Collectives received the funding, were guided by the grants contract and 'equal ops', employed the workers and ran the funded organisations.

(c) Effects on lesbian/feminist collectives

Most funded collective organisations complained that too much of their work involved administration connected with their grant. Certainly, a great deal of Anne's time was taken up preparing the Archive's annual application for renewal of funding. But funding also introduced other changes in collectives. Structural alterations, such as the introduction of employees and formal administration systems was one; the imposition of the structure of the GLC itself was another: as 'anti-establishment' as it tried to be, the laws under which the GLC had to operate meant it remained a state institution. A third change was the GLC's enforcement of its own approach through its grant contract, which were at odds with many lesbian feminists' perspectives.

Amongst other things, this created a gap in communication between many groups and the GLC (cf. Raine and Webster, 1984, p. 37). A major source of the lack of understanding between grants officers, who were often the only contact lesbian feminists had with their grant aid body, and collectives was the grant contract itself. This document bore little relation to the working practices of collectives. It also, incidentally, often worked against the intentions of the GLC, which frequently complained about the way grants contracts had to be legally drafted (cf. GLC (1986), p. 90). Thus both the GLC and the groups they funded often ended up with a contract neither wanted.

For lesbian feminist collectives, the contract could hardly have contrasted more with their intentions. The underlying philosophy of collectives was that they should avoid formal structures; that organisation should be based on mutual agreement; that everyone working should be treated as an equal member rather than as an 'employee'. In contrast, the GLC contract required formal incorporation, audited accounts, record-keeping, policy statements, rules on employment of staff, Articles of Association and constitutions. Furthermore, certain policies and principles of the GLC would have to be adhered to – particularly in relation to 'equal ops'. Collective members of lesbian feminist organisations were forced to become directors of companies, registered in Companies House along with every other business in Britain.

It was possible, for short periods, to disregard the implications of the contract. Once the company was founded and Articles and Memorandum of Association drawn up, they were usually put in a file somewhere to collect dust. But if serious conflict arose in the collective, the lack of any established methods of resolving disputes exposed the structural conditions generated by the formal rules. This is eventually what happened in the Archive dispute.

That dispute revealed the significance of the structural changes in collectives, particularly the introduction of employees and the emergence of a role for 'brokers' as a result of the communication gap. 'Brokers' (my term, not theirs) were women who established contacts with grants officers and who 'translated' the desires and interests of the collective into 'local government-ese'. Brokers thus had considerable indirect power, which led to an obvious and formal structural imbalance in the ideally equal status of all collective members. The broker was usually one of the workers, most likely the finance worker, if there was one.

Employees also presented another structural problem. In theory, the collective formulated policies for the organisation, and workers were employed to execute these decisions. In practice, especially if workers were members of the collective (as in the case of the Archive), they often contributed more to the decision-making process than the rest of the collective, since they had more working knowledge of the organisation. And since workers were recruited for their affiliation with the group as well as their skills, they had as much 'local' knowledge as the other collective members, and therefore felt they had as much of a right to suggest policies.

This set up a potentially divisive structure, in which workers could resent having their opinions ignored, and collective members could resent being told what to do by workers. A worker who additionally had a special relationship with the grant-giving body was in a particularly strong, and therefore threatening, position. Thus funding set up structures which could lead to conflicts, and the Archive was a good example of this in action (see Section 7 below).

6. AFTER THE GLC: FUNDING CONDITIONS IN THE LATE 1980s

By late 1987, equal ops and the structures created during the GLC period remained, but funding dropped seriously. After the GLC was abolished in April 1986, the Government partially covered GLC grant-aid commitments with the London Boroughs providing the rest (Table 8). The final transition year was 1990, and any grants thereafter were funded by boroughs alone. The London Boroughs Grants Scheme (LBGS), set up to administer what money there was, found itself with fewer funds every year.

Table 8   Funding for Voluntary Groups After GLC Abolition[115]

Year	DoE	Borough/District
1986/87	£15 million	£5 million
1987/88	£10 million	£10 million
1988/89	£10 million	£10 million
1989/90	£5 million	£15 million

Severe deficits had accumulated in many Labour Boroughs, as ever tighter controls were imposed by the Government on local rates, and as Government subsidies declined annually.[116] Moreover, legislative changes had heavily controlled London Boroughs' political activities.[117] It was difficult enough for stigmatised 'minority' groups to retain funding, and the late 1980s was an ideal time to 'drop the lesbians and gays' – support for whom had frequently been used as an indication of the 'loony-ness' of the 'Loony Left'.[118]

The late 1980s was thus a period of transition. The majority of funded organisations were still in existence, but it was becoming increasingly difficult to retain funding. There were few new funded organisations appearing, and a number had merged together to pool resources. Organisations and buildings were rapidly closing down, or restricting their services or activities.

The dependence upon local government for increasingly scarce funds was acknowledged as causing stress and demoralisation. As one worker in a lesbian organisation put it:

> When I came to work here, both the workers that left were totally demoralised by the constant fear of losing funding – they wouldn't work – what was the point if it was all going to go down the tubes next year? [...]
>
> Part of the problem was local government. In the past, when Labour boroughs were 'raising our consciousness' about these issues, they were willing to fork out the money to pay for it, but they're not any more. It's like blood out of a stone these days. The GLC set a model – it gave permission to local boroughs to recognise and pay for these issues. But now there isn't any money. Like Hackney being broke and so on...

By the time I moved to London in May 1988, the Archive and LESPOP, amongst others, had recently been informed their funding would not be renewed. The political climate had changed – often referred to as the 'backlash' during fieldwork,[119] meaning a shift in popular opinion to the right, and the steady erosion of local authorities' ability to implement their 'radical' policies, most especially by spending money on them.

After funding cuts at the Archive, the two workers, Paula and Anne, found other posts, but continued to work at the Archive. Anne devoted her time to preparing the Archive's appeal against loss of funding, and she also tackled with renewed urgency the organisation of the Lesbian Summer School. It was now the only short-term source of income to pay the rent in Wesley House if, as expected, the appeal failed (the fact that it succeeded was undoubtedly due to Anne's ability to give the LBGS appeal committee what it required). It was notable that Jean, who frequently had much to say about the doings of the Archive, had very little to say, and no involvement in, the fight to retain funding. The significance of this difference in attitude towards grant aid will become clearer as the Archive dispute is recounted below.

7. THE ARCHIVE DISPUTE

Anne was the 'broker' in the Archive, due to her contacts with the LBGS grants officer. Apart from organising the appeal, she suggested and arranged most of the fund-raising events, and had all the information, contacts and time to organise agendas. Paula, though she spent as much time in the office as Anne, did not have the same 'broker' role nor the same contacts.

Anne's role was not controversial while she was perceived as an executive who made non-contentious suggestions and carried them out efficiently. However, once perceived as attempting to dictate the political approach of the Archive against other collective members' interests, conflict was inevitable. When this happened it was seen as a dispute between Jean and Anne, though the whole collective was involved. Jean was regarded as the main definer of the Archive's political stance – having little to do with the practical running of the Archive (least of all the grant), but instead monitoring its politics. When she began to feel that Anne was offering – and implementing – an alternative position, serious conflict occurred.

The distinction between Anne's and Jean's political views, although subtle, had their roots in the GLC's political project. Crucially, Anne was pursuing the GLC's approach towards 'equal ops', whereas Jean was antagonistic towards that approach. This constituted a fundamental difference on 'identity politics' between the two women, and ultimately the entire purpose of the Archive's existence.

(a) Background: organisation and representation

Until the dispute occurred, the Archive collective paid little attention to the rules contained in its Memorandum and Articles of Association drawn up in 1984. No formal rules were made about how the collective should be organised, its members preferring to make decisions on a consensus basis.

This continued until June 1987, when the collective passed a resolution stating that the workers would be included in a new 'management committee' called the 'Lesbian Archive Collective.' This decision was based on the principle that the collective should be a 'non-hierarchical system of decision-making whereby workers and other collective members would take equal responsibility.' The following year in April, all collective members were made directors of the Archive's umbrella company, Orinda Limited – except the workers, who could not legally be directors, and instead became Secretaries of the company. This was a cosmetic exercise, however; collective meetings never mentioned the role of directors, and the fact that collective meetings were, in legal terms, company directors' meetings was ignored until the dispute erupted. Collective meetings were still run on a consensus basis – no votes were taken, no formal rules were applied.

The Archive's published policy statements reflected the GLC's 'equal ops' more than radical/revolutionary feminist politics – which was, of course, a requirement of the grant. The Archive newsletter stated, under the heading 'Policy', that:

> The Lesbian Archive and Information Centre (LAIC) collects information about lesbians of all ages, classes, race [*sic*] and cultures and about disabled and able-bodied lesbians. We aim to celebrate the diversity of lesbian experience. We do not seek to collect materials which represent lesbians and women in negative ways, which are pornographic or sado-masochistic or which are racist, anti-semitic, ableist or ageist. (*News from the LAIC*, February 1988, no page)

However, there was in practice little emphasis on 'identity politics' either in collective meetings or daily activity. The one exception was the organisation of the Summer School, in which strenuous efforts were made to ensure black, disabled and older women's presence. This was due to three factors: first, the Summer School depended on several grants, all of which required the implementation of equal ops; second, it was no longer acceptable to hold conferences which did not provide disabled access and content of interest to 'minorities'; third, Anne was in charge of organising the Summer School. She was not only well-acquainted with equal ops, but she also agreed with its aims. Jean did not.

(b) The sources of conflict

The problems started on 22 June, 1988. The funding having been restored (to everyone's surprise), a collective meeting was held to discuss Anne's and Paula's re-employment. Paula, who wanted to keep her new job, said she would to return on a part-time basis, and suggested this was a good opportunity to hire a black worker. In response, Jean argued the collective must be certain to recruit a worker with 'the right politics', and it was agreed that 'essential qualities' of a new worker should include 'a positive attitude to separatism'. Two other collective members asked about the definition of 'black', which led to a long discussion, ending in a decision that it should be self-defined.

The tension between 'equal ops' and radical/revolutionary feminism was directly faced in deciding the wording of the job advertisement. To say that the vacancy was open *only* to black women would prioritise 'equal ops'; conversely, to say that a black woman was *preferred* (implying that if a black woman with the 'right' politics failed to apply, then a white woman could be employed) separatism was prioritised. Anne was in favour of the former and Jean in favour of the latter, which was eventually adopted. There was also a suggestion that one of the interviewing panel be a black woman 'borrowed from another project' (as the Archive had no black collective members), but at the next meeting, one member said it was not a good idea to involve women from outside the Archive.

It was therefore of considerable significance that Anne and another collective member produced a job advertisement making it clear that black women *only* need apply. The advertisement said,

> A Blackworker would be encouraged and assisted in setting up a Black lesbian support group and Black lesbians and other minority group lesbians would be welcome to join the Collective and to become involved in helping to develop the LAIC.

At the following meeting, Jean was angry that Anne had omitted the term 'preferred', and demanded it be rephrased. Anne did not attend that meeting, unusually for her, and when she heard about it, she said the advertisement would stay as it was. Paula and several others agreed with her.

As the Summer School was imminent, the meeting decided to defer the issue until after the conference. This proved unwise, for at the Summer School, another serious dispute erupted. Briefly, it involved accusations that two tutors and some participants at the event were 'libertarian' and 'pro-S/M', and that the Summer School organisers had allowed the showing of an 'S/M' lesbian 'pornographic film' in lesbian feminist 'space', thus rendering it 'unsafe', and the Summer School organisers, particularly Anne, were held responsible. The Archive collective members were split on the issue, with Emma, Pat, Gillian and Mary siding with Jean; and Paula, Ellen and Vera siding with Anne. Although Mary had rarely attended collective meetings before, she became centrally involved following the Summer School affair. Monica and Rachel had yet to make up their minds, but rapidly Monica sided with Jean, and Rachel, though she objected to the showing of the film, decided she wanted none of the dispute and left the collective. Towards the middle of the dispute, Emma and Pat also resigned.

Those who disagreed with the showing of the film argued that the reputation of the Archive was now at stake, and Anne would have to answer for that. But the 'blackworker' issue was still fresh in people's minds, for which Anne was also being challenged. The collective meeting to discuss these issues, held on August 4th 1988, was not at all like previous meetings. Mary, who had the previous week called everyone to make sure they would attend (a very unusual action), asked for the discussion to be taped, which was agreed. Normally, collective meetings began in a relaxed atmosphere, and to suggest taping would have seemed extremely out of place. Thereafter, all collective meetings were taped. Anne's behaviour was also markedly different. She looked extremely nervous, and sat a little apart from the group. Though she spoke a lot, she was not directing this collective meeting as she usually did – she was responding to accusations, and was anxious and angry about it.

The 'consensus' in the collective had gone, and it was never to return. A tense debate ensued about whether the showing of the film contravened Archive policy on 'S/M'. Those who argued it did emphasised how many women had been upset by seeing the film in what was supposed to be 'safe space'. Those who argued it did not suggested the film was not 'S/M' and in any case, showing a film in a teaching context was not the same as condoning its content. They also suggested that some revolutionary feminists' threatening behaviour during the conference had rendered it 'unsafe space' quite as much as the film.

The realisation that the collective had no procedure for resolving disputes when no consensus could be reached brought everything to a halt for a time. The problem was deferred by agreeing that all collective members should see the film before further discussions. This was arranged, and it was agreed that collective members could bring along their lovers for support. Most did so. However, seeing the film did not solve the problem.

The next collective meeting, on 10 August, continued the debate over the Summer School for a time, but soon the debate turned back to the hiring of the black worker. Jean repeated that someone of the 'right' politics must be hired and it would be a 'problem' if the Archive hired 'a black lesbian in preference to politics'. Ellen said this would be asking a black lesbian to prioritise her lesbianism over her black consciousness, which was unacceptable. Anyway, she argued, the Archive had to reflect the diverse lesbian community. Jean replied that, 'the Archive is not in a local government employment situation'. In fact of course, it was.

Jean proposed a new job description which altered the word 'black' to the word 'ethnic'. Paula became involved in this debate, arguing that the Archive should provide 'black lesbian only' events, and therefore a black worker was needed. Jean repeated her view that 'the first priority is a good worker for the Archive, and so a black lesbian is not absolutely crucial'. This was unacceptable to Anne's supporters.

At the meeting of 25 August, having finally resolved the advertisement wording by stating that a 'black or ethnic minority lesbian' was 'pre-ferred', the next argument concerned class. The job application form (which Anne also drew up) included the question: 'How would you describe yourself in terms of race, ethnicity, class? Are you physically challenged in any way?' This was clearly gleaned from similar questions on GLC application forms.

Jean led the debate again, at one point saying 'I'd be absolutely horrified by anybody that put class into a job advert. I think it's loony poli-tics' – a direct reference to the 'Loony Left' – and argued, 'This is a total change of Archive politics.' Anne argued that class simply represented another identity, as did age and disability, saying to Jean:

> I know that you do not want to recognise class as a political issue, because I presume you think that it detracts from a revolutionary and radical feminist perspective, but this is not what we are arguing. We are arguing about whether it is important to know about the person applying for a job here. Who they are, their background…

Jean retorted,

> This is just crazy. You can't just suddenly form policy for the Archive and expect it to go through on the nod, something that has never been discussed – and we're not even having a meeting on that issue. […] Criteria in politics are being worked out for the Archive, I think, in a private way.

This revealed the crucial structural issue: Jean was not only concerned about socialist feminist ideas 'creeping in' to the Archive, she was con-cerned that Anne was attempting to undermine the collective's revolution-ary feminist perspective by using her position as a worker. And she associated the *manner* in which Anne was doing this with local govern-ment approaches to 'identity politics'. She clearly saw this as a battle to keep GLC ideology out of the Archive, which Anne was attempting to 'slip' past the collective. Anne protested that she was not doing anything sly, and she quoted from 'equal ops' policies concerning the importance of recognising 'that some categories of people are discriminated against'. Jean immediately retorted that 'we are a feminist archive. We do not necessarily follow the priorities of local councils and other such organisations.'

This debate went on for some time, in the same vein. Finally, the critical difference between Jean and Anne was made crystal clear:

Jean:　　This is a contentious issue. It is a particular politics to use that word [class]. There is no doubt about it.

Anne:　　I think the politics in the Archive around recognising difference is *exactly* what we need to be talking about tonight. In relationship to the film and all other issues. [...] What this Archive means to working class lesbians, to black lesbians – and every other different kind of lesbians. I thought that was what this Archive was about. Recognising the whole lesbian community. It's obviously no longer that.

(c) Structural weaponry

Once the insurmountable divide had been reached, both sides turned to structures, for there were no longer any social relations. And the grant conditions provided plenty of those. They were first used on October 4, 1988. A collective meeting had been planned. At the beginning, one of the collective members on Jean's side stated that the 'Management Committee' (MC) wished to have a meeting without the workers. No mention of a 'management committee' had been made before.

Paula argued it was not a dispute between workers and non-workers, but between one half of the collective and the other. Jean's side, however, insisted that the issue was the workers: Jean suggested that 'the workers are going on as if there was not a collective around'. Various arguments ensued about the legalities of creating a workerless management committee overnight, and whether, even if it was legal, it was feminist practice to have a 'hierarchical organisation' like that where the workers have no say.

Anne again mentioned the responsibility the Archive had towards the grant funding body, suggesting that if the Management Committee (MC) decided to freeze the blackworker job as was being proposed, then this indicated a refusal to abide by the LBGS Equal Opportunities Policy. Jean replied that if Archive policies did not agree with those of the LBGS, then the Archive would be better off with no workers and no funding. The point

Figure 11: Sketch of the Archive Dispute

Sketch drawn about the Archive dispute by one of the collective members, who was on Anne's side. Anne is depicted holding a grant aid form and worker's contract, with Paula next to her. Note also the references to class and race, the attempt of black women to enter the office, and in the insert, showing how some public discussions of the dispute were damaging the Archive's reputation by accusations of 'S+M'.

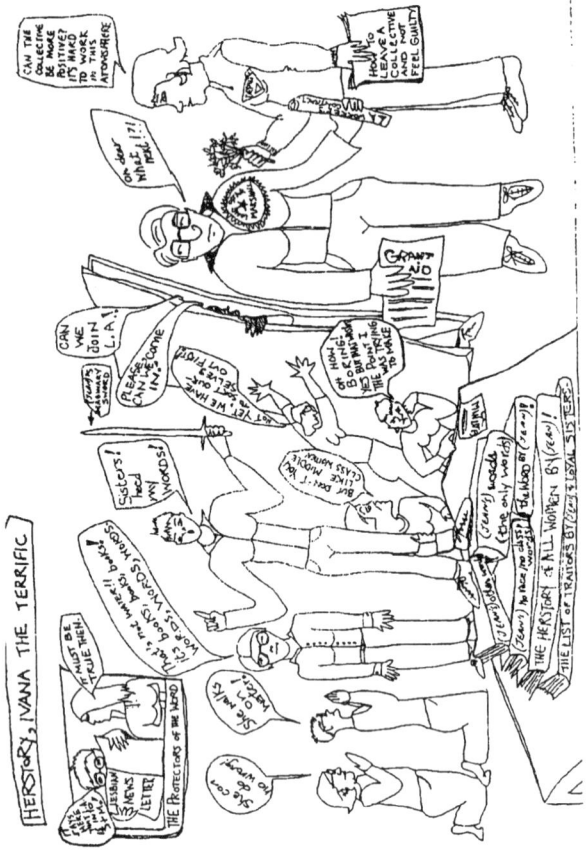

was clear: Jean perceived the LBGS as an unwelcome controlling force and saw Anne as the agent of that control.

There was only one more full collective meeting, on November 2, 1988. Jean's side continued to assert it was a dispute with the workers, and so they continued to hold MC meetings, not attended by Anne's supporters on the collective. The MC sent a number of formal memos both to the workers and other collective members, suggesting tightening of all rules concerning workers, collective members, grievance procedures, decision-making processes and the position of the Directors and Secretaries of Orinda Limited.

The collective thus suddenly began to act like the board of directors of a company (which legally it was). The language used in the memos no longer showed any concern about egalitarianism. They spoke, for example, of 'serious breaches of professional confidentiality' and 'disciplinary procedures'. As these were the only structures for dispute resolution to hand, they were fully implemented, but the motive for doing so was still a dispute over the Archive's politics:

> We...sense that the workers are attempting to change the politics of the Archive unilaterally...ignoring the fact that the Archive was founded on the basis of revolutionary/radical feminist politics – something which until recently we had no reason to believe had changed. (12 October, 1988)

Anne also used all the resources at her disposal. In addition to exploring the legal potentials of company law, she initiated a campaign within the community via friendship networks, her links with other funded organisations and the gay press. And whereas Jean's group chose to represent the dispute as being about worker misconduct and the events at the Summer School (i.e., an issue of feminist politics), Anne's group represented it as being about hiring a black worker (i.e., an issue of 'equal ops'). For example, Anne and her supporters prepared a petition protesting against the freezing of the post. A report prepared by Anne for that final collective meeting on 2 November stated that:

> The Lesbian Archive has been funded over the past four years to provide a resource for the *whole lesbian community*. In accordance with the grant conditions set down by the GLC and now LBGS, funded groups are required to implement an Equal Opportunities Policy....It is because of these policies that we are funded at all....The failure of some members of the Collective to support *positive action* to employ a Black worker and to thereby change the all-white membership of the collective, contravenes our policy of anti-racism. (original emphasis)

Jean's side of the collective also brought along their document to be discussed (an extract of which was quoted above).

Anne's side of the collective left this meeting early. Jean's side remained and drew up a list of 7 decisions, which involved sending formal warning letters of dismissal to the two workers, removing their names from Archive bank accounts and adding their own, stating that the MC was now in charge of the Lesbian Archive, and seeking legal advice.

The MC then wrote to the two workers requesting that they turn up for disciplinary hearings on 30th November. On 23 November, Anne organised a meeting with lesbian feminist friends and supporters, in order to create an 'LAIC Caretaking Group'.

Anne and Paula sent legal representatives to the disciplinary hearing, but did not appear themselves. These representatives were turned away, and the workers were 'sacked' by the MC. The MC then added another lock on the office door of the Archive, so that only its members could enter.

This was the moment of the ending of the Archive collective. From then on, the dispute was carried out between the two sides entirely separately. Anne's group had many more contacts at their disposal for publicity and were much more willing to use them than Jean's group. The gay press became interested, but Jean's group often refused interviews, whereas Anne's group positively solicited them. Both groups had by this time consulted lawyers, and Anne's side had started a support fund to help pay for the legal costs.

The MC asked the workers to come to the Archive on December 7 and collect their belongings. The rest of Anne's group came along. They turned up early to meet and discuss company law with a barrister in another room in the building, and then went to the Archive. There was a short, sharp confrontation at the door between the two groups, with mostly Anne and Jean speaking. Anne asked why she could not attend the collective meeting – even though she was sacked, she was still a collective member. She was told it was not really a collective meeting, since the collective had broken down. Jean complained bitterly about Anne's publicity campaign on the issue. After a few more ripostes, it became clear that Anne's group were not going to be allowed to enter, and they left.

After being informed by the barrister that the Memorandum and Articles of Association stated that a maximum of 30 directors was permitted for Orinda Limited, Anne's group decided to hold an Extraordinary Director's meeting the following evening to elect 16 new directors, giving Anne's side an absolute majority. Formal letters, required by law, announcing the meeting were sent to Jean's side (predictably, none turned up).

The 16 new directors were elected from the Caretaker's Group and minutes were sent to Jean's side saying the workers had not legally been sacked, and that keys were required so they could go to work. Jean's group responded on 15 December by serving injunctions in the High Court of Justice on all directors at the extraordinary meeting, preventing them from changing the locks on the Archive door, announcing that the director's meeting was unconstitutional, and demanding that the financial books (which Anne had kept) be handed over.

This set in train a series of legal wrangles, the details of which do not need to be given here. A number of public meetings were arranged by Anne's group, one of which attracted over 250 women – a measure of Anne's success in publicising the incident. Eventually, independent mediators were brought in to work out a solution. In the end, all the old collective members agreed to resign. Jean's group took the company, some profits from the Summer School and some archival materials. A caretaking group was then formed to restructure the Archive along strict 'equal ops' lines, outlining minimum percentages of the collective to be composed of various minority groups. The Archive was closed down for three months while the dispute was being resolved.

Visiting the Archive again in March 1989 after it had re-opened, I found several black women present working at the central tables, and Anne still there, for someone from the old collective had to show the new women how to run the place. A research project was being carried out by a black lesbian to find out what black women wanted out of the Archive, and what they thought about it (L. King, 1989).

The Archive had become something quite different. Its walls had been given a new coat of political paint, even to the extent that there would no longer be a collective running it. The change was not obvious in the publicity literature, as that had always reflected the 'equal ops' approach; the difference now was that the organisation itself reflected those views. The discursive battle had been won by Anne's side, even though neither side remained in the Archive.

This sort of dispute, though perhaps less explosive in other cases, occurred time and again within the 'community'; throughout the 1980s, one player in the battle was always 'equal ops', and amongst the weapons were the structures and rules contained in the grant-aid conditions.

Without Ken Livingstone's GLC, the Archive would not have existed in the form it did, for the women involved would not have been able to afford it; without the GLC, the organisation's structures and stated aims would not have been so much at odds with the motivations of the women who founded it; without the GLC, the terms of the debate over such issues as race, sexuality and class would have been different. It was a bizarre state of affairs, when one half of a lesbian feminist collective chose to use company law and the High Court of Justice against the other half. It was not a situation that either the GLC or the Archive could have predicted or desired; but the articulation between the two, during this particular historical moment in London, eventually led to it.

The dispute, particularly with relation to the Summer School, brought out other issues as well. The 'community', never remaining in one place for long, was shifting the terms of the debates concerning gender, sexuality and race, away both from the radical/revolutionary feminist perspective and the GLC perspective, though informed by both. This is where the various references I have made to 'libertarians' and the 'politics of difference' comes in. Having looked at where the 'community' was, it remains to consider where it was going as the 1990s drew on.

6 Difference and Desire: The Sexuality Debates

The debates concerning 'libertarians' and 'S/M dykes' brought radical/revolutionary lesbian feminists into direct conflict with other elements of the community. The Summer School was a key moment, bringing together many lesbian feminists who normally moved in differing circles, exposing and crystallising changes in approach within the 'community'. By the end of the 1980s, a new constituency of 'urban amazons' emerged, whose perspectives were fundamentally opposed to those of the radical and revolutionary lesbian feminists.

Beyond the overt political disagreements were wider implications of the debate which neither fully addressed: the deconstruction of the idea of the 'individual' possessed of a discoverable, authentic and fixed identity, and the coherence of the individual's antithesis: society. The possibility that these two conceptual bedrocks were crumbling was the most serious challenge to the 'community' as a whole, threatening as it did both the loss of identity, purchased at such cost, and a political standpoint. The continual use of the term 'fragmentation' not only referred to the breaking up of political unities and alliances, but to the breaking up of their theoretical basis – a new doubt about the 'authenticity' of gendered and sexual identities, through unravelling how they are culturally constructed. The unravelling effectively implied that lesbian feminist critiques of hetero-patriarchal society in fact retained many of those (western) society's assumptions.

The central 'western' assumption retained was the notion of the opposition of the individual and society, seen as a force constraining the individual.[120] For lesbian feminists, 'society' was equivalent to 'hetero-patriarchy' and 'hetero-patriarchy' was based on the antagonistic binary opposition between men and women. With the unravelling of the basis upon which 'men' and 'women' were constructed as a binary pair (i.e., the idea that maleness and femaleness were essential, and opposite, identities), the whole edifice of the construction was challenged. It was not enough for lesbian feminists simply to add race and class to their analysis: it could be asserted that their whole analysis was gleaned from, and thus had the effect of reinforcing, that to which they were ostensibly opposed.

The sense that a theoretical change was underway, but that what it meant was uncertain was often referred to in the late 1980s. Janice's comments on the debates going on in the 'community', for example:

> I think it's about racism and power and not letting other people in. And it's about having different philosophies – and there's one kind of philosophy that has a tendency towards exclusion – of black women, for example, which is racist. And class, all those things [...] It's not just about race or class, it's about...[pause] how can I say this? I think those issues come into it strongly, but I also think there's more to it than that. But I'm not sure what it is.

Parallel changes exist in current literature on the deconstruction of western gender, sexuality and identity, though such literature frequently goes much further than anything in the 'community', perhaps because of its more abstract, rather than practical character.[121] One can only guess at the nature of the connection. There was, as I have shown, an interactive process within the community between different perspectives and changing social and political conditions in London, which may also be reflected in the literature.

In any event, the radical feminist focus on women's personal experiences as the basis for their political analysis exposed many differences between women (race, age, disability, class, etc), which eventually questioned the unitary nature of the category 'woman'. And the social overlaps between lesbian feminists and the lesbian and gay community inevitably exposed the complexity of how sexuality is related to gender in practice. Furthermore, the practical organisation of community organisations introduced another dimension of conflict which exposed the inevitable reality that many women held a variety of political views simultaneously, not all of which were based on radical/revolutionary feminist principles, and in some cases contradicted them. And finally, the trend towards discovering ever-more differences between women began to dove-tail with postmodernist thought and some wider social and political trends towards a particular kind of individualism – the kind which argues that everyone is a minority of one and has the right to create and continuously recreate themselves.[122] That marked a shift from 'identity politics'- the recognition that different groups are discriminated against on the basis of their ascribed group identity – to the 'politics of diversity' – the assertion that no difference is authentic, but created, and therefore freedom involves giving people the means to construct their own differences, using whatever cultural *bricolage* they see fit.

The debates over sexuality and sexual desire during the late 1980s was the main 'location' of the conflict between the different perspectives which illustrates this transformation within the community.

1. THE CHALLENGE OF DIFFERENCE

The 'libertarian' and 'S/M dyke' issues as they were discussed during the late 1980s were concerned with relations and politics *within* the community.[123] Where much lesbian feminism had focused on hetero-patriarchy, thus defining lesbian feminist existence by what it rejected, the 'libertarian' *debate* (as opposed to 'libertarianism' per se) focused on the community itself; and the 'S/M dyke' debate considered the limits of its boundaries. The experiences of women since becoming part of the community were considered, taking stock of the effects of feminism on their lives, reviewing issues previously assumed to be settled (such as 'butch-femme') and more controversially, touched on subjects which had been 'taboo'. These centred on sexuality – not, as before, on a male or male-defined sexuality and its oppressiveness for women, but on *women's* sexuality, and more specifically, lesbian sexuality.

The 'libertarian' side of the debate made much of the 'taboo' nature of such topics, and many 'libertarian' events were given titles which deliberately reflected this emphasis. For example, the 'Making It Public' series of talks and screenings, which centred on discussions about lesbian sexuality and sexual practice. The flier advertising it was intentionally 'breaking taboos' (Figure 12): they were covered with images of women that not only depicted explicit sexual activity, but also other images seemingly calculated to offend radical/revolutionary feminists: these included a 'butch-femme' couple and a black woman dressed in black leather jacket and trousers with a heavy metal belt, white shirt and pencil-thin leather tie. The titles of each event emphasised this further: 'Serious Pleasure Taboos'; 'Top/Bottom, Butch/Femme, Ki-Ki, Lifestyle Lesbians'; 'Across Cultures – Ethnic Identity on the Lesbian Scene'; 'Serial Monogamy, Non-Monogamy, the Single Lesbian'; and 'Fantasies'. The imagery and language used left no doubt that it was intended as a challenge to radical/revolutionary feminism. Indeed, at the first of the meetings, one of the organisers, Dana, explicitly referred to the Summer School (at which she had been a tutor) and the attitudes of radical/revolutionary feminists as the reason she helped organise this series:

The process which led me to start to articulate discussions around taboo issues culminated in an incident at the Lesbian Summer School last year [...]. [That incident] led me to assess my place within the so-called lesbian community, and led me to question my assumptions about lesbian feminism and the joys of sisterhood. [laughter from audience]

[...] What it has made me realise in addition is that our attempts to create an alternative vision are only justified if we can do so through honesty. However, it seems to me that by trying to subvert the dominant heterosexual culture, we are creating our own dogma. [...] Just as in society there's a split between good women, bad women – the madonna/whore syndrome – within our subculture, there's the good lesbian, who's politically correct, and the bad lesbian, who's not really a lesbian. To create an alternative vision, we need to be able to break this cycle. [...] We cannot grow if we suppress our truths, however painful. It's all very well to create a lesbian heaven, but we must live with the world, and we must deal with it.[124]

This sort of statement, common during such debates, made two important assertions: first, that the 'community' did not, as had been assumed, differ from the 'outside' in intellectual form – one 'dogma' was being replaced by a new 'dogma'; and second, that radical and revolutionary feminists were not being truthful about lesbianism. They were being idealistic and refusing to face 'reality'. The focus was squarely on the community's politics, with the added implication that the 'truth' lay in breaking the sexual taboos of the lesbian feminist community.

The 'Making It Public' series was at one extreme (separatist events were at the other). But there were many events which did not pin their perspectives so firmly to their masts. Among these were the 'Celebrating Lesbian Sexuality', 'Lesbian as Rebel' and 'Lesbian History' courses discussed in Chapter 2. The tutors were all feminists and lesbians, and all the participants were also lesbians, at least sympathetic to various hues of feminism.

What these courses had in common with the 'Making It Public' series was an investigation of the concepts upon which the category 'lesbian' was based. Repeatedly, the concepts of gender, sexuality and identity and their interconnections were explored. Repeatedly, the differences between women, whether due to cross-cutting categories such as class, race and age, or due to differences in individual experiences, were discussed. Here, I will focus on the starker distinctions between 'libertarianism' and revolutionary feminism to clarify the transformations underway.

Figure 12:   Making it Public Publicity
The flier adverstising the 'making It Public' series. Note the three symbols on the
bottom right hand corner of the second page, one for GLA (Greater London Arts),
one for the London Borough Grants Scheme and one for Hackney Council. The
organisation which set up the series, the Women's Media Resources Project, was
funded by all these bodies.

The debate centrally involved 'difference', that somewhat shadowy
word which appears to mean everything and nothing, but which (not unco-
incidentally) is also a central term in postmodernist debate. At a basic
level in this context, 'difference' meant the differences between women
felt to have been ignored in the universalising tendencies of radical/
revolutionary feminism.[125] Alice described her views on the matter:

> I began to have problems with separatism…when it comes to talking
> about *difference*, there often seems to be a real resistance to that….
> [T]here's also a politics of an elimination of difference, which seems to
> be the politics of the revolutionary feminists now….It's a symbolic
> annihilation of black women very often, and any other kind of difference

that might exist in the lesbian community....So I've had to rethink my separatism.

However, the 'libertarian' approach also had its own universalising character. Establishing that gender was more complex and diverse than previously assumed did not exclude the possibility that at some (pre-social) level, all people have an essential 'core', an 'authentic' uniqueness of their own. Onto this, diversity could be imprinted by a variety of social, political and historical conditions with which the 'authentic self' interacts, creating (socially-generated) categories of people. The implication of this was to permit the continued existence, underneath all the cultural construction, of an 'authentic' individual who could, in theory, be unearthed, given adequate release of the constraints which prevented such self-discovery.

This 'core self' was rooted, for 'libertarians', in a fundamentally Freudian idea: that sexual desire is 'always already', to use a phrase coined in feminist psychoanalysis.[126] This notion was replacing gender as the 'authentic' source of the self. The interest lay in how this self was expressed, moulded and manipulated by social and historical conditions.

For example, in renewed debates on 'butch-femme', the main question was whether lesbians had managed to escape a socially-imposed gender dichotomy in their dress and behaviour since feminism's critique of it, or whether they had merely 'tinkered' without going outside the paradigm. Three examples make the point.

During the 'butch-femme' discussion of the 'Making It Public' series, several extracts of films were shown. One of these concerned a young woman who wanted to enter an all-male journalism college. With some careful tuition from her brother, she learned how to look, behave, walk, dress and speak like a man. In the final scene of the extract, the transformed young woman is shown walking across the college campus: she is wearing smart men's trousers, a starched shirt, dark sunglasses and has close-cropped hair, and is walking with a long stride, looking assertive and confident. On seeing this shot, the audience (all lesbians and part of the 'community') burst into laughter.

As the discussion afterwards made clear, the young woman's attempt to pass as a man was indistinguishable for this audience from a 'designer dyke': the clothing, the hair style, the physical 'presence' (taking up maximum 'space') all reminded the audience of many lesbians they knew – indeed, of many lesbians in the room at the time. The question one of the tutors asked was, 'Why did we all laugh on seeing that clip? What do the styles we wear say about us, as lesbians?'

In the second example, taken from one of the 'Celebrating Lesbian Sexuality' meetings, the tutor asked participants for examples of famous lesbians they took as 'role models'. The question confused some participants, and many said they were unaware of using 'role models'. One participant said the way she felt about herself had not changed since she became a lesbian; what had changed was how others perceived and treated her. Along with many others, she felt that being a lesbian did not alter the 'self' in any fundamental way – what it altered was her position in the 'gender order',[127] and how others thought of her and behaved towards her.

The tutor then pointed to the clothing participants were wearing, suggesting that their styles might in other contexts be taken to be 'butch' – not the exaggerated 1950s type of 'butch', which parodied masculine style and behaviour, but more of a rejection of the feminine. So was what lesbianism meant, and its connections to gender, being constructed here?

The third example, taken from the 'Lesbian History' course, occurred during a discussion about historical constructions of lesbianism. The 'butch' model of 'lesbian', the tutor suggested, had been used both by sexologists and in literature to define 'lesbianism' in the early twentieth century, asserting that lesbians were more man than woman in a biological sense. Second-wave feminism, the tutor argued,[128] had permitted lesbians to be 'women' once again, and allowed them to think that there was no incompatibility between lesbianism and womanhood – on the contrary. But again, as in the 'Celebrating Lesbian Sexuality' course, the tutor pointed to the clothing and styles of the participants. Out of context, was it not like 'male' clothing and style? Had modern-day lesbians really managed to escape historically constructed gender dichotomies and their connections with sexuality?

All these examples involved discussions of Anglo-Saxon culture and its representations. A number of other discussions looked more closely at cross-cultural divisions within the 'community', asking to what extent the gender dichotomies being discussed in the 'butch-femme' issue was a western cultural construction which excluded lesbians of other cultural backgrounds. Black lesbians in the 'community', for example, wore a much wider range of styles and, some argued, had a very different experience of 'feminine' and 'masculine', because these categories had been defined differently for them – both by the white Western culture in which they lived, and by their own cultures.[129] In what sense, then, were they 'women' in the sense white women were 'women' – or lesbians, come to that? Thus the idea of an unchanging, homogenous, gendered or sexual identity, defined by an overarching 'society', and based on some underlying and fundamentally human 'essence', was being challenged here.

There might in fact be no single measure of qualities such as gender and sexuality.

These discussions were different from radical/revolutionary feminist approaches in that they did not prioritise relations *between men and women* as their object of analysis, and the major concern was not women's oppression at the hands of men *per se*, but the nature of women in and of themselves, most especially as they related to one another within complex social, historical and political contexts. The new approach undermined gender dichotomies, creating a plurality of genders (the concern now being differences within categories rather than between them). And that implied that the apparently universal differences between men and women asserted by lesbian feminists might simply be re-asserting the (western) ideology they were attempting to challenge. Let me expand on this briefly.

The libertarian debate during the late 1980s centred around the nature of lesbian desire, power relations and the sources of identity (all of which were seen as thoroughly interlinked). Of particular concern was whether and how these factors differed for lesbians, and whether labels such as 'heterosexual' and 'lesbian' were meaningful in any cross-cultural, cross-temporal and cross-class terms. These sorts of questions – about the social construction of gender and sexuality and its effect in women's lives – had always been present within radical and revolutionary feminism. The difference in this debate was the focus on lesbian experience and destabilising the idea of a fixed, 'authentic' gender, which existed independently of their context.

This kind of essentialism had previously occurred, it was argued, due to a circular argument incorporating ethnocentric assumptions: lesbian feminism assumed that all contexts were pre-determined by the 'hetero-patriarchy'. But hetero-patriarchy had been defined using western notions of gender identity – which the (western) 'hetero-patriarchy' had constructed. This locked the western conception of gender into the lesbian feminist conception of hetero-patriarchy. Thus 'western' assumptions about what determined gender were incorporated into lesbian feminist analyses of all contexts, with the consequent loss of the possibility that 'man' and 'woman' might mean different things in different contexts. Thus 'differences' between *women in practice*, the focus of the more recent discussions, went to the heart of assumed connections between gender, sexuality and identity and was seriously destabilising them.[130]

The women interested in the 'libertarian' approach, which focused heavily on 'difference' as a construction, were labelled 'libertarians' by opponents because the approach was perceived as *laissez-faire* with regard to sexual practice. This perspective was, to many radical and revolutionary feminists, an apolitical, hedonistic, 'do what you want and forget feminism' one. The approach was not regarded as new, seen instead as a repetition of 'patriarchal' arguments against feminist campaigns to alter sexual relations ('sexual desire is natural, don't mess with it').[131] Far from escaping or challenging 'western' constructions, it was argued, 'libertarians' were reinforcing them in a depressingly familiar way.[132] It was also seen as the same kind of attitude gay men in the 'community' were promoting: that the way to alleviate discrimination against 'sexual minorities' was to have all rules on sexual behaviour relaxed. The implications of this (i.e., do not judge the nature of sexual relations) was something radical/revolutionary feminists had been fighting against for years. What was new in the 'libertarian' debate was that the arguments were now coming from other lesbians (even ones saying they were feminists) within the community and even worse, claiming for women the kind of 'desire' to which men had been 'subjecting' women for centuries. The 'libertarians' appeared to be deliberately destroying all that lesbian feminists had done within the community, eliminating the 'safe space', the 'patriarchy-free zone' they had worked so hard to create.

This brief discussion makes it clear that these debates must be placed in their social context. There were two sides to this: relations within the community, and socio-political conditions in which the community existed – in particular, dominant ideas about sexuality and gender current at the time.

2. THE 'COMMUNITY' CONTEXT

The distinction between opposing groups (pro- and anti-libertarian) was sometimes not as clear cut as the differences in the arguments. Although both sides saw themselves in a condition of 'battle' with one another, some women publicly known as 'libertarians' had recently been part of the 'other side', and most insisted they were still committed feminists. Such women objected to the 'hijacking' of the term feminism by those opposing them, and complained that they were made to feel 'pariahs' of the lesbian 'community'. Many said they felt frightened by the hatred they believed was directed at them for speaking out on lesbian feminist 'taboo' subjects. For those 'libertarians' who had been members of radical/revolutionary feminist groups, had been the friends and lovers of the women who now opposed them, the 'hatred' they felt was not therefore purely about differences in beliefs: it was also to do with a sense of personal betrayal, on both sides.

This was the case for Charlotte, who had been an active revolutionary feminist until recently. After publicly denouncing some of her earlier beliefs at a revolutionary feminist meeting (because she had concluded that many issues could not be explained by a revolutionary feminist approach alone), she was ostracised and subjected to, as she put it, 'a character assassination' by her old friends. She felt this was a betrayal of friendship; they felt she had betrayed their trust in her.

To revolutionary feminists in particular, there could be few greater betrayals than to become a 'libertarian'. Revolutionary feminists responded to 'libertarian' accusations of 'hijacking' feminism by saying that if (radical/revolutionary) feminism was not about understanding and attacking a patriarchally-defined sexuality for women, it was about nothing at all, so anyone who did not question certain kinds of sexual practice was not a feminist. 'Libertarians' were now, radical/revolutionary feminists suggested, trying to assert that lesbian sado-masochism was an acceptable feminist practice. And they also felt frightened of the 'libertarians', of the violence they associated with it and what they believed to be a (patriarchal) hostile use of power in sexual relations.

There was something to this suggestion, as a number of women making 'libertarian' arguments did not take issue with, and indeed occasionally promoted sado-masochism.[133] However, the majority in my experience did not, and many argued that the radical/revolutionary feminist concentration on 'S/M dykes' was a 'red herring', detracting from more fundamental points being made concerning the authenticity of gendered and sexual identities. But to anti-libertarians, libertarianism represented nothing less than the re-imposition of hetero-patriarchy within the lesbian 'community' and a theoretical justification for sado-masochism.

Connected to this is a second point: many women in the 'community' felt peripheral to these debates, and that their concerns were not being expressed. Many felt issues such as S/M were of little interest to them personally, and many also believed the issues were being debated in too 'local' a manner, concerning only community relations, and detracting from the more widely relevant feminist project. One woman said she had joined a group called the 'Deckchairs' as a protest: the Deckchairs were so-called because its members felt the debates in the community were like re-arranging the deckchairs on the Titanic as it was sinking – that is, wilfully ignoring the immediate crisis at hand, the backlash against feminism to which Susan Faludi (1992) refers. Anyway, several women said, the two sides of the debate would never resolve their differences, so the whole argument was not only missing the point, it was a waste of time.

Women making these comments were generally participants at meetings and events rather than speakers or organisers. Their interest in the debates were concerned with, on a theoretical level, the underlying implications of 'difference' and, on the level of experience and practice, with relations between women which were not about 'S/M' or pornography, but about more common experiences in lesbian relationships, which nevertheless involved discussing issues such as power and desire. They felt the debates had been 'exoticised' beyond their own experience.

The third social aspect of this debate was a 'generation gap'. This refers to actual age differences between the women involved, but also to a perception of the 'age' of the ideas: radical/revolutionary feminism was often cast as 'dated', refusing to accommodate changing conditions and new perceptions, and as being overly-judgemental in their attitudes towards sexuality. The accusation of 'prudishness' was not new,[134] but in the context of the 'community', where younger women felt attacked by older women for their behaviour, it took on an ironic aspect: the women who had rejected 'patriarchy' (the 'rule of the Father') were being cast as domineering parents themselves. They were not allowing younger women to 'have fun', to dress as they pleased, to go out to the clubs they chose, to express their sexuality in the way they wanted, to speak about sexual matters in the way they wanted. Although the women writing 'libertarian' theory and setting up meetings were a similar age to their opponents, those it attracted were frequently young women in their early to mid-twenties.

As in many cross-generational conflicts in Euro-American cultures, the question of style was a major point of argument. Within the community, women's styles were seen by lesbian feminists as an indicator of wearer's political perspective (or lack of it). This is understandable in the context of feminist critiques that (male-defined) style sexually objectifies women's bodies within 'hetero-patriarchy'; but to many younger women (who, as lesbians, felt men had nothing to do with their styles), criticisms came too close to stereotypical parental admonishments on the same topic, and they deeply resented it. For some, their styles were expressions of their individuality; for others, they marked deliberate confusion of symbolic meaning. The idea was that no clothing or style lacked symbolic meaning, and therefore women could use the symbols to undermine themselves: by wearing strongly 'feminine' clothing (for example, a mini-skirt) with strongly masculine clothing or footwear (for example, a leather biking jacket and/or steel-toed work boots) the divergent symbolism would clash and the wearer could not be classed either as 'feminine' or 'masculine' in the stereotypical sense. This sort of gender-bending with symbols was common among libertarians.[135]

Furthermore, wearing the 'wrong' clothes in this context could become the same mark of rebellion it had been outside the community. Certain 'politically incorrect' styles (which included the wearing of black leather) became fashionable on the 'scene', and developed as the mark of a 'baby dyke' (see Plate 8): a young, outspoken, strident lesbian who was not afraid to confront either the 'politically correct brigade' within the community nor the admonishments of people outside it, and refused to be made to feel guilty about it.

This 'generation gap' was not lost on radical and revolutionary feminists, and there was concern about the appeal of 'libertarianism', particularly in terms of style, for younger women. For example, Clara, a revolutionary feminist with a teenage daughter, described her view:

A lot of the young women who are trolling around in black leather and studs are just doing it for rebellion. And they're not actually involved in any kind of S/M practice necessarily. But it does worry me in terms of young women joining the movement...that seems to be where they start off....The girls [*sic*] in black and studs...they're on the whole very young....I think there is a generation gap, I think there's a big one.

The 'generation gap' was noted by most interviewees over thirty. Vera for example, in discussing how a large number of younger women had joined the 'community' in recent years, mentioned the difference between them and herself:

They really see things differently than I see them. And I've had to withhold my anger in trying to explain to them certain things, because they'll see me as somebody trying to lecture them. That's a danger. And I don't know if they'll ever see things as I see them – there's obviously a difference in the way they see life and the way I see life.

The Summer School reflected this emerging split between 'young' and 'old'. Conflicts during Jean's courses and the screening of the film (the rest of the conference went relatively smoothly) were seen as a battle between a group of younger participants and a group of older ones. On the question of style, for example, the way some younger women were dressed at the Summer School caused considerable conflict. Several were wearing mini-skirts and make-up (along with heavy men's work boots and thick black tights), which many older women found deeply offensive. The younger women found this incomprehensible, and were certainly not going to back down or apologise. There were no means for the older women to force the younger women to do any such thing in any event: because of the commitment to egalitarianism and 'sisterhood', there were no formal methods of establishing seniority or authority – and nor, for that matter, were there any formal means of exclusion.

This inability to assert seniority or to have the automatic power to exclude is relevant to the way in which much of the 'libertarian versus revolutionary' debate was conducted. The tactic used instead of appeals to seniority, by women on both sides of the debate, was basically 'witchcraft accusation',[136] even to the extent of accusing opponents of being 'evil' – or of being under the influence, consciously or not, of something evil, such as 'internalised hetero-patriarchy', 'internalised racism' or some other form of delusion. As noted before, the accusation of being an 'S/M dyke' or of being 'pro-S/M' was sufficient grounds for exclusion from lesbian feminist spaces. Had the younger women at the Summer School been wearing black leather, and anything resembling chains or studs, they would not have been allowed to enter the conference at all, for that was unambiguously 'S/M gear' and had been explicitly banned from the conference. 'Witchcraft *accusation*' came into play when a woman's previously unquestioned status as a member of the 'community' came under scrutiny. At the Summer School, women eventually identified as 'libertarians' by their opponents were also labelled 'S/M dykes' and/or 'pro-S/M', which the accused women hotly refuted – though they did not deny being 'libertarians', saying that they did not understand what the term meant.

As discussed before, Anne and several other Summer School organisers were asked to account for their actions. Of particular concern was how the film, *She Must Be Seeing Things*, had been permitted to be shown. Anne and two other women had viewed the film several weeks before the Summer School, and had not drawn strong attention to its controversial nature.

Paula, who until then was accepted as a revolutionary feminist separatist, said ruefully, several days before the collective meeting to discuss the organisers' actions, that she felt it was a 'witch hunt', and there was little Anne or the others could do to dispel their 'guilt'. What they were expected to do, Paula suggested, was atone for their actions, and she was sure Anne and the others would refuse (this prediction was correct). As in witchcraft accusation, the accusation itself undermined the value of anything the accused had to say, and one accusation was often sufficient to damage a woman's reputation. Anne's reputation had been damaged beyond repair as far as Jean's side was concerned; many women had been condemned for far less.

Cally, for example, a woman who peripherally helped organise the Summer School, had been accepted as a lesbian feminist. She did not involve herself in either side of the Archive dispute that followed the

Summer School, but it became known that she supported the showing of the film. Following this, rumours started to go around that Cally had been seen at the Fallen Angel wearing black leather from top to bottom. I do not know the truth or otherwise of the accusation, but that was hardly relevant. The accusation itself was enough for some of Cally's old colleagues to decide that she had become 'pro-S/M' (or maybe had been all along). Cally was amongst the women who subsequently attended the taboo-breaking Making It Public series.

The response to these accusations of being 'S/M' or 'pro-S/M' during the dispute was to produce a counter-accusation: racism, expressed through focusing on the Archive black worker issue.

The fourth social aspect of the debate concerned ethnic composition. A number of women regularly accused of being 'libertarians', and who helped organise meetings and events were black, whereas this was rare among revolutionary feminist organisers. The 'libertarian' approach paid closer attention to the *details* of ethnic diversity than did revolutionary feminists, looking at the complexity of cultural differences, rather than discussing racism *en bloc*. Again, this related to the divergent perspectives on the issue of 'difference'. The 'libertarian' approach tended towards 'celebrating' differences between women, whereas radical/revolutionary feminism tended towards underemphasising them, or interpreting them (through the lenses of racism, classism, ageism, etc) as products of patriarchy and therefore bad. The 'libertarian' approach argued the differences between women did not automatically mean 'inequality', whereas the revolutionary perspective tended to imply that they did. The differences created between women along the lines of race, according to this view, were based on inequalities generated by patriarchy and must be resisted rather than redefined and then 'celebrated' as differences.

However, in practice, the arguments against 'libertarianism' were directed mostly at the issue of sexual practice, and almost never at 'difference'. Indeed, the two issues were seen by most 'anti-libertarians' as entirely separate. Although some revolutionary feminists argued that the 'libertarian' emphasis on 'difference' was a cover for promoting hetero-patriarchal sexual practice ('difference' being seen here as inevitably involving asymmetric power relations, which within patriarchy are based on the constructed asymmetries of heterosexual relations), most women distinguished debates about sexual practice from those about cultural diversity. Following the GLC experience and the anti-racist campaigns from ethnic groups, almost all radical feminists, and many revolutionary feminists, were incorporating ideas about 'difference' between women, in terms of cultural diversity at least. But they insisted they had their own analysis on that issue, in partnership with black feminists but quite independently of the 'libertarians'. Many were also annoyed at Jean, who, they felt, was giving revolutionary feminism a bad reputation. Jean's name became the shorthand for referring to the revolutionary feminist side of the debate, and she was perceived as a charismatic and somewhat frightening leader of that side. This association was a source of irritation to many radical/revolutionary feminists who disagreed with her views on 'difference', even if they were sympathetic to her campaigns against 'libertarian' views on sexual practice.

That, in brief, was the complex situation I encountered during the late 1980s in London. Behind the debate were three questions which concerned both 'libertarians' and radical/revolutionary feminists. First, how were different aspects of the community associated or separated and who was to be included and excluded? A variety of representations co-existed within the 'community' and within individuals' own perspectives, despite being in some cases contradictory. The question was whether, as a lesbian feminist, 'membership' of the lesbian/gay 'community', based as it was on sexual identity rather than gender identity, was to be denied, curtailed or somehow incorporated. This was an issue of identity expressed as a challenge to its coherence: can one's identity simultaneously be all about gender and all about sexuality? Second, the nature of gender and its relation to sexuality: if 'woman' was no longer a meaningful universal term, then how is lesbianism related to gender, given that lesbianism itself is culturally and historically specific? This was an issue of identity expressed as a challenge to its 'authenticity' and the individual's 'ownership' of it. If these identities changed over time in line with dominant conceptions and conditions, then in what sense was being a lesbian either 'alternative' *or* self-created, authored as it were, by the self? And third, within the context of the unravelling of central concepts such as gender and sexuality, what is the relation of the individual to the community? Does the community have any right to dictate to or define the individual? This was an issue of identity expressed as a challenge to the perceived opposition between autonomy and sociality: what are the criteria for membership to this community, and did these involve somehow constraining difference or autonomy? If it did not, then can one speak of 'a community' at all, or just diverse individuals who occasionally form alliances and coalitions because of some specific and temporary overlapping interests? But if this is the case, then on what is a woman's individually created gender and sexuality based? Where does the 'stuff' used by individuals to construct their gender and sexuality come from?

This third point was to some extent a retreat from the implications of the first two, a reassertion of identity as 'authenticity' and 'ownership', and it was continually referred to in 'libertarian' discussions. Many expressed resentment at the constraint on autonomy in lesbian feminism: at having definitions of womanhood and lesbianism imposed on them; at the denial of difference and individuality they saw in lesbian feminism; at being ostracised for expressing views perceived as anti-feminist; at the imposed 'silencing' of issues important to them; and most of all, resentment about being made to feel guilty and afraid of their own feelings. These were not only battles against other women; they were also internal battles.

This came up repeatedly in the Making It Public series, particularly the meetings on 'taboos' and 'butch-femme'. In the former, many participants said they felt their sexual experiences and desires contradicted what their feminist beliefs suggested they should be; in the latter, many discussed how the restrictions on style and self-expression experienced through feminism made them feel guilty about wanting to be more feminine, saying they were made to believe this was 'internalised hetero-patriarchy' rather than, as they now proposed, an expression of themselves.[137]

Not only 'libertarians' were troubled by these issues. The conflict between autonomy and community affected most women as frequently mentioned, and the relations between lesbianism, feminism, gender and identity were continually being reworked, often painfully. The insistence from feminism that the sources of desires and beliefs *should* be investigated – combined with the new direction of the debates over gender and sexuality – meant that nothing was certain any longer. Labels such as 'radical feminist', 'revolutionary feminist', 'libertarian' and so on did not mean a great deal for women's self-identification. The 'libertarian versus revolutionary' depiction of the debate, emphasising the extremes of the opposing sides, suggested a static position for each perspective and belied the more seriously destabilising implications of the debates. Challenging the idea of an 'authentic' identity, when previous alliances had been founded on that idea, was leading women increasingly to question whether they could be identified by *any* political label, or whether everyone constituted a minority group of one.

More cynical observers called this anti-authenticity and anti-community trend 'super-individualism', the outcome of the 1980s swing to the right. Many older women in the community suggested Margaret Thatcher's message had influenced younger women: while believing they were radical in their lifestyles, they were in fact reinforcing a conservative creed: 'I stand alone and unique in the world as an individual; I have no responsibilities to others for my actions, and others have no right to interfere with my choices.' The problem with this approach for many lesbian feminists was the assumption that choices individuals make somehow emerge out of the ether, or a person's 'inner soul', untainted by oppressive ideologies, power regimes, social and economic structures, etc. One woman suggested that this 'super-individualism' prevents analysis of how and why people make the choices they do. The answer appears to stop at, 'because it is an expression of individuality'. As far as many lesbian feminists were concerned, there was no critical analysis if one simply accepted difference as just 'difference' – fragmented and unconnected with anything else in the world.

Yet it is clear that women were not dealing with these issues in a vacuum. The very terms of the debate strongly echoed wider social conditions and perspectives, and many debates concerned whether ideas expressed by the opposing groups were in fact re-phrased 'dominant ideology'. The question of whether it was possible to become a different kind of 'other', not the kind defined by the wider culture in which the debate arose in the first place, continually emerged in these debates. Much of the 'libertarian versus revolutionary' conflict was based on this issue.

Three persistently tackled issues make this clear: first, in claiming that lesbianism was something more than and different from a feminist political standpoint, to what extent was lesbianism being defined by popular notions of it as an identity? Second, in claiming that styles originally designed to be 'feminine' could be imbued with different types of meaning (as 'libertarians' suggested was possible), to what extent was the original meaning of the clothing being utilised and therefore perpetuated? Third, in claiming that lesbian desire could be defined separately from dominant cultural ideas about it, to what extent are those notions really escaped? So in order to understand the parameters of this debate, those wider cultural notions about gender and sexuality as they existed outside the community in London in the late 1980s need to be briefly investigated.

3. THE WIDER CONTEXT

In attempting to understand more popular notions about gender and sexuality in London during the late 1980s (as opposed to academic notions), the Clause 28 legislation proved particularly instructive. Clause 28, which prohibited the 'promotion of homosexuality', emerged out of a concern that certain Labour-controlled local authorities and education authorities (mostly in London) were in the business of 'social engineering'.[138] The legislation was intended to stop the GLC-influenced 'positive images' and 'anti-discrimination' campaigns on behalf of lesbians and gay men.[139] Such campaigns were seen as 'unspeakable' by their opponents because they constituted a dismantling of the negative symbolic effect of 'homosexuality' by providing it with positive content. Clause 28 (a piece of legislation first unsuccessfully attempted in 1986, shortly after GLC abolition), reflected one kind of response to the GLC's policies on homosexuality: an effort to put what the GLC had started back in a 'closed box'.[140] The advocates of Clause 28 were concerned not so much about the 'proper' representation of homosexuality as they were concerned about the 'proper' representation of social existence as a whole. Let me briefly expand on this assertion.

The pro-Clause 28 lobby did not have any positive perception of homosexuality, and in fact such perceptions are not widely available in the media or popular culture.[141] The most positive statements outside gay liberation and lesbian feminism tend to be of the 'live and let live' and 'I don't mind as long as they do it in private' nature. What homosexuality represents in a popular symbolic sense is the opposite of what 'normal' sexuality and gender should be, one means of establishing the way heterosexuality should be practised by contrasting it to an opposite. The concept says nothing about how you 'should' behave as a homosexual, for you should not be a homosexual at all if you want a 'correct' social identity.

Thus the contents of the category homosexual in popular understanding is based not on what a homosexual *is*, but on social definitions of *heterosexual* behaviour. The contents of what constitutes homosexuality could therefore vary, according to changes in views about what constitutes a 'normal' (heterosexual) social being. Examples of such 'normality' which use the *category* 'homosexual' (as opposed to its practice in reality) to provide the negative instance include: sexual practice should not include sodomy and one should not be promiscuous or attracted to children; men should not act in effeminate ways, and women should not act in masculine ways; assertiveness is 'correct' for men, it is 'incorrect' for women; emotional behaviour is 'correct' for women, it is not 'correct' for men. And so on. Whether the negative characteristics are genuinely more common among homosexuals than heterosexuals is hardly the point. Such assertions about the right and wrong ways to be a person do change, and therefore the 'content' of the category 'homosexual' changes along with what most concerns people about the nexus of sexuality, desire, gender and social identity.

One further implication emerges from this: there is a 'gap' in popular culture concerning a positive definition of homosexuality, in the sense of what 'it' is, rather than what heterosexuality is not. Those labelled 'homosexual' are left with nothing but the idea that they are not a 'correct' social person. Thus lesbian feminism, gay liberation and more latterly 'libertarianism' could be seen in part to be filling that gap, using homosexuals as the referent, rather than a notion of 'ideal social being'. The 'positive images' campaign could be seen in much the same light. But to do this undermines the 'Otherness' of homosexuality, it removes its use as a dumping ground for what is 'bad' about gendered and sexual personhood. In many respects, the same could be said of Edward Said's undermining of the notion of 'Orientalism' (Said, 1991).

Looked at in this way, the assertions of those supporting Clause 28 become somewhat more comprehensible. They saw the 'promotion' of homosexuality as an extremist socialist tactic intended to undermine the 'moral fabric' of British life – including family relations, children's education, the mental and physical health of the people and ultimately, the very survival of British 'society' itself.[142] Two pro-Clause 28 statements from Parliamentary debates illustrate the point:

> Undermining the common standards of society, flaunting behaviour that the overwhelming majority of those brought up in this country and its traditions find revolting, unsettling the minds of the coming generation is one way [...] of changing the society in which we live. (Dr. Rhodes Boyson MP, Minister for Local Government, 8 May 1987, *Hansard*, c.1002).

> [promotion of homosexuality] will lead to the ultimate breakdown of family life, upon which the whole tenor of this country and its ways have been formed for generations and which the whole civilised world has been formed and based. (Lord Swinfen, 18 December 1986, *Hansard*, c.326).

These were strong claims indeed – the assertion that the whole of society rested upon maintaining a negative image of homosexuality. The opposing side argued that such assertions were completely unwarranted. For example:

> Why is there this emphasis on homosexuality? Why are some people so obsessed with it? What is the evidence that homosexuality is threatening to others or to society as a whole? I have not heard a word on that.... Let me remind the Noble Lords that most sex crime is heterosexual; most child abuse is heterosexual. Are we asked to believe, quite against the facts, that homosexuals are, as it were, generally less law abiding than the rest of society? Are we asked to believe that homosexuals are

less useful to society than the rest of us? Indeed, I ask myself [...] whether the proponents of this clause [...] actually have the faintest idea of what they are talking about. (Lord Peston, 11 January 1988, *Hansard*, c.995).

So those opposing the clause made their case using a different tack: that of civil liberties, describing instances of discrimination against homosexuals as a result of 'intolerant' and 'bigoted' attitudes towards a minority. Anti-Clause 28 speakers drew out the implication that using homosexuals as a category of 'abnormal' to promote a notion of 'normal' goes against the rule of equality under the law. For example, Allan Roberts MP asked the Minister for Local Government for a clarification of the statement in the Clause that local authorities and schools must not allow teaching of the 'acceptability' of homosexuality as a 'pretended family relationship':

The Minister [...] said that 'acceptability' meant not putting forward the view that homosexuality was the norm. Will the Minister tell us what he means by 'the norm'? Does he mean that only a minority of people are homosexuals, so it is not the average or typical, and they are not the majority? Or does he mean that it is abnormal and that makes it inferior or wrong? (Allan Roberts MP, Standing Committee A, 8 December 1987, c.1228).

The debate can thus be seen, once again, as a conflict of interests between 'society' and the 'individual'. The pro-Clause lobby were arguing that the interests of 'society' (as they defined it) were paramount; the anti-Clause lobby were arguing that the rights of individual autonomy and choice were paramount. There was much which was topsy-turvy about this debate: the right wing side were arguing that homosexuality was a 'choice' (and therefore could be 'promoted'), and the left wing side were arguing that it was not (and therefore could not be 'promoted'); the right wing side were arguing that the state must restrict individual freedom in this instance (and thus protect 'society'), and the left wing side were arguing that it must not (and thus protect autonomy and freedom from dis-crimination). The *form* of the debate – a dispute about autonomy versus society – was the same in Parliament as it was in the community. The *content* of the debate was different in the two spheres, but underlying aspects of the concepts of sexuality, gender and identity had the same reference points.

One example, that of the nature of male and female sexuality, and the different approaches towards it, outlines the complexity of this. In Parliament, the debates on Clause 28 concentrated almost solely on male

Figure 13: The Civil/Human Rights Approach to the Campaign against Clause 28
Some examples of the 'civil/human rights' approach to the campaign against
Clause 28 – from an article on the Archbishop of York's statement in the House of
Lords and from the Stop The Clause lobbying group.

homosexuality, referring only occasionally to lesbianism (as has always been the case in parliament this century).[143] The pro-Clause lobby assumed that men were the active partners in sexual activity, and therefore any threats to 'society' would naturally come from male, not female, homosexuals. This was explicitly said on occasion:

> Homosexuals, in my submission, are handicapped people....I think particularly of male homosexuals because, as I think the noble Earl, Lord Halsbury, brought out, lesbians are no danger. (Lord Longford, *Hansard*, 18 Dec 1986, c. 316)

Why 'handicapped people' should be a 'danger' was not made clear by Lord Longford, but in any event this reflected the view that (a) homosexuality is about sexual practice, and (b) sexual practice is male-defined and enacted; men are the actors (subjects), women the receivers (objects). This argument (as expressed by pro-Clause 28 MPs and Peers) suggested a male-defined sexuality is biologically given, and therefore would never change; what had to be controlled was 'unnatural and immoral' use of this sexuality.

As has been seen, lesbian feminism agreed that sexual practice in this society is male-defined and enacted, but argued that there was nothing 'natural' (or 'moral') about this, but was instead the result of hetero-patriarchal ideology.[144] Lesbian feminists therefore argued that the 'threat' to 'society' (a hetero-patriarchal society) came not from male homosexuality, but from lesbianism, based on the assertion that lesbianism undermined male-defined sexual practice. What was assumed as given by the pro-Clause lobby was for lesbian feminists precisely the point of attack: male-defined sexuality, they argued, was at the root of the entire corpus of representations in this society concerning gender and identity which worked so thoroughly against the interests of women. It is interesting to note that this lesbian feminist approach was not expressed in Parliament by either side; the 'anti-Clause' lobby avoided it because it implied that homosexuality (lesbianism) not only could but *should* be promoted, and the reason for promoting it was indeed to undermine the 'moral fabric of society', which could only be a good thing for women, as far as lesbian feminists were concerned.

The gay liberation perspective was different again, arguing that there was nothing innately moral or immoral about different sexual practices between consenting individuals, and therefore it was wrong to discriminate against them. 'Positive images' was to be welcomed because it helped to dispel the discrimination against homosexuals based on incorrect beliefs about their character and behaviour (precisely what the pro-Clause lobby objected to about 'positive images').

This variety of representations, both in form and content, were deeply involved in the disagreements between 'libertarians' and revolutionary feminists. The 'libertarian' appeals to greater autonomy from the 'restrictions' imposed on them by lesbian feminism were seen by lesbian feminists as attempts to remove the political relevance of lesbianism and redefine it as an 'individual choice', masking its true source in heteropatriarchal ideology. The 'libertarian' argument was thus interpreted with reference to the wider perspective – just as revolutionary feminist arguments were interpreted by libertarians – so that in effect both were addressing the wider discourse and, most importantly, using its form.

That wider discourse contained three cross-cutting assertions: 1) that gender identity (what constitutes maleness and femaleness in individuals) is closely linked to sexual orientation and sexual practice; 2) that there is 'normal' and 'abnormal' desire, which has implications both for the individual and for society; 3) that at some level, whether ascribed or achieved, sexual orientation is an 'authentic' individual identity, and defines individuals in a fundamental way. The fact that on an analytical level these three characteristics could contradict one another detracts little from their being utterly intertwined in practice. Identity always implies gender and sexuality and has social implications – for individuals, for the state, for family structures and so on. All three, gender, sexuality and identity, refer back to one another, become both cause and symptom, source and justification for the others: they cannot be separated within this construction.

The debate between 'libertarians' and radical/revolutionary feminists indirectly began to break this self-referential intertwining: not as a Kuhnian paradigm shift (Kuhn, 1962), a sudden and complete break, but in the muddied and partial way shifts occur in the everyday practice of living. In this community new ideas did not usually replace old ones, they were *added*; in the doing of theory rather than in the thinking of it, much more contradiction is tolerable. The break implied in denying both gender dichotomies and an interlink between sex and gender should have, analytically speaking, led to a break in the notion of an 'authentic' identity; but in practice, it had not, by the end of the 1980s in this community, occurred, at least not explicitly. In everyday life, 'womanhood' and 'lesbianism' still had an authenticity, even if the 'scene' had become more diverse, and even if political campaigns now spoke of alliances, coalitions and diversity rather than groups, identities and unity. The acceptance of a partial and multiple, never-completed, continually changing identity – the loss of some underlying 'authenticity' – was too great a demand, greater even than the previous radical/revolutionary feminist demand of 'perfect womanhood'. To lose that in the fragments was, by the end of the 1980s at least, asking too much.

Furthermore, although the 'community' generated the conditions to make the unthinkable thinkable – expressing the possibility that there was no 'authenticity' of the self to be revealed, but simply more cultural construction – the practical world in which these women lived belied this. Stark distinctions between men and women in material, structural and symbolic terms, and between heterosexuals and homosexuals still continued in everyday lived experience.

This made the conclusions of the debate for most women in the 'community' if not in-credible, then im-practical. The discrimination directed against lesbians and gay men was real; the line between 'gay' and 'straight', 'man' and 'woman' was real; and as important, conflicts within the community which were threatening to tear it apart were real. These realities may be based on a collection of cultural constructions, a slanted view based on Euro-American assumptions, but they had concrete effects nevertheless. As Dana put it, 'we must live with the world, and we must deal with it.'

So despite the radical changes in ideas encouraged by 'libertarian' debates, the social, political and material world in which the 'community' existed had not changed nearly as radically, and until it did, the thinkability of a partial, fragmented and forever incomplete identity could only be a 'reality' set against a concretely-experienced 'fiction'. No amount of intellectual recognition of the fiction could remove women from their everyday experience of a world which constantly reasserted notions about gender and sexuality as fixed and authentic individual identities.

This was the wider context in which 'difference' entered the debate. The following section illustrates how this was experienced in various confrontational moments, using the Summer School and its aftermath as examples of how the conflict was played out.

4. SOME MOMENTS IN THE BATTLE: THE SUMMER SCHOOL AND ITS AFTERMATH

The problems at the Summer School began on the first day. The first overt confrontation occurred when Jean gave a talk in the afternoon, entitled 'The eroticisation of women's subordination'. She outlined the argument that the notion of sexual pleasure was defined under 'male supremacy' to mean violence against women, which women were supposed to enjoy. The two tutors of the video course, Samantha (a white woman) and Dana (a black woman), attended this talk, and began to question Jean. In particular, they were concerned that Jean was not incorporating 'difference' into her analysis, and they felt Jean's analysis of both power (based solely on gender dichotomies) and women's sexuality (defined solely through their oppression by men) was inadequate.

Some weeks after the event, Samantha recalled what happened:

> When I went to [Jean's] talk with [Dana], I'd never heard her speak before, and I was really interested in what her line was. But I was so outraged that it was so – almost white purist – I couldn't stand that. And I said, 'wait a minute, you're talking about lesbian desire becoming like heterosexual desire. It's not. And what about difference? What about black women and white women?' I mean, she thought I went in there to deliberately stir it up, and I didn't....And [Dana] was accused of bringing up race as a diversionary tactic, like, 'we're here to talk about sex, stop talking about race.' And [Dana] was saying, 'it defines me as much as your patriarchy defines you.' And [Jean] kept saying, 'No. Patriarchy defines you more.' And [Dana] was saying, 'wait a *minute.*' You know.

The debate went on for some forty minutes, during which time tempers began to flare among Jean's supporters in the audience. After the meeting broke up, several of these women went to the Archive office and complained about Samantha and Dana's behaviour. They suggested that the two women were 'libertarians' and 'pro-S/M' and demanded to know why they had been allowed to attend the Summer School, let alone teach a course at it. Objections were first raised here about the proposed showing of extracts of the film, *She Must Be Seeing Things*, by Samantha and Dana as part of their course.

This confrontation set the tenor for the following disputes. Dana and Samantha's actions were interpreted by Jean's supporters as a personal (and planned) attack against Jean; the incident also 'revealed' the tutors as 'libertarians', and signalled the presence of such women at the conference.

Trouble had also begun in the morning, however. Jean had given the first part of her course entitled 'Lesbian Sexuality', and although no serious altercations occurred, a number of women (most quite young) had been surprised by what Jean had said. They expected a discussion about lesbian sexual practice, and had instead heard a lecture on 'male supremacy' and shown slides of 'hard core' and 'soft core' pornography to indicate exactly what that meant. Jean made it explicit that she intended to show there was no real distinction between the 'libertarian' approach and the more standard male-produced and consumed pornography. This touched a nerve with many women present, who had come expecting to be able to discuss their own sexual desires in conditions where they would not feel condemned for 'admitting' them.

There are two points to note here: first, there was a serious misunderstanding between a good portion of the audience and Jean about the nature of the discussion expected in the course; and second, Jean had shown a lot of explicit sexual material in her presentation, to which many women reacted badly. Jean said during the first meeting that it had to be seen in order to understand the true nature of what feminists were up against.

Over the next two days, the confrontations in Jean's courses became more fraught, and women increasingly interrupted Jean's lectures to question her on the way she had structured the debate. They felt she had 'polarised' the issues to such a degree that few people in the room could identify with either side.

These challenges drew continual responses from revolutionary feminists in the audience, who began to accuse these women of being 'pro-S/M'. At the third meeting, Jean was sufficiently concerned about the challenges that she felt she had to outline her perspective again:

> As I understand it, sexuality under male supremacy is constructed around the subordination of women – meaning that for women, the subordination of women is sexy and exciting and pleasurable. And for men the subordination of women is sexy, pleasurable and exciting. [...] Inequality in and of itself is sexy. [...]
>
> If this is the case, then [...] the fact that inequality is sexy becomes the very air we breath under male supremacy. It's very difficult to separate off a form of sex which is not about eroticised power difference, but is about equality. The definition that I gave of eroticising power difference on Friday was – I called it heterosexual desire. [...] For me, the aim is [...] to eliminate heterosexual desire, which is created from the power difference that exists in male supremacy between men and women.

After explaining this a little further, Jean offered women the chance to comment. One member of the audience, after stating she felt she must speak because she and several others had been so upset by Jean's presentation in the previous two days, said:

> There's a lot about what's being presented, and the analysis, that I don't disagree with. However, I think the way it is being presented means you either agree with that analysis completely or you're an S/M dyke [...] And I'm very unhappy about that. [...] I've got to the point where I was

thinking, 'Hold on. I'm not a feminist anymore, because I don't like what you're saying.'

After some more discussion, Jean returned to the original topic she had planned for the third meeting, which was about the re-introduction of 'butch-femme' relationships in lesbian communities. Several women again objected to the way Jean presented the material, one woman saying,

> Whether you wear a jacket or a dress isn't automatically some kind of butch and femme position. I mean, I'm a bit concerned – I think it's really offensive. [...] We ought to recognise that women have a freedom – or should have – to dress the way they want to dress and look the way they want to look, without having to be automatically butch or femme.

There was a great deal of discussion about the meaning of style during this meeting, during which a split between 'young' and 'old' perspectives was fully discussed. Jean repeated several times that because younger women had not experienced the 1950s, they did not realise the true power of the styles they were now choosing to wear.

At one point, a woman attempted to interrupt Jean's discussion, but was cut short by another member of the audience with the comment, 'If women want to talk about it, there's plenty of space in the building.' The first woman responded with:

> Well thanks a lot. I'm really tired of being marginalised in this meeting. A woman here has just walked out because she's intimidated. She's too frightened – don't 'tut' at *me* – she is too frightened to stand up and say why she is feeling marginalised and I think a lot of women are feeling like that here. [...] I don't want to be told that what we are doing is projecting our pornography. [...] We should be able to come here and talk about ourselves, and not be told that we're not proper feminists [...] Why are we continually being put down and silenced?

After the third meeting, which broke up in considerable acrimony, Jean herself had become so upset by the challenges that she refused to attend the fourth meeting, and another tutor took over.

At the same time as Jean's course, Samantha and Dana had been presenting their course in another room (entitled 'Film and Video'), with few of the confrontations which had occurred in Jean's course. This might seem surprising, as the content strongly reflected the emerging perspective which had caused such acrimony when offered by members of the audience in Jean's course. The first part of the course focused on the way lesbians view film, and 'how lesbians have appropriated popular female icons in order to intervene in dominant film narrative.' It involved looking at instances where lesbians had viewed 'mainstream' film and television characters as images of lesbianism. The second part looked at how black lesbian sexuality had been represented in film. Dana argued that these representations had more to do with the 'fantasies and fears' of 'white directors or black male directors' than with 'reality'. The course also considered black women's writing on sexuality 'where desire and sex can be represented from a perspective of power and control.'

In short, the video course was looking – in a language suffused with irony, humour and the vocabulary of postmodernism – at all those issues concerning 'difference' between women and its relation to sexuality, gender, identity and their cultural construction discussed above. That the course did not cause confrontation can be explained by the fact that the committed revolutionary feminists were all attending Jean's course instead of the film course, and that Samantha and Dana were touching on issues many women in the 'community' were beginning to want to discuss: a focus on themselves, rather than 'hetero-patriarchy'; images of themselves, rather than those of 'pornographers'; their own sexuality and its complexity as it was experienced, rather than what it 'should be'. Had the women attending the video course felt it was being 'anti-feminist' there would undoubtedly have been strong objections. As lesbian feminists, many had spent years challenging others in public. That other women attending the conference felt both the tutors and their perspective were profoundly anti-feminist is therefore an indication of the emerging divergence in perspective which had been developing for some time in the community.

As the conference went on, there were increasingly vociferous demands that the proposed showing of the film be cancelled. This was refused, on two grounds: first, that showing the film was not intended as an endorsement of its content, but the basis for a discussion within a 'safe space'; and second, that Jean had shown far more explicit and potentially offensive material in her course. The protestors said it was not the same thing at all – first because Jean made it clear that she opposed the pornographic images she had been showing; second because *She Must Be Seeing Things* had been made by 'pro-S/M' lesbians who endorsed 'lesbian pornography'; and third because the tutors showing it had already proven to be 'libertarians' themselves.

The difference, then, between the slides shown by Jean and the film was that the film was a representation of lesbian relationships, made by lesbians, and the tutors intended to discuss the film in terms of the audience's own experiences. The film was about two women, one black and one white. The black woman was cast as the more aggressive, stronger woman, more 'butch', and the white woman as the more feminine, less assertive 'femme'. The black woman was plagued by the belief that her lover was having affairs with men, and she went to some efforts to 'compensate' for not being a man, even at one point visiting a sex shop to see if there was something she could get there which would help. But being disgusted by what she saw, she left without buying anything.

On the day the film was to be shown, opponents took control of the building's tannoy and denounced the film. They also set up a room as a 'pornography free zone' where women could go as an alternative to seeing the film. Several also stood at the entrance to the hall appealing for women not to enter.

Samantha and Dana, by now extremely nervous, started to set up the projector and other equipment. One protestor got up and, in her effort to stop this preparation, almost toppled the projector. She was restrained by another woman, and the showing of the film began. As with Jean's third course, which occurred on the same day as the showing of the film, this event broke down in disarray.

By this time, the atmosphere in the building was electric. The fourth day involved long discussions between many people – participants, tutors, organisers – about the previous day and what it had meant, and that the organisers were going to have to account for their actions. Some younger women were upset at having been labelled 'S/M dykes' by revolutionary feminists, and felt they had been 'trashed and degraded'. Others were upset at the showing of the film, and felt they would not recover from seeing it for many months.

Once the Summer School ended, the repercussions began to reverberate around the 'community'. Reports on the event began to appear in various journals,[145] the women involved discussed the issues within their networks of friends, and discussions about the Summer School started to emerge in courses and groups, analysing what had happened. Thus the rifts and changing perspectives began to cohere, having been so clearly exposed. In the background, there had been the anxiety over attracting black women to the event, concern over ticket prices, previous disputes over issues involving race, class, disability, power, sexuality and their relations. During the Summer School all of this came to the fore. Following the conference, events such as Making It Public, and on the opposing side, groups such as the London Separatist Group were formed, and with it a 'siege mentality' increasingly developed.

The Summer School was not all that occurred that summer and the following autumn in the London 'community'. There was also Joan Nestle's visit to London to promote her book, *A Restricted Country* (1987), and a collection of lesbian erotica entitled *Serious Pleasure* was published (Sheba, 1988), followed closely by the launch of a lesbian erotica journal entitled *Quim*.[146] Furthermore, a one-day conference, entitled 'The SM Debate', intended to bring together 'S/M dykes' and their opponents for a discussion was arranged. Revolutionary feminists had initially agreed to attend, but on seeing that the 'S/M dykes' had arrived in 'S/M gear', they set up an alternative meeting elsewhere in the building.

Some women against 'S/M' were in the audience, and two on the panel, but they were vastly outnumbered by those in favour. The event became an expression of the view of 'S/M dykes'. They argued that both their practices and styles were 'reclaiming' power for women, they lifted the 'repression' on sexual expression enforced by both society and radical/revolutionary feminists. It was, they argued, the most 'revolution-ary' of acts, the most undermining of the status quo.

There was a considerable difference between this approach and that of the 'libertarians'. So far as 'libertarians' in my experience discussed 'S/M' in their own meetings and events (which they did not do often, because of the continual accusation that this was all they were interested in), it was to analyse how the constructions of power and desire came to be associated with one another in that particular way in this culture. To revolutionary feminists, however, the 'S/M dyke' position was at the end of a very short continuum from 'libertarian' approaches.

As a result of this collection of meetings and publications by the 'libertar-ian and pro-S/M contingent', some radical/revolutionary feminists responded in kind. There was a feeling amongst many lesbian feminists that the 'sexual-ity debates' had been dominated by the 'libertarian' viewpoint and the lesbian feminist view was either being silenced or 'trashed'. Several months after the end of my time in London, on 20 January 1990, a conference was held at Wesley House organised by the London Separatist Group, entitled the 'London Lesbian Sex and Sexuality Day'. Its intention was to refute 'lib-ertarian' accusations that separatists were 'anti-sex', and to attempt to deal with the issues that had been brought up in 'libertarian' debates.

In the introductory talk to this conference, an organiser said it was 'important to claim an active sexuality for lesbians against S/M', which was 'an alternative perspective to S/M'. There was an appeal that there should be no 'labelling' by participants, because the event was there for open discussion about sexuality and sexual politics. It was added that no racism or disablism would be tolerated, and if anyone at the conference behaved in a persistently 'oppressive' manner, they would be asked to leave.

During the sessions, the emphasis was on problems in lesbian relationships – for example, physical and emotional violence and abuse, the difficulties presented by interracial and inter-class relationships, the problems of alcoholism, and the problems of women who were 'survivors of sexual abuse'. Even the session entitled 'What sex means to us', though it started as a positive discussion, ended with an extremely emotional debate over whether rape was possible in lesbian relationships.

In all these debates, women often said it was the first time they had discussed such issues in public. It was also frequently suggested that the problems were the result of 'internalised hetero-patriarchy', the imagery constantly provided by 'hetero-patriarchy' and women's experiences at the hands of men, which had been brought into lesbian relationships and the 'community'. It had not been possible, in other words, to leave the 'hetero-patriarchy' outside the door of the 'community'.

This was a quite different emphasis from the Making It Public series. Even though that series dealt with problems in lesbian relationships – and one of the most tense sessions was the meeting about interracial relationships – there was no emphasis on abusive relationships. Rather, there was an analysis of what were considered 'ordinary, everyday' relationships, and a re-analysis of sexual practices and desires which had been deemed to be 'oppressive' and 'patriarchal'. The London Lesbian Sex and Sexuality Day looked at the things which had gone 'wrong' in the 'community' – in effect, the failure, as yet, of the lesbian feminist ideal to achieve egalitarian relations between women. In contrast, the Making It Public series was questioning whether the basic premises of that ideal were correct. Again, the Sex and Sexuality Day was ultimately based upon, and continually referred to, the asymmetric relationship between men and women as the source of problems for women. The Making It Public discussions did not refer to this at all, but rather the wider field of representations of gender and sexuality between women.

What can be seen here is the emerging transition, bitterly fought, from a structural and social view of the way power and inequality operates, to a cultural and individualistic view of it. In academic debates, this has been marked as a shift from a determinist and/or essentialist perspective to one which emphasises difference and a lack of any 'authentic' truth. Within the community, both perspectives claimed the moral high ground on several levels: lesbian feminism through its insistence on keeping a focus on the constructions of power and their attendant representations of gender which led to women's oppression; and the new 'politics of difference' approach by saying that power was a diverse and complex thing which could not leave anyone innocent of its implementation and reproduction.

However, the way the whole debate was experienced in practice in this community can only really be understood when the specific historical context in which it occurred, London in the late 1980s, is taken into account. In many ways, what lesbian feminists objected to were the trends towards self-interest and constructions of self through consumption (of knowledge, of style, of technology), containing an underlying assumption that somehow if you 'just let go', your true self would emerge, through the way in which you choose to construct yourself. To lesbian feminists, this was the sign of an increasingly conservative social and political context, and it was allowing hetero-patriarchy to express itself without any critical analysis.

Many women in the community felt peripheral to the substantive content of these debates, not identifying particularly with either side, even though they felt important conceptual issues needed to be addressed. To conclude, then, are some comments from such women about their thoughts on the changes underway in their community. They record a wide range of perspectives, and reveal the sense of uncertainty and change. They also reveal the continual necessity of 'having to live in the world, and having to deal with it.'

5. CHANGING PERSPECTIVES

The first two women, Suki, a 20-year old Chinese woman, and Dawn, an African (Ghanaian) woman of 19, were both fairly new to the 'community'. So their views represent some aspects of younger women's perspectives. Suki had begun working for women-only and lesbian organisations, first voluntarily and then as a salaried worker. She deliberately avoided reading any 'lesbian erotica' or 'S/M' literature. Dawn had very recently become involved with the 'community' at the time of the interview, having sought it out because she concluded she was a lesbian. Unlike Suki, she was interested in the 'sexuality debates' and had read some of the more recent 'erotica' publications with some interest.

Suki (20)

I object to that politics of having someone tell you what it's all about, being a lesbian – I feel I don't need to be told, because I am a lesbian.

We're all individuals anyway, and our experiences are different, you can't define it in only one way.

As regards what feminism is, at the end of the day, I would leave it up to other women to define themselves. Because how I define feminism or lesbianism may not be how others define it.... A lot of women who call themselves feminists assume that because we're all women, we're all equal, all the same; and therefore, we face similar oppressions – which I think is totally bullshit.

Lesbianism has affected parts of my life, but other things have affected other parts – being Chinese, young, poor, homeless and so on.

Dawn (19)

I think as black women, we're really marginalised, ignored and kept apart or whatever in feminist and lesbian circles...and yet it's funny, because in the company of black women – not black lesbians – I feel intimidated...I feel more threatened telling a black woman I'm a lesbian than telling a white woman. Don't know why, really.

I don't see myself as fitting into any particular label. I just am. I don't like to categorise myself like that, y'know.

When I caught the tube back from the Pride march this year, I had all my Lesbian and Gay Pride march badges on. And all the gay men got off at Stockwell. And I was just standing there on my own...and I looked around, and the whole carriage was full of men. I quickly crept down to the bottom of the carriage and I took all the badges off – and I felt so *ashamed* that I should have to do that....That spoiled the whole day for me – having to come back into a heterosexist world.

Clara (33)

For me, being a separatist has got to be being a lesbian. To be able to live as a lesbian without being oppressed as a lesbian....But of course, different women have different reasons for being separate – for example, black women – and I do involve myself in mixed anti-apartheid campaigns. But I only compromise my politics so far, otherwise I'd lose my integrity, you know.

[At a London Separatist Group meeting] women were talking about what one can do about all this so-called sexual liberation, S/M type business....Separatism was given a bad name, it was accused of being racist, it was accused of being intransigent, it was accused of being the thought police...and I think a lot of women shied away from it....But I actually believe that it's a cornerstone...it's fundamental and if you get too far away from the basic bits, you lose track of where you're going.

Vera (40)

The collective dispute I was involved in at the [...] Women's Centre was both about racism and lesbianism.... It really was an education to me about racism...I learned how people proceed when they want to block black women. And there was – there always is – anti-lesbianism, but that didn't matter, because that only matters to the lesbians. Even in this dispute, it only mattered to the lesbians.

If you'd asked me whether it was important to be a lesbian in order to be a feminist three years ago, I would have said yes. Now I'm not so sure. I kind of miss the unity of the WLM, I do miss it.

S/M is about power and sexuality and sex – and hate. I think it's challenged in the wrong way – it's repetitious, so I'm bored with it. And I think on both sides of the fence it's very polarised....

There are times when I just don't want to be around feminism, feminists. I just want to relax and not have to think.

I wish there were more actions these days – less actions against things like *She Must Be Seeing Things*, which was just a stupid movie.

Ruth (47)

I used to call myself a radical feminist, but I think these terms are outmoded now, because there's been too much fighting over the demarcation lines.... Now I'm so often told that I'm a libertarian that I get too personally distraught.... I don't really know how I would define myself. I'm not sure that I want to.

I myself don't think that the question of butch and femme and sadomasochism are the most important issues of our time.... You can't just say yes or no to S/M, you have to establish what you're talking about.

Mandy (39)

I actually got into libertarianism *first*, and then moved into lesbian feminism. That kind of gay lib, 'anything goes' philosophy.

I think I used to feel that all men basically hated women...but I was never very clear on where that hate came from....I saw it as institutionalised in patriarchy and the rule of fathers. If I had to really push myself now, I would actually still agree with a lot of that. But the implications aren't the same any longer, and also the sense of inevitability isn't the same.

I think I put up a lot of resistance at first to any suggestion that my politics might somehow be directly related to my being white and middle class...for a few years, I still felt very threatened by the issue of race diluting the strength of revolutionary feminism....

Nicola (30)

You see, I went through a big crisis...because revolutionary feminism doesn't take into account things like racism and classism and anti-semitism and that sort of thing...I mean, there was a time when I was a strict, strict feminist separatist.... Now I think, where was my head?

Two things happened...sisterhood stopped being wonderful, and women had to start taking on board differences between us. And the way that came about was that women who were different...just got fucked off with being left out....

Alice (29)

I always knew somehow that lesbianism was very, very subversive, even before I was a feminist...so in an unformulated way, I've always experienced lesbianism as subversive.

I guess the otherness, the difference, always seems to be a problem, because it's almost like...because we're a community under siege, to admit difference sometimes makes it feel insecure, and seems to weaken our resistance.

The S/M debate seems to me – although the S/M dykes claim it's about difference, it seems to me to be more about how that group is the same. I mean, they all look the same to me.

Charlotte (30)

I don't think there can be a single definition of lesbianism, because there's a difference between your feelings and your identity, isn't there? I would define myself as a feminist and as a socialist these days...I've been quite linked, I suppose, to radical feminism.... But in some ways, I feel I'm too libertarian to quite fit in. There are some radical feminists who annoy me intensely – who are still very didactic and narrow.

A friend and some other women and I met to discuss the issues raised by Joan Nestle's book, and we were hoping to meet her, because we all defined ourselves as femme in some ways...we felt that was rather embarrassing, really, we felt ashamed of it....And I had to tell my friends that I'd been to this thing – and they were clearly scandalised and didn't know what to say next....But it was an opportunity to say that we felt quite alienated on the lesbian scene – we felt it, it was real for us.

In the end, I don't think it's much of an alternative to lesbian feminist denunciations if all you can say is, 'I do what I like'. You know, we are still supposed to be feminists as well – we are still supposed to have some recognition of the social construction of sexuality....But I don't know quite where to draw the line any more.

Penny (33)

I don't tend to define myself much anymore. I mean, I still define myself as a lesbian and a feminist. But there was a time when I would have called myself a revolutionary feminist and a separatist...the change came slowly, and after a time it became clear that those titles weren't appropriate anymore.

Yes, lesbians are talking more about sexuality these days, talking about all sorts of difficult things, things that we would have said challenged lesbianism in the past....And it seems strange, because societally, we're not any safer now than we were then...

I think that the new lesbians, the young lesbians, seem to have totally different – I don't know what goes on for them at all....All I can say is that it seems like a whole new thing, and I don't know what's going on [laughs].

Samantha (29)

I found the Summer School really terrifying – partly because I had no control over what people were thinking about me – making me into this monster, someone who used to be a good feminist, and who had now gone bad. There was also a woman who said I was an S/M dyke...it was horrible. I was extremely hurt by it.

I think if you've already given up the privileges of heterosexuality, you're taken into a family called 'lesbian feminism', and you discover a movement and a place where you can be accepted, then it's quite frightening to think that...you won't be acceptable there – because then you'll be out the door twice. I think I was frightened of that....But I suppose with me and [Dana] being the *enfants terrible* anyway...we had nothing to lose.

I started off as a socialist feminist and then I became a radical feminist and now I don't know what my label is, I don't think I have one – generally feminist.

Jane (38)

Ah, the delights of being in the women's movement. Although I still talk about being in the WLM, I tend to do it in a historical sense, cos' I actually don't think it exists now, except in the hearts and minds of those who want it to exist. Do you know what I mean?

Beverly (40)

I do think I experience a different kind of atmosphere now...now, in a way, it's harder to express the complexity of the issues....I think that's happened a lot in the polarisation of issues around sexuality and stuff: if you're not pro something, you're assumed to be anti it....I find that very difficult and saddening, in a way.

I *think* I would say I was a lesbian radical feminist. I think these terms are hard to – they've got increasingly hard to understand, really.

I think the mainstream in Britain is classist, racist, bigoted, igno-rant, mean-spirited – though the trouble with defining the mainstream is that you perpetuate their power. I think *we're* the mainstream [laughs].

CONCLUSION

The intellectual means had been created, out of the conditions of the com-munity within the context of London, to completely re-organise the notion of both the individual (in the possibility of becoming 'dividual') and the individual's relationship to society. The possibility of the former had been predicted as long ago as 1938 by Marcel Mauss, in his discussion of the Western category of the person:

Who knows whether this 'category', which all of us here believe to be well founded, will always be recognised as such? It is formulated only for us, among us....With us the idea could disappear. (Mauss, 1987 [1938], p. 22)

By the end my time in London, however, 'society' had not changed enough to make it either possible or desirable to self-destruct, as it were. Accepting that both 'authenticity' and 'community' are products of the cultural and social ideologies which lesbian feminism was seeking to escape meant the necessity of accepting that there was no 'core' to dis-cover in the self, no 'authentic identity' for the 'community', only what was created, recreated, illusory. But that shadowy entity I have called a 'community' was women's lived reality, based on friendship networks and on divisions and alliances generated from the divisions and alliances existent in the wider contexts of London and Britain. And so the politics of gender, sexuality and identity marched on, albeit somewhat altered by the experience of being exposed to the harsh light of day.

Appendix A
Section 28 of the Local Government Act, 1988 ('Clause 28')

28. –(1) The following section shall be inserted after section 2 of the Local Government Act 1986 (prohibition of political publicity)–

"Prohibition on promoting homosexuality by teaching or by publishing material.

2A.–(1) A local authority shall not–

(a) intentionally promote homosexuality or publish material with the intention of promoting homosexuality;

(b) promote the teaching in any maintained school of the acceptability of homosexuality as a pretended family relationship.

(2) Nothing in subsection (1) above shall be taken to prohibit the doing of anything for the purpose of treating or preventing the spread of disease.

(3) In any proceedings in connection with the application of this section a court shall draw such inferences as to the intention of the local authority as may reasonably be drawn from the evidence before it.

(4) In subsection (1)(b) above "maintained school" means,–

(a) in England and Wales, a county school, voluntary school, nursery school or special school, within the meaning of the Education Act 1944; and

(b) in Scotland, a public school, nursery school or special school, within the meaning of the Education (Scotland) Act 1980."

(Local Government Act 1988, Part IV, 'Miscellaneous and General', c. 9, p. 1163).

Appendix B
Subjects Covered in Life History Interviews

1 Age, nationality, amount of time spent in London
2 Family background
3 Past and present occupations
4 Education
5 Details of housing in London
6 Reading habits and music listened to, and any changes in these over time.
7 Development of interest in feminism, definitions of feminism, and changes in attitudes towards feminism.
8 Lesbianism, its definition, its relation to feminism, how interviewees came to define themselves as lesbians, and effects on their lives as a result of being lesbian feminists.
9 Attitudes towards men.
10 Spirituality
11 Involvement with and experience of lesbian feminist groups, organisations and collectives.
12 Whether there is, in the minds of the interviewees, a 'community' to which they belonged, and if so, how the community is defined, interviewees' connections with and experiences of the community.
13 Friends and lovers
14 Economic conditions
15 The use of resources in the community and concepts of 'safe space' within the community.
16 Current disputes and debates within the community.
17 Attitudes towards children
18 Knowledge of recent feminist and lesbian feminist history and interest in lesbian history.

Notes to pages 1–16

1. *Local Government Bill*; Parliamentary Debates, House of Commons Official Report, Standing Committee A, 29th Sitting, December 8, 1987; London: HMSO, c.1199.
2. See for example, Alderson and Wistrich, 1988.
3. Foucault, 1987 [1976]
4. In Judith Butler's terms, this was an attempt at using performance as a means of revealing the 'abjected beings' created at the same time as a 'normative' subject is created (Butler 1993, p. 3), and as a means to challenge that normative subjectivity. See also Chapter 6 in this volume.
5. *Women Like Us*, 1988 and *Women Like That*, 1991, Clio & Co. Productions for Channel 4 Television. See also Neild and Pearson (1992).
6. There are many texts which reflect these ideas. As radical feminist theory developed within a political movement, some of the most useful come from earlier second wave feminist writings based on women's experiences of the movement. These include Millett, 1971; Morgan, 1970; Levine *et al*, 1973; Sarachild, 1978 and Bunch, 1987. See also Gunew, 1991, Part IX. Alice Echols (1989) has written a detailed historical account of the radical feminist movement in America, in which she skilfully describes the roots and development of the theory there. A British version does not yet exist, but Echols' description of later radical feminist ideas reflected those I found during fieldwork. She distinguishes this later perspective by calling it 'cultural feminism', but I retain the term 'radical feminism', as this was the term used during fieldwork. Other useful secondary sources include Eisentstein, 1984 and Spender, 1985b. There is no generally available description of revolutionary feminism's development. Revolutionary feminist theory can be gleaned, however, from its use in, for example, Leeds Revolutionary Feminist Group, 1981; Jeffreys, 1985 and 1990; Hoagland and Penelopc, 1988; Rhodes and McNeill, 1985; and Trebilcot, 1986.
7. See for e.g. Barrett, 1988, Segal, 1988 and Rowbotham, 1989, though Barrett in particular has revised her approach, and gives 'patriarchal ideology' more autonomy from particular modes of production/reproduction than she had done earlier.
8. See for e.g. Mitchell (1974), Chodorow (1978), Gallop (1982), Irigaray (1985), Moi (1985), Marks and de Courtivron (1981), Sayers (1986) and Brennan (1989).
9. See, for example, Dworkin, 1981; Brownmiller, 1975; Caputi, 1988; Griffin, 1981; Hanmer and Saunders, 1984; Hanmer and Maynard, 1987; Jeffreys, 1982a and 1982b; Kappeler, 1986; Rhodes and McNeill, 1985; and Ward, 1984.
10. See, for example, Rhodes and McNeill, *op. cit.,* Jeffreys, 1990 and Stanko, 1985.
11. See, for example, Daly, 1979; Frye, 1983; and Smart and Smart, 1978.
12. Of course, the idea that women are the 'other' was suggested earlier by de Beauvoir (1953).

13. The phrase 'woman-identified-woman' was coined by Radicalesbians (1973). There is an interesting parallel with this analysis and Ardener's (1975) notion of 'muted groups'.
14. See, for example, Abbott and Love, 1972; Johnstone, 1973; Ettore, 1980; and Raymond, 1986. This analysis is clearly based on Western constructions of sexuality. See Bell, 1987, for very different reasons for women's separatism amongst Australian aborigines.
15. See, for example, Faderman, 1985, Jeffreys, 1981 and 1985 and Lesbian History Group, 1989.
16. See, for example, Leeds Revolutionary Feminist Group, 1981.
17. This point has also been noted by Strathern (1988, pp. 26–27), though I am making a stronger distinction between feminisms here than she does.
18. This is what Strathern (1988, p. 25) refers to as the 'ethnicist vision' of feminism.
19. The argument that multiple genders exist has been made in other contexts. See, e.g., Connell (1987), Riley (1988) and Butler (1990). See also Alcoff (1988) for a discussion of the problems the 'deconstruction of woman' poses for feminism in general.
20. In some respects, this is a very different argument from those which formed the basis of the 1960s and 1970s 'anti-establishment' communes in northern European and northern American countries, where the overall impression was an attempt at suppressing the individual in the interests of the social whole. However, one could also see these communes as an attempt to erase the *impersonal* or anonymous aspects of public life by merging the public into the private. In any event, it would seem that such communes experienced the same ambivalence in balancing the social and the individual as has been described above. See, for example, Abrams and McCulloch (1976) and Kanter (1972).
21. See Dumont (1986); Carrithers, Collins and Lukes (eds, 1987); Morris (1991); Heller, Sosna and Wellerby (eds, 1986); Bordo (1987) for discussions of the development of individualism in the West. See Lukes (1973) for descriptions of different forms of individualism within western philosophical traditions.
22. See Ardill and O'Sullivan, 1986, for a detailed summary of the history of the LLGC dispute over 'S/M'.
23. *GLC Women's Committee Bulletin*, Issue 19, September 1984.
24. Male to female transsexuals were not accepted as 'women' and could not therefore be lesbians. Stories occasionally circulated in lesbian circles of a transsexual attempting to 'pass' as a lesbian and how the 'deceit' had been unmasked.
25. There was also, of course, myself as a member of the collective. I have not included a description of myself for two reasons: firstly, the collective understood that I was present mostly for research purposes, and therefore I would not be contributing to the group in the way that others did. And secondly, I feel that my own character is stamped across the entirety of this text and needs no further elucidation.
26. My breaking of this rule here is due to the fact that the Archive collective no longer exists in this form, and now has a much more open-book policy. See Chapter 5.

27. At the time, e-mail and the internet were not widely known about or used. In more recent years, this has been a major new source of networking for groups such as lesbian feminists, and has considerably expanded, and somewhat altered, the conceptual 'space' of such communities. This will have to remain a subject for a future publication.

28. Bourdieu defines 'doxa' as a moment when 'there is a quasi-perfect correspondence between the objective order and the subjective principles of organisation [...where] the natural and social world appears as self-evident. This experience we shall call *doxa*, so as to distinguish it from an orthodox or heterodox belief implying awareness and recognition of the possibility of different or antagonistic beliefs.' (Bourdieu, 1987, p. 164)

29. For discussions on the experiences of lesbian mothers in custody disputes, see for example, ROW Lesbian Custody Group, 1986; Hanscombe and Forster, 1982; Bottrill, 1988; Allen and Harne, 1988.

30. Discussions of CR groups can be found in Echols, 1989 and Eisenstein, 1984.

31. See Grau (1995), esp. pp. 1–15.

32. In 1991, the pub changed its name to 'The Angel'; the upstairs rooms became the offices of the *Pink Paper*, and were therefore no longer available for meetings.

33. It has now changed hands, but still has the same character.

34. See Ardill and O'Sullivan (1986) for a discussion of the dispute over lesbian S/M at the LLGC.

35. See Green (1991) for a more detailed analysis of the 'style wars' between different groups within the community.

36. Blackman and Perry (1990) also noted this. See Green (1991) for a more detailed discussion.

37. For a particularly detailed and poignant description of the historical importance of 'spotting' to lesbians in the USA, see Faderman (1992).

38. See, for example, Waters (1977).

39. This is a point also made by Connell (1987) concerning how gender regimes vary according to context.

40. See 1981 census, GLC Special Table DT 1286

41. See Egerton (1990), Anlin (1989) and Austberry and Watson (1983) for more details on difficulties lesbians in particular experienced in finding housing.

42. London Research Centre, October 1989, *London Housing Statistics 1988*, Statistical Series Number 70, p. 34.

43. See, for example, Ponse (1978) especially Ch. 3, on differing levels of secrecy about sexual orientation.

44. See Carpenter, 1988 for an example of the effects of lesbianism in the workplace.

45. See also Allen and Harne, 1988.

46. See also the collection of papers in Moore and Meyerhoff, 1975, for a cross-cultural view of communal ideology.

47. See Hui, 1988, for a similar view from a Chinese perspective.

48. The conflation of these ideas can be seen in Lillian Faderman's work (1985) and that of Sheila Jeffreys (1985), who both argue for a feminist motivation in some women's rejection of men in western history (see also Jeffreys,

1984, for a discussion of whether sexual practice between women was necessary in order for them to be called lesbians). Raymond (1986) also suggests that this is cross-culturally true.

49. The 'Chicago School' spatial analysis of cities, in terms of the 'mosaic' pattern of communities, the 'concentric circles' notion and the 'melting pot' theory were not accurate representations for London, in my view (cf. Park, Burgess and McKenzie, 1967; Wirth, 1956; and Zorbaugh, 1929 for examples of 'Chicago School' urban theory).

50. There is a wealth of writing by lesbian feminists on the subject, but few are context-specific -e.g., Hoagland, 1986a and 1986b; Jeffreys, 1986, 1989 and 1990; Evans, 1989; Dykewomon, 1989; Jennings, 1986; Trebilcot, 1986; Amazones d'Hier, Lesbiennes d'Aujourd'hui, 1986; and Silveira, 1988.

51. See, for example, Shepherd, 1987; Herdt, 1984; Nadelson, 1988, Greenberg, 1988 and Blackwood, 1985a. See Blackwood 1985b on the absence of discussions of lesbianism in anthropology. See Strathern, 1988, for a discussion of Melanesian studies on ritualized homosexuality, especially pp. 208–221.

52. A comprehensive list can be found in Greenberg, 1988.

53. See Hawthorne, 1991, for an expression of this distinction.

54. *ibid*, p. 139. This view of lesbianism is shared by a number of lesbian feminist theorists, although they reject a class analysis. See, for example, Wittig, 1980 and 1981; Jeffreys, 1985 and Faderman, 1985.

55. Wolf (p. 98), Lockard (p. 86), Krieger (p. 6), Barnhart (p. 90) and McCoy and Hicks (1979, p. 65). Ettore's suggested that some lesbian feminists during the 1970s became territorial in London (pp. 151–154).

56. Wolf, p. 98, Lockard, p. 86, Castells, p. 140, Barnhart, p. 90.

57. cf. Dominy, Lockard, Wolf, Krieger, Barnhart.

58. cf. Castells (*op.cit.*), Fitzgerald (1986).

59. cf. Wolf, Lockard, Krieger, Barnhart. See also Ross, 1990. An added feature in the American studies was the popularity of sports teams – especially softball, soccer and pool.

60. Dominy (1983, p. 109), Wolf (p. 162), Ettore (1980, p. 60), Barnhart (p. 92) and Krieger (p. 60).

61. Dominy (pp. 109–111), Lockard (p. 93), Ettore (p. 60), Krieger (p. 60). Wolf's interpretation was at variance with all other studies.

62. In Barnhart's case, the emphasis on friendship with ex-lovers was far stronger than in London (Barnhart, 1975, p. 94). See also Becker, 1988, for a study on lesbian ex-lover relationships.

63. See for example, Dominy 1983, p. 102

64. See particularly Ponse, *op. cit.,* Chapter 3, and Warren, 1974.

65. cf. Vance, 1984, and Martin and Lyon, 1983, p. 301.

66. See also Linden *et al*, 1982 and Leidholdt and Raymond, 1990.

67. See SAMOIS (1987) and Linden *et al* (1982), both suggesting that 'S/M dykes' had been in existence for some years.

68. cf. Cohen (1985) and Anderson (1987).

69. See, Schutz, 1970; Berger and Luckmann, 1967; Garfinkel, 1967 and Bourdieu, 1987 (especially p. 72) for discussions of 'taken-for-grantedness'.

70. Fuss, 1989, Ch.6. See Altman *et al*, 1989, for examples of this trend in gay theory and the problems it has generated, particularly the papers by Weeks,

Vance and Vicinus. See also Rabinow (1987), Boyne (1990), Butler (1990 and 1993) and Weedon (1987).

71. As a movement in Britain, 'first wave' feminism began with the suffrage campaign in 1866 (Tuttle, 1987, p. 369). See also Faderman (1985 and 1992).

72. These 'subcultures' were what I have referred to as 'scenes'–essentially social spaces consisting of bars and clubs (cf. Weeks, 1983 and 1987, Greenberg, 1988, Ch. 7).

73. See, for example, Katz, 1976; Weeks, *op. cit.*, McIntosh, 1968, D'Emilio, 1983, Halperin, 1986, Plummer, 1981 and Greenberg, 1988. A recent exception is Faderman (1992), which does look at the overlap between the lesbian feminist and lesbian and gay communities.

74. See, for example, Raymond, 1986; Jeffreys, 1981, 1982b, 1985; Jackson, 1983, 1987 and Auerbach, 1978.

75. See Faraday, 1981.

76. See Caplan, 1987b; Weeks, 1983 (Ch. 1) and 1987 and Fuss, 1989, p. 108. Faderman (1992) places it later, at about the end of the nineteenth century.

77. Foucault's argument is based on an analysis of 'dividing practices' (see Rabinow, 1987, Introduction). The term was used particularly in *The Birth of the Clinic* (1986b) and *Discipline and Punish* (1985).

78. Certainly, terms for different sexualities were coined by doctors and sexologists such as Karl Ulrichs (1860s, 'Uranians'), Karoly Benkert (1869, 'homosexuality', 'inversion' and 'perversion'), Krafft-Ebing (1886, a whole series of labels, including 'sadism', 'masochism', 'transvestism', 'urolagnia', 'necrophilia' and 'antipathic sexual instinct', his term for homosexuality), Havelock Ellis (1975 [1897] and 1936 [1910–1913]) and Magnus Hirschfeld (1914) ('sexual inversion'), Edward Carpenter (1908, 'intermediate sex'). See Weeks, 1985, Ch. 4 and 1987, p. 33, and Greenberg, 1988, Ch. 9.

79. E.g. Faderman, 1992, for the most detailed account available thus far; Weeks, 1983, Ch.7; D'Emilio, 1984, p. 145, and Anon., 1982.

80. See, for example, Faderman (1992) Ch. 7; Davis and Kennedy (1986); Sawyer (1965); Newton (1984); Lorde (1979); Martin and Lyon (1983) and D'Emilio (1983). See also Bannon (1986a and 1986b) and Mushroom (1983). The continued existence of 'butch-femme' role-play in the USA is documented in, for example, Vance (1984) and Nestle (1987).

81. For example, Havelock Ellis (1975).

82. In fact, women were represented as finding sex distasteful (unless they were 'whores'). First wave feminist campaigns against the male sexual 'drive' strongly reflected these views. See Jeffreys, 1987.For qualifications of this claim, see Gay, 1984. This is not of course a universal cross-cultural belief. See, for example, Goodale (1989) and Nadelson (1988).

83. See Neild and Pearson (1992).

84. cf. Faderman, 1992; D'Emilio, 1983; Katz, 1976; Weeks, 1983.

85. Jeffreys, 1985, Ch. 7.

86. Faderman, 1985, Part IIIA, Ch. 5, and see particularly Jeffreys, 1989. In her 1992 volume, Faderman considerably moderates this view.

87. The 'working class' status of most of the women who frequented the bars was also suggested by Davis and Kennedy (1986) and by Faderman (1992,

Ch. 7). As in the USA, the 'bar scene' in London was clearly separated from the middle class literati crowd in London's 'bohemia' and 'Bloomsbury set' (cf. Hanscombe and Smyers, 1987).

88. See also Jeffreys, 1987, and Raymond, 1986. Vicinus in Altman *et al*, 1989, criticises both the Jeffreys/Faderman approach and the Nestle approach by arguing they present an ahistorical view of lesbian 'authenticity'.

89. See Rich (1980), Auchmuty (1989) and Raymond (1986). The earlier exception was de Beauvoir (1953).

90. See also Breines, 1982, for a description of the 'new left' movement in the USA.

91. This was reported by many women in London and is documented in Ettore (1980, pp. 145–147).

92. D'Emilio, 1983, p. 236; Alderson and Shulman, 1983; Dixon, 1988, p. 75.

93. See also Echols, *op. cit.*, pp. 210–241 for the USA; Alderson and Shulman, 1983, for Britain.

94. Tuttle, 1987, pp. 290–291 and pp. 179–180.

95. Two early texts were Abbott and Love (1972) and Johnstone (1973).

96. See Barth (1970) and Cohen (1974) for example. This issue is generally covered more adequately by studies of the city, rather than ethnic groups or communities within cities (see, for example, Hannerz, 1980; Pahl *et al*, 1983 and Castells, 1977 and 1983).

97. See, for other examples of urban communities, Burton (1978) and Young and Willmott (1962). However, both these cases were marked by territoriality and strong, unifying connections seen as crucial to the existence of the 'community'.

98. cf. Hannerz, 1980, p. 115*ff*.

99. See also Anderson (1987).

100. See also Becker, 1967.

101. This point is also noted by Talai (1986) for the Armenian community in London.

102. See, for example, Epstein, 1978; Abner Cohen, 1974 and Glazer and Moynihan, 1978.

103. An interesting exception is Talai's research on the Armenian community in London (1986).

104. Bourdieu (1987), Chapter 2. Bourdieu argues that practice (how one behaves) tends to be limited by 'habitus', which he defines as 'the strategy-generating principle enabling agents to cope with unforseen and ever-changing situations.' (p. 72).

105. For summaries of the drive to abolition, see O'Leary, 1987; Carvel, 1987; Flynn *et al*, 1985; Forrester *et al*, 1985; GLC, 1986; Young, 1984; D. King, 1989.

106. For Britain, see Bryan *et al* (1985), p. 164 *ff*.; Sisters in Study (1988); Centre for Contemporary Cultural Studies (1982); for the USA, see Hooks (1990); Moraga and Anzaldúa (1983); Combahee River Collective (1986) and Smith (1983). On black lesbianism, see Lorde (1982); Cornwell (1983); and Roberts (1981).

107. cf. GLC, 1986, p. 94 and O'Leary, 1987.

108. An 'irrational' fear of and prejudice against homosexuals; cf. Kitzinger, 1987, especially pp. 154–162.

109. See Alderson and Wistrich, 1988.
110. Sources: GLC Internal Reports: Community Relations Projects Group Women's Committee Capital and Revenue Estimates 1983–1984, 1984–1985 and 1985–1986.
111. Sources: figures for June 1982 to October 1983 were provided in issue 13 of the *GLC Women's Committee Bulletin* (Jan/Feb 1984); the figures for the remainder were compiled from groups named in the lists provided in issues 10 to 26 of the same *Bulletin*, and have been divided into the categories supplied in issue 13. Issue 24 (March 1985) was unavailable, so figures are incomplete.
112. Source: Raine and Webster (1984, p. 28)
113. This was not a novel idea in local government at the time. See Cockburn (1980), Ch. 4.
114. GLC Internal Report S527 (regarding Equal Opportunities) stated that the aim was to 'formulate positive action policies to redress existing imbalances' (p. 5).
115. Source: GLC *Women's Committee Bulletin*, August/September 1985.
116. See Forrester et al, 1985, ch.4; Carvel, 1987, Chs. 10 and 11; Flynn *et al*, 1985; D. King, 1989, p. 468; Livingstone, 1987, Ch. 9.
117. cf. in particular the Local Government Act, 1986.
118. See Tobin, 1990, pp. 55–56 and Carvel, 1987.
119. See also Bindel, 1988, p. 50.
120. See Strathern (1987) and (1988), which outlines the 'western' character of the 'society vs the individual' dichotomy.
121. Two excellent examples are Butler, 1990 and 1993. See also Diamond and Quinby, 1988, and Nicholson, 1990, and Flax (1987). See Tress, 1988 and Lovibond, 1989 for critiques of the new developments.
122. See, for example, Bordo (1993) and Shilling (1993).
123. See Sawicki (1988, pp. 177–178), Rich (1986) and Ferguson (1984, p. 107) for similar USA examples.
124. This quote is from a tape transcript.
125. See Echols, 1984; Hollibaugh and Moraga, 1984; and Ardill and O'Sullivan, 1986, for examples of this kind of critique.
126. See Moi (1985), Brennan (1989) and Butler (1990) for a critique of the essentialist character of 'always already'.
127. The phrase is taken from Connell (1987).
128. Using Faderman's work (1983 and 1985).
129. See Blackman and Perry (1990) for a discussion of this issue.
130. See Barrett (1987) for a discussion on the different uses of the term 'difference' in gender theory literature.
131. See Kappeler (1986), pp. 135–45 and 149–66, and Dworkin (1981), Ch. 3 for roots of the term 'libertarian'. See also Leidholdt and Raymond (1990) for a critique of the 'libertarian' approach.
132. See Cooper and Herman, 1990, for an example of this argument.
133. See, for e.g., Rubin (1981 and 1984).
134. See Chester and Dickey (1988) and Norden (1990) for a discussion of differences in opinion on censorship; Snitow *et al.* (1984) and Vance (1984) for critiques that radical/revolutionary feminists are 'anti-sex', and Lederer (1980) for radical feminist defences against this charge.

135. This trend in 'deviant dress' has also been noted by Wilson, 1990.
136. I am using the term in its anthropological sense: see Evans-Pritchard, 1937.
137. See also Faderman (1992), esp. Chapter 10.
138. For example, Max Hastings of the *London Evening Standard*, referred to Livingstone and his colleagues as a 'fungus growth of social engineers, of the undemocratic democrats controlling vast resources and major public platforms' (quoted in Forrester *et al*, 1985, p. 50).
139. The two major publications outlining these campaigns can be found in GLC, 1985 and GLC Women's Committee, 1986. See also Ryan and Spragg 1988, and London Strategic Policy Unit, 1988.
140. Local Government Act 1986 (Amendment) Bill [H.L.], *Hansard*, 18 Dec. 1986, c.310 *ff*. This was not a unique legislative effort. For the USA, see Fitzgerald (1986, p. 65); Castells (1983, p. 144). In any event, Britain does not have a good record on gay rights compared to Europe (Tatchell, 1990).
141. See Armitage *et al* (1987) for a survey of the media's treatment of homosexuality and Rutledge, 1988 for a selection of quotations about homosexuals.
142. See in particular Tingle, 1986.
143. See Faraday, 1988.
144. See Dworkin (1981) and Jeffreys (1990) as good examples of this argument.
145. Including *Square Peg* (seen as 'libertarian', e.g. Anon., 1988), *Feminist Review* (seen as socialist feminist and 'pro-libertarian' – e.g. Ardill and O'Sullivan, 1989) and the *Lesbian Information Service Newsletter* (LISN), seen as revolutionary feminist, e.g., L.I.S., 1988).
146. Later, there would be publications on the opposing side responding to these, such as Sheila Jeffreys' *Anticlimax* (1990) and from the USA, an anthology of papers entitled *The Sexual Liberals and the Attack on Feminism* (Leidholdt and Raymond, 1990).

Bibliography

Abbott, Sidney and Barbara J. Love, 1972. *Sappho Was a Right-On Woman: A Liberated View of Lesbianism*. New York: Stein & Day.

Abrams, P. and A. McCulloch, 1976. *Communes, Sociology and Society*. Cambridge: Cambridge University Press.

Adam, Barry, 1985. 'Structural foundations of the gay world'. *Comparative Study of Society and History*, vol. 27, no. 4 (October), pp. 658–671.

Alcoff, Linda, 1988. 'Cultural feminism versus post-structuralism: the identity crisis in feminist theory'. *Signs* vol. 13, no. 3, pp. 405–436.

Alderson, Lynn and Sheila Shulman, 1983. 'Writing Our Own History I: When Lesbians Came Out in the Movement'. *Trouble and Strife* (Winter), pp. 51–56.

—— and Harriet Wistrich, 1988. 'Clause 29: radical feminist perspectives'. *Trouble and Strife* no. 13 (Spring), pp. 3–8.

Ali, Tariq, in conversation with Ken Livingstone, 1984. *Who's Afraid of Margaret Thatcher? In Praise of Socialism*. London: Verso.

Allen, Sue and Lynn Harne, 1988. 'Lesbian mothers – the fight for child custody'. In Cant and Hemmings, pp. 179–194.

Altman, Dennis, Carole Vance, Martha Vicinus, Jeffrey Weeks *and others*, 1989. *Homosexuality, Which Homosexuality? Essays from the international conference on lesbian and gay studies*. London: GMP Publishers.

Amazones d'Hier, Lesbiennes d'Aujourd'hui, (Collective), 1986. 'Radical Lesbianism', trans. Denise Blais. *Gossip* no. 4, pp. 21–26.

Anderson, Benedict, 1987 [1983]. *Imagined Communities: Reflections on the Origin and Spread of Nationalism*. London: Verso.

Anlin, Sandra, 1989. *Out But Not Down*. London: Homeless Action.

Anon., 1982. 'Lesbians in pre-Nazi Germany'. *Connexions* (Winter), No. 3, pp. 16–19.

Anon., 1988. 'Lesbian Summer School'. *Square Peg* no. 21, pp. 22–23.

Ardener, Edwin, 1975. 'The Problem Revisited'. In *Perceiving Women*, Shirley Ardener (ed), London: Dent, pp. 19–27.

Ardill, Susan and Sue O'Sullivan, 1986. 'Upsetting an Applecart: Difference, Desire and Lesbian Sadomasochism'. *Feminist Review* no. 23 (June), pp. 31–57.

——, 1989. 'Sex in the summer of '88'. *Feminist Review* no. 31 (Spring), pp. 127–134.

Armitage, Gary, Julienne Dickey and Sue Sharples, 1987. *Out of the Gutter: A Survey of the Treatment of Homosexuality by the Press*. London: Campaign for Press and Broadcasting Freedom.

Auchmuty, Rosemary, 1989. 'By Their Friends We Shall Know Them: The lives and networks of some women in North Lambeth, 1880–1940'. In Lesbian History Group, pp. 77–98.

Auerbach, Nina, 1978. *Communities of Women*. Cambridge Mass.: Harvard University Press.

Austberry, Helen and Sophie Watson, 1983. *Women on the Margins: A Study of Single Women's Housing Problems*. London: Housing Research Group, The City University.

Bannon, Anne, 1986a [1959]. *I Am A Woman*. New York: Naiad Press.
——, 1986b [1962]. *Beebo Brinker*. New York: Naiad Press.
Barnhart, E., 1975. 'Friends and Lovers in a Lesbian Counterculture Community'. In Glazer Malbin (ed.) pp. 90–115.
Barrett, Michèle, 1987. 'The Concept of "Difference"'. *Feminist Review* vol. 26 (Summer), pp. 29–41.
——, 1988 [1980]. *Women's Oppression Today: The Marxist/Feminist Encounter*. (Revised edition). London: Verso.
Barth, Fredrik, 1970 [1969]. Introduction to *Ethnic Groups and Boundaries: The Social Organisation of Culture Difference*, F. Barth (ed.). London: George Allen & Unwin, pp. 9–38.
Beauvoir, Simone de, 1953. *The Second Sex*. (Trans. and ed. H. M. Parshley). New York: Knopf.
Becker, Carol S., 1988. *Unbroken Ties: Lesbian Ex-Lovers*. Boston: Alyson Publications.
Becker, Howard S., 1967. *Outsiders: Studies in the Sociology of Deviance*. New York: The Free Press.
Bell, Diane, 1987. 'The politics of separation'. In M. Strathern (ed.) pp. 112–129.
Berger, P., and T. Luckman, 1967. *The Social Construction of Reality*. London: Penguin.
Bindel, Julie, 1988. 'The State of the Movement'. *Trouble and Strife* no. 13 (Spring), pp. 50–52.
Blackman, Inge and Kathryn Perry, 1990. 'Skirting the Issue: Lesbian Fashion for the 1990s'. *Feminist Review* no. 34 (Spring), pp. 67–78.
Blackwood, Evelyn (ed.), 1985a. *Anthropology and Homosexual Behavior*. New York: The Haworth Press.
——, 1985b. 'Breaking the Mirror: The Construction of Lesbianism and the Anthropological Discourse on Homosexuality'. In Evelyn Blackood (ed.) pp. 1–17.
Bordo, Susan R., 1987. *The Flight to Objectivity: Essays on Cartesianism and Culture*. New York: State University of New York Press.
——, 1993. *Unbearable Weight: Feminism, Western Culture and the Body*. London and Berkeley, CA: University of California Press.
Bottrill, Ruth, 1988. 'Compulsory Heterosexuality, Lesbian Mothers and Education'. Unpublished M.A. Dissertation, University of London Institute of Education.
Bourdieu, Pierre, 1987 [1977]. *Outline of a Theory of Practice*. Cambridge: Cambridge University Press.
Boyne, Roy, 1990. *Foucault and Derrida: The Other Side of Reason*. London: Unwin Hyman.
Breines, Wini, 1982. *Community and Organization in the New Left: 1962–1968*. New York: Praeger.
Brennan, Teresa (Ed.), 1989. *Between Feminism and Psychoanalysis*. London: Routledge.
Brown, Rita Mae, 1976. *A Plain Brown Rapper*. Baltimore: Diana Press.
Brownmiller, Susan, 1975. *Against Our Will: Men, Women and Rape*. New York: Simon and Schuster.
Bryan, Beverley, Stella Dadzie and Suzanne Scafe, 1985. *The Heart of the Race: Black women's lives in Britain*. London: Virago.

Bunch, Charlotte, 1987. *Passionate Politics, Essays 1968–1986*. London and New York: Longman.

Burton, Frank, 1978. *The Politics of Legitimacy: Struggles in a Belfast Community*. London: Routledge and Kegan Paul.

Butler, Judith, 1990. *Gender Trouble: feminism and the subversion of identity*. New York, London: Routledge.

——, 1993. *Bodies That Matter: On the discursive limits of 'sex'*. London: Routledge.

Cant, Bob and Susan Hemmings (eds), 1988. *Radical Records: Thirty Years of Lesbian and Gay History, 1957–1987*. London: Routledge.

Caplan, Pat (ed.), 1987a. *The Cultural Construction of Sexuality*. London: Tavistock.

——, 1987b. 'Introduction'. In Caplan (ed.), pp. 1–30.

Caputi, Jane, 1988. *The Age of Sex Crime*. London: The Women's Press.

Carpenter, Edward, 1908. *Intermediate Types Among Primitive Folk*. London: Mitchell Kennerly.

Carpenter, Val, 1988. 'Amnesia and antagonism: anti-lesbianism in the youth service'. In Cant and Hemmings, pp. 169–180.

Carrithers, Michael, Steven Collins and Steven Lukes (eds), 1987 [1985]. *The Category of the Person: anthropology, philosophy, history*. Cambridge: Cambridge University Press.

Carvel, John, 1987. *Citizen Ken*. London: Chatto & Windus.

Castells, M., 1977. *The Urban Question*. London: Edwin Arnold.

——, 1983. *The City and the Grassroots: A cross-cultural theory of urban social movements*. London: Edwin Arnold.

Centre for Contemporary Cultural Studies, 1982. *The Empire Strikes Back*. London: Hutchinson.

Chester, Gail and Julienne Dickey (eds), 1988. *Feminism and Censorship: the current debate*. Bridport: Prism Press.

Chodorow, Nancy, 1978. *The Reproduction of Mothering*. Berkeley: University of California Press.

Cliff, Tony, 1984. *Class Struggle and Women's Liberation*. London: Bookmarks.

Cockburn, Cynthia, 1980 [1977]. *The Local State: Management of Cities and People*. London: Pluto Press.

Cohen, A. P., 1985. *The Symbolic Construction of Community*. London: Tavistock Publications.

——, (ed.), 1986. *Symbolising Boundaries: Identity and Diversity in British Cultures*. Manchester: Manchester University Press.

Cohen, Abner, 1974. Introduction to *Urban Ethnicity*, A. Cohen (ed.). London: Tavistock.

Combahee River Collective, 1986. *Black Feminist Organizing in the 70s and 80s*. New York: Kitchen Table, Women of Colour Press.

Connell, R. W., 1987. *Gender and Power*. Cambridge: Polity Press.

Cooper, Davina and Didi Herman, 1990. 'Turning Us Off'. *Trouble and Strife*, no. 19, pp. 14–18.

Cornwell, Anita, 1983. *Black Lesbian in White America*. New York: Naiad Press.

Course Students, 'Uncovering Lesbian History 1800–1970', c.1986. *For Those Who Would Be Sisters: Uncovering Lesbian History, Work in Progress Number*

2. London: Information Bureau, Centre for Extra-Mural Studies (University of London).

Cousins, Mark and Athar Hussain, 1985 [1984]. *Michel Foucault.* London: Macmillan Education.

Curb, Rosemary and Nancy Manahan (eds), 1985. *Breaking Silence: Lesbian Nuns on Convent Sexuality.* London: Columbus Books.

D'Emilio, J., 1983. *Sexual Politics, Sexual Communities: The Making of a Homosexual Minority in the U.S., 1940–1970.* Chicago: University of Chicago Press.

——, 1984. 'Capitalism and Gay Identity'. In Snitow *et al.*, pp. 140–152.

Daly, Mary, 1979. *Gyn/Ecology: The Metaethics of Radical Feminism.* Boston: Beacon Press.

——, 1987. *Webster's First New Intergalactic Wickedary.* London: Women's Press.

Davis, Madeline and Elizabeth Lapovsky Kennedy, 1986. 'Oral History and the Study of Sexuality in the Lesbian Community: Buffalo, New York, 1940–1960'. *Feminist Studies* vol. 12, no. 1 (Spring), pp. 7–26.

Diamond, Irene, and Lee Quinby (eds), 1988. *Feminism and Foucault: Reflections on Resistance.* Boston, MA Northeastern University Press.

Dixon, Janet, 1988. 'Separatism: A look back at anger'. In Cant and Hemmings (eds), pp. 69–84.

DOE, (Depratment of Environment), 1983. *Streamlining the Cities: Government Proposals for reorganising local government in Greater London and the Metropolitan counties.* (October) London: HMSO, CMND 9063.

Dominy, Michele Denise, 1983. 'Gender Conceptions and Political Strategies in New Zealand Women's Networks' (unpublished Ph.D. dissertation). Cornell University .

——, 1986. 'Lesbian-Feminist Gender Conceptions: Separatism in Christchurch, New Zealand'. *Signs: Journal of Women in Culture and Society* vol. 11, no. 2 (Winter), pp. 274–289.

Douglas, Mary, 1966. *Purity and Danger: an analysis of concepts of pollution and taboo.* London: Routledge & Kegan Paul.

Drude, and Dahlerup, 1986. *The New Women's Movement: Feminism and Political Power in Europe and the USA.* London: Sage.

Dumont, Louis, 1986. *Essays on Individualism: Modern Ideology in Anthropological Perspective.* Chicago and London: University of Chicago Press.

Dworkin, Andrea, 1981. *Pornography: Men Possessing Women.* London: The Women's Press.

——, 1983. *Right-wing Women.* New York: Perigree Books.

Dykewomon, Elana, 1989. 'Lesbian Theory and Social Organization: The Knots of Process'. *Sinister Wisdom* no. 37, pp. 29–34.

Echols, Alice, 1984. 'The Taming of the Id: Feminist Sexual Politics, 1968–83'. In Vance (ed) pp. 50–72.

——, 1989. *Daring to be Bad: Radical Feminism in America, 1967–1975.* Minneapolis: University of Minnesota Press.

Egerton, Jayne, 1985 [1981]. 'Prudes and Puritans'. In Dusty Rhodes and Sandra McNeill (eds), pp. 211–214.

——, 1990. 'Out But Not Down: Lesbians' Experience of Housing'. *Feminist Review* no. 36 (Autumn), pp. 75–88.

Eisenstein, Hester, 1984. *Contemporary Feminist Thought*. London: Unwin Paperbacks.

Ellis, Havelock, 1936. *The Psychology of Sex (two volumes)*. New York: Random House.

Ellis, Havelock, 1975 [1897]. *Sexual Inversion*. New York: Arno Press.

Epstein, A. L., 1978. *Ethos and Identity: three studies in ethnicity*. London: Tavistock.

Ettore, E. M., 1978. 'Women, urban social movements and the lesbian ghetto'. *International Journal of Urban and Regional Research* vol. 2, no. 3, pp. 499–520.

——, 1980. *Lesbians, Women and Society*. London: Routledge and Kegan Paul.

Evans, Lee, 1989. 'The Spread of Consumerism: Good Buy Community'. *Sinister Wisdom* no. 37, pp. 9–19.

Evans-Pritchard, E. E., 1937. *Witchcraft, Oracles and Magic Among the Azande*. Oxford: Oxford University Press.

Faderman, Lillian, 1983. *Scotch Verdict: Miss Pirie and Miss Woods v. Dame Cumming Gordon*. London: Quartet.

——, 1985. *Surpassing the Love of Men: Romantic Friendship and Love between Women from the Renaissance to the Present*. London: Women's Press.

——, 1992. *Odd Girls and Twilight Lovers: A History of Lesbian Life in Twentieth-Century America*. Harmondsworth: Penguin.

Faludi, Susan, 1992. *Backlash: the undeclared war against women*. London: Vintage.

Faraday, Annabel, 1981. 'Liberating Lesbian Research'. In Plummer (ed); London: Hutchinson, pp. 112–129.

——, 1988. 'Lesbian Outlaws'. *Trouble and Strife* no. 13 (Spring), pp. 9–16.

Ferguson, Ann, Ilene Philipson, Irene Diamond, Lee Quinby, Carole S. Vance and Ann Barr Snitow, 1984. 'Forum: The Feminist Sexuality Debates'. *Signs* vol. 10, no. 1, pp. 106–135.

Fitzgerald, Frances, 1986. 'The Castro'. *The New Yorker*, July 21, pp. 34–70 and July 28, pp. 44–63.

Flax, Jane, 1987. 'Postmodernism and Gender Relations in Feminist Theory'. *Signs* vol. 12, no. 4, pp. 621–643.

Flynn, N., S. Leach and C. Vielba, 1985. *Abolition or Reform? The GLC and the Metropolitan County Councils*. London: George Allen & Unwin.

Forrester, Andrew, Stewart Lansley and Robin Pauley, 1985. *Beyond Our Ken: A Guide to the Battle for London*. London: Fourth Estate.

Fortes, Meyer, 1945. *The Dynamics of Clanship among the Tallensi*. Oxford: Oxford University Press.

Foucault, Michel, 1985 [1977]. *Discipline and Punish: The Birth of the Prison*. (tr. Alan Sheridan) Harmondsworth: Penguin.

——, 1986a [1980]. *Power/Knowledge: Selected Interviews and Other Writings 1972–1977 by Michel Foucault*. (ed. Colin Gordon). Brighton: Harvester Press.

——, 1986b [1973]. *The Birth of the Clinic*. (tr. Alan Sheridan) London: Tavistock.

——, 1987 [1976]. *The History of Sexuality: An Introduction*. (tr. Robert Hurley) London: Peregrine Books.

Frye, Marilyn, 1983. *The Politics of Reality: Essays in Feminist Theory*. Trumansburg, NY: Crossing Press.

212   *Bibliography*

Fuss, Diana, 1989. *Essentially Speaking: Feminism, Nature and Difference*. London: Routledge.

Gallop, Jane, 1982. *Feminism and Psychoanalysis: The Daughter's Seduction*. London: Macmillan.

Gay, Peter, 1984. *The Bourgeois Experience: From Victoria to Freud*, Vol. I, 'The Education of the Senses'. Oxford: Oxford University Press.

Garfinkel, Harold, 1967. *Studies in Ethnomethodology*. Englewood Cliffs: Prentice Hall.

Geertz, Clifford, 1983 [1975]. *Local Knowledge: further essays in interpretive anthropology*. New York: Basic Books.

Glazer Malbin, N. (ed.), 1975. *Old family/New Family*. New York: Van Nostrand Press.

Glazer, Nathan and Daniel P. Moynihan (eds), 1978 [1975]. *Ethnicity: Theory and Experience*. Cambridge, MA and London: Harvard University Press.

GLC, 1985. *Changing the World: A Charter of Gay and Lesbian Rights*. London: GLC.

——, 1986. *The Future of London's Government: research and consultation project by the Greater London Council*. (March) London: Howard Jones Ltd..

——, Women's Committee, c.1986. *Tackling Heterosexism: A Handbook of Lesbian Rights*. London: GLC.

Goffman, Erving, 1968 [1963]. *Stigma: Notes on the Management of Spoiled Identity*. London: Penguin.

——, 1987 [1959]. *The Preservation of Self in Everyday Life*. London: Penguin.

Goodale, Jane C., 1989 [1980]. 'Gender, Sexuality and Marriage: a Kaulong model of nature and culture'. In MacCormack and Strathern, pp. 119–142.

Gossip, 1986–1988. *Gossip: A Journal of Lesbian Feminist Ethics*. London: Onlywomen Press; Volumes 1–6.

Grau, Günter (ed.), 1995. *Hidden Holocaust? Gay and Lesbian Persecution in Germany 1933–45* (with a contribution by C. Schoppmann; tr. P. Camiller). London: Cassell

Green, Sarah, 1991. 'Marking Transgressions: The use of style in a women-only community in London.' *Cambridge Anthropology*, vol. 15, no. 2, pp. 71–87.

Greenberg, David F., 1988. *The Construction of Homosexuality*. Chicago and London: University of Chicago Press.

Grewal, Shabnam, Jackie Kay, Liliane Landor, Gail Lewis and Pratibha Parmar (eds), 1988. *Charting the Journey: Writings by Black and Third World Women*. London: Sheba Feminist Publishers.

Griffin, Susan, 1981. *Pornography and Silence*. London: Women's Press.

Gunew, Sneja (ed.), 1991. *A Reader in Feminist Knowledge*. London and New York: Routledge.

Hall, Radclyffe, 1982 [1928]. *The Well of Loneliness*. London: Women's Press.

Halperin, David, 1986. 'One Hundred Years of Homosexuality'. *Diacritics*, vol. 16, no. 2 (Summer) pp. 34–45.

Hanmer, J. and S. Saunders, 1984. *Well-Founded Fear*. London: Hutchinson.

——, and Mary Maynard (eds), 1987. *Women, Violence and Social Control*. London: Macmillan.

Hannerz, Ulf, 1980. *Exploring the City: Inquiries Toward an Urban Anthropology*. New York: Columbia University Press.

Hanscombe, Gillian and Jackie Forster (eds), 1982. *Rocking the Cradle: Lesbian Mothers-a Challenge in Family Living*. London: Sheba Feminist Press.

——, and Virginia L. Smyers, 1987. *Writing for their lives: the Modernist women, 1910–1940*. London: The Women's Press.

Hardy, Dennis, 1979. *Alternative Communities in Nineteenth Century England*. London: Longman.

Harriss, Kathryn, 1989. 'New alliances: socialist-feminism in the eighties'. *Feminist Review* No. 31, pp. 37–52.

Hawthorne, Susan, 1991. 'In Defence of Separatism'. In Gunew, pp. 312–318.

Heller, Thomas C., Morton Sosna and David E. Wellerby (eds), 1986. *Reconstructing Individualism: Autonomy, Individuality and the Self in Western Thought*

Hennessy, Rosemary, 1993. 'Queer Theory: A review of the *Differences* Special Issue and Wittig's *The Straight Mind*'. *Signs*, vol. 18, no. 4, pp 964–973.

Herdt, Gilbert H., 1984. *Ritualized Homosexuality in Melanesia*. Berkeley, LA, London: University of California Press.

Heresies, 1981. *Sex Heresies*, Issue 12, Vol. 3, No. 4.

Hirschfeld, Magnus, 1914. *Die Homosexualität des Mannes und des Weibes*. Berlin: Louis Marcus.

Hoagland, Sarah Lucia, 1986a. 'Lesbian Ethics: Some Thoughts on Power in Our Interactions". *Lesbian Ethics* vol. 2, no. 1, pp. 5–31.

——, 1986b. 'Lesbian Separatism: An Empowering Reality'. *Gossip* no. 6, pp. 24–36.

——, and Julia Penelope (eds), 1988. *For Lesbians Only: A Separatist Anthology*. London: Onlywomen Press.

Hollibaugh, Amber and Cherríe Moraga, 1984. 'What We're Rollin Around in Bed With: Sexual Silences in Feminism'. In Snitow *et al*, pp. 404–414.

Hooks, Bell, 1990 [1982]. *Ain't I a Woman*. London and Winchester, Mass.: Pluto Press.

Hui, Yik, 1988. 'Living on the fringes – in more ways than one'. In Cant and Hemmings (eds), pp. 108–115.

Irigaray, Luce, 1985. *The Sex Which Is Not One*. (tr. C. Porter with C. Burke). Ithaca, NY: Cornell University Press.

Jackson, Margaret, 1983. 'Sexual Liberation or Social Control? Some aspects of the relationship between feminism and the social construction of sexual knowledge in the early Twentieth Century'. *Women's Studies International Forum* vol. 6, no. 1, pp. 1–17.

——, 1987. '"Facts of life" or the eroticization of women's oppression? Sexology and the social construction of heterosexuality'. In Pat Caplan (ed.) pp. 52–81.

Jeffreys, Sheila, 1981. 'The Spinster and Her Enemies: Sexuality and the Last Wave of Feminism'. *Scarlet Woman* no. 13, Part 2, (July), pp. 22–27, 45.

——, 1982a. 'The Sexual Abuse of Children in the Home'. In *On the Problems of Men*, Scarlet Friedman and Sarah Elizabeth (eds); London: The Women's Press.

——, 1982b. 'Free from the Uninvited Touch of Man: Women's Campaigns Around Sexuality, 1880–1894'. *Women's Studies International Forum* vol. 5, no. 6, pp. 629–645.

——, 1984. 'Does it matter that they did it?'. *Trouble and Strife* no. 3, (Summer) pp. 25–29.

——, 1985. *The Spinster and Her Enemies: Feminism and Sexuality 1880–1930*. London: Pandora.

Jeffreys, Sheila, 1986. 'Sado-Masochism: The Erotic Cult of Fascism'. *Lesbian Ethics* vol. 2, no. 1, pp. 65–81.

——, (ed.), 1987. *The Sexuality Debates*. London: Routledge & Kegan Paul.

——, 1989. 'Butch and Femme: Now and Then'. In Lesbian History Group (eds) pp. 158–187.

——, 1990. *Anticlimax: A Feminist Perspective on the Sexual Revolution*. London: The Women's Press.

Jenkins, Helen, 1984. 'Lesbian Strength and Gay Pride Week, June 1984'. *GLC Women's Committee Bulletin* no. 17, pp. 7–8.

Jennings, Paula, 1986. 'Lesbian Liberation Later'. *Gossip* no. 3, pp. 77–81.

Johnstone, Jill, 1973. *Lesbian Nation: The Feminist Solution*. New York: Simon & Schuster.

Kanter, R. M., 1972. *Commitment and Community: Communes and Utopias in Sociological Perspective*. Cambridge Mass.: Harvard University Press.

Kappeler, Suzanne, 1986. *The Pornography of Representation*. Cambridge: Polity Press.

Katz, Jonathon, 1976. *Gay American History*. New York: Avon.

Keyes, Charles F. (Ed.), 1981. *Ethnic Change*. Seattle, London: University of Washington Press.

King, Desmond S., 1989. 'Political Centralization and State Interests in Britain: the 1986 abolition of the GLC and MCCs'. *Comparative Political Studies* vol. 21, no. 4 (January), pp. 467–494.

King, Linda, 1989. *We Have Always Been Here: A Report by Linda King, Black Worker, and the Lesbian Archive and Information Centre*. London: LAIC.

Kitzinger, Celia, 1987. *The Social Construction of Lesbianism*. London: Sage.

Knight, Barry and Ruth Hayes, 1984 (May). *Government and the GLC: views from voluntary organisations-a survey*. London: London Voluntary Service Council.

Koedt, Anne, 1973. 'The Myth of the Vaginal Orgasm'. In Levine *et al*, pp. 198–207.

Krafft–Ebing, R. von, 1965 [1886]. *Psychopathia Sexualis*. New York: Putnam.

Kramer, Ralph, 1981. *Voluntary Agencies in the Welfare State*. Berkeley, London: University of California Press.

——, 1990 (February). *Voluntary Organisations in the Welfare State: on the threshold of the '90s*. London: LSE, Centre for Voluntary Organisation.

Krieger, Susan, 1982. 'Lesbian Identity and Community: Recent Social Science Literature'. *Signs* vol. 8, no. 1 (Autumn), pp. 91–108.

——, 1983. *The Mirror Dance: Identity in a Women's Community*. Philadelphia: Temple University Press.

Kuhn, Thomas S., 1962. *The Structure of Scientific Revolutions*. Chicago: University of Chicago Press.

L.I.S., and others, 1988. 'Treachery at the Lesbian Summer School'. *Lesbian Information Service Newsletter* vol. 13 (August), pp. 5–9.

Labour Campaign for Lesbian and Gay Rights, 1986 (August). *Legislation for Lesbian and Gay Rights: A Manifesto*. Manchester: LCLGR.

Leach, Edmund, 1954. *Political Systems of Highland Burma*. London: Bell.

Leat, Diana, Sue Tester and Judith Unell, 1986. *A Price Worth Paying? A study of the effects of government grant aid to voluntary organisations*. (No. 651), London: Policy Studies Institute.

Lederer, Laura (ed.), 1980. *Take Back the Night: Women on Pornography*. New York: William Morrow.

Leeds Revolutionary Feminist Group, The, 1981. 'Political Lesbianism: The Case Against Heterosexuality'. In Onlywomen Press pp. 5–10.

Leidholdt, Dorchen and Janice G. Raymond (eds), 1990. *The Sexual Liberals and the Attack on Feminism*. New York: Pergamon Press.

Lesbian History Group, The, 1989. *Not a Passing Phase: Reclaiming Lesbians in History 1840–1985*. London: The Womens Press.

Levine, Ellen, A. Koedt, and A. Rapone (eds), 1973. *Radical Feminism*. New York: Quadrangle Books.

Linden, Robin Ruth, Darlene R. Pagano, Diana E. H. Russell and Susan Leigh Star (eds), 1982. *Against Sadomasochism: A Radical Feminist Analysis*. San Francisco, CA: Frog In The Well.

Livia, Anna, 1986. *Accommodation Offered*. London: Women's Press.

Livingstone, Ken, 1987. *If Voting Changed Anything, They's Abolish It*. London: Collins.

Lockard, Denise, 1985. 'The Lesbian Community: An Anthropological Approach'. In Evelyn Blackwood (ed.) pp. 83–95.

London Strategic Policy Unit, Lesbian and Gay Working Party, 1988. *Lesbian and Gay Issues: Policy Development and Legislation, 1967–1987*. London: London Strategic Policy Unit.

Lorde, Audrey, 1979. 'Tar Beach'. *Conditions* no. 5, pp. 34–47.

——, 1982. *Zami: A New Spelling of My Name*. New York: Persephone Press.

Lovibond, Sabina, 1989. 'Feminism and Postmodernism'. *New Left Review* (Nov/Dec), No. 178, pp. 5–28.

Lukes, Steven, 1973. *Individualism*. Oxford: Blackwell

MacCormack, Carol and Marilyn Strathern (eds), 1989 [1980]. *Nature, Culture and Gender*. Cambridge: Cambridge University Press.

Marks, E. and I. de Courtivron, 1981. *New French Feminisms*. Brighton: Harvester Press.

Martin, Del and Phyllis Lyon, 1983. *Lesbian/Woman*. New York: Bantam.

Mauss, Marcel, 1987 [1938]. 'A category of the human mind: the notion of the person; the notion of self' (tr. W. D. Halls). In Carrithers *et al*, pp. 1–25.

——, 1990 [1950]. *The Gift: the form and reason for exchange in archaic societies*. (tr. W. D. Halls) London: Routledge.

McCoy, Sherry and Maureen Hicks, 1979. 'A Psychological Retrospective on Power in the Contemporary Lesbian-Feminist Community'. *Frontiers* vol. IV, no. 3, pp. 65–69.

McIntosh, Mary, 1986. 'The Homosexual Role'. *Social Problems* (Fall), Vol. 16, No. 2.

Millett, Kate, 1971. *Sexual Politics*. New York: Avon Books (Fourth Printing).

Mitchell, Juliet, 1974. *Psychoanalysis and Feminism*. London: Allen Lane.

Moi, Toril, 1985. *Sexual/Textual Politics: Feminist Literary Theory*. London: Methuen.

Moore, Henrietta, 1988. *Feminism and Anthropology*. Cambridge: Polity Press.

Moore, Sally Falk and Barbara G. Meyerhoff (eds), 1975. *Symbol and Politics in Communal Ideology: Cases and Questions*. New York: Cornell University Press.

Moraga, Cherríe and Gloria Anzaldúa, 1983. *This Bridge Called My Back: writings by radical women of colour*. New York: Kitchen Table, Women of Colour Press.

Morgan, Robin (ed.), 1970. *Sisterhood is Powerful: An Anthology of Writings from the Women's Liberation Movement*. New York: Random House.

Morris, Brian, 1991. *Western Conceptions of the Individual*. Oxford: Berg

Mushroom, Merrill, 1983. 'Confessions of a Butch Dyke'. *Common Lives, Lesbian Lives* no. 9 (Autumn).

Nadelson, Leslee, 1988. 'Pigs, women, and the men's house in Amazonia: An analysis of six Mundurucú myths'. In Ortner and Whitehead (eds), pp. 240–272.

Neild, Suzanne and Rosalind Pearson, 1992. *Women Like Us*. London: The Women's Press.

Nestle, Joan, 1987. *A Restricted Country*. London: Sheba Feminist Publishers.

Newton, Esther, 1984. 'The Mythic Mannish Lesbian: Radclyffe Hall and the New Woman'. *Signs* (Summer), no. 9, pp. 557–75.

Nicholson, Linda J. (ed.), 1990. *Feminism/Postmodernism*. London: Routledge.

Norden, Barbara, 1990. 'Campaign Against Pornography'. *Feminist Review* no. 35 (Summer), pp. 1–8.

O'Leary, Brendan, 1987. 'Why was the GLC abolished?'. *International Journal of Urban and Regional Research* vol. 11, no. 2, pp. 193–217.

Onlywomen Press, 1981. *Love Your Enemy? The Debate Between Political Lesbianism and Heterosexual Feminism*. London: Onlywomen Press.

Ortner, Sherry B. and Harriet Whitehead, 1988 [1981]. *Sexual Meanings: The Cultural Construction of Gender and Sexuality*. Cambridge: Cambridge University Press.

Pahl, R. E., 1970. *Patterns of Urban Life*. London: Longman.

——, R. Flynn and N. H. Buck, 1983. *Structures and Processes of Urban Life*. (2nd ed.) New York: Longman.

Park, R., Burgess and McKenzie, 1967 [1925]. *The City*. Chicago University of Chicago Press.

Pearson, Roger, 1990. 'Court overturns lesbian mother custody decision'. In *The Independent* (25 August), p. 5.

Plummer, Ken (ed.), 1981. *The Making of the Modern Homosexual*. London: Hutchinson.

Ponse, B., 1978. *Identities in the Lesbian World: The Social Construction of Self*. Westport, CT: Greenwood Press.

Poster, Mark, 1984. *Foucault, Marxism and History: Mode of Production versus Mode of Information*. Cambridge: Polity Press.

Rabinow, Paul (ed.), 1987 [1984]. *The Foucault Reader: An introduction to Foucault's thought*. Harmondsworth: Penguin.

Radicalesbians, 1973. 'The Woman Identified Woman'. In Levine *et al* (eds) pp. 240–245.

Raine, John and Barbara Webster, 1984. *Strategy, Choice and Support: a review of grant-aid to voluntary and community organisations from the London Borough of Camden*. (February) Birmingham: Institute of Local Government Studies, University of Birmingham.

Rasmussen, Stein E., 1960. *London: the unique city*. London: Harmondsworth.

Raymond, Janice, 1986. *A Passion for Friends*. London: Women's Press.

——, 1988. 'Putting the politics back into lesbianism' (first presented as a paper at the Lesbian Summer School, London, July 1988). *Lesbian Information Service Newsletter* vol. 16 (Nov.), pp. 11–14, vol. 17 (Dec.), pp. 15–18.

Reiter, Rayna R. (ed.), 1975. *Toward an Anthropology of Women*. New York: Monthly Review Press.

Rhodes, Dusty, and Sandra McNeill (eds), 1985. *Women Against Violence Against Women*. London: Onlywomen Press.

Rich, Adrienne, 1980. 'Compulsory Heterosexuality and Lesbian Existence'. *Signs* vol. 5, no. 4 (Summer), pp. 631–660.

Rich, Ruby B., 1986. 'Feminism and Sexuality in the 1980s'. *Feminist Studies* vol. 12, no. 3 (Fall), pp. 525–561.

Rights of Women, Lesbian Custody Group, 1986. *Lesbian Mothers' Legal Handbook*. London: The Women's Press.

Riley, Denise, 1988. *Am I That Name? Feminism and the category of 'women' in history*. London, New York: Macmillan.

Roberts, J. R., 1981. *Black Lesbians: An Annotated Bibliography*. New York: Naiad Press.

Ross, Becki, 1990. 'The House that Jill Built: Lesbian Feminist Organizing in Toronto, 1976–1980'. *Feminist Review*, no. 35 (Summer), pp. 75–91.

Ross, Ellen and Rayna Rapp, 1984. 'Sex and Society: a research note from social history and anthropology'. In Snitow *et al*, pp. 105–126.

ROW Lesbian Custody Group, 1986. *Lesbian Mothers' Legal Handbook*. London: Women's Press

Rowbotham, Sheila, 1989. *The Past is Before Us: Feminism in action since the 1960s*. Harmondsworth: Penguin.

Rubin, Gayle, 1975. 'The Traffic in Women: Notes on the 'Political Economy' of Sex'. In R. Reiter (ed.) pp. 157–210.

——, 1981. 'The Leather Menace: Comments on Politics and S/M'. In SAMOIS (ed.) pp. 192–227.

——, 1984. 'Thinking Sex: Notes for a Radical Theory of the Politics of Sexuality'. In Vance (ed.) pp. 267–319.

Rutledge, Leigh W., 1988. *Unnatural Quotations: a compendium of quotations by, for, or about gay people*. Boston: Alyson Publications.

Ryan, Brona and Julie Spragg, 1988. *Being Gay: A Booklist and Information Guide for Lesbians and Gay Men*. London: Islington Council.

Said, Edward W., 1991 [1978]. *Orientalism: Western Conceptions of the Orient*. Harmondsworth: Penguin.

SAMOIS, (eds), 1987 [1981]. *Coming to Power: Writings and Graphics on Lesbian S/M*. 3rd edition, Boston: Alyson Publications.

Sarachild, Kathie (ed.), 1978. *Feminist Revolution*. New York: Random House.

Sawicki, Jana, 1988. 'Identity Politics and Sexual Freedom: Foucault and Feminism'. In Diamond and Quinby (eds) pp. 177–191.

Sawyer, Ethel, 1965. 'A Study of a Public Lesbian Community'. *Anthropology Essay Series* (Washington University) (September) pp. 9–20.

Sayers, Janet, 1986. *Sexual Contradictions: Psychology, Psychoanalysis, and Feminism*. London: Tavistock.

Schutz, Alfred, 1970. *Reflections on the Problem of Relevance*. New Haven and London: Yale University Press.

Schwimmer, E., 1972. 'Symbolic Competition'. *Anthropologica* XIV (2), pp. 117–155.

Sebestyen, Amanda, 1988. *'68, '78, '88: From Women's Liberation to Feminism*. Bridport: Prism Press.

Segal, Lynne, 1988 [1987]. *Is the Future Female? Troubled Thoughts on Contemporary Feminism.* London: Virago.

Sharpe, L. J., 1984. 'The Debate on Metropolitan Government: the functional dimension'. In *Governing London*, Papers and Proceedings of the conference arranged by members of University College London and the London School of Economics, April 6, 1984. pp. 1–18.

Sheba, Collective (eds), 1989. *Serious Pleasure: Lesbian erotic stories and poetry.* London: Sheba Feminist Publishers.

Shepherd, Gill, 1987. 'Rank, gender and homosexuality: Mombasa as a key to understanding sexual options'. In Caplan (ed.), pp. 240–270.

Shilling, Chris, 1993. *The Body and Social Theory.* London: Sage.

Silveira, Jeanette (ed.), 1988. *Lesbian Ethics.* Albuquerque, NM: Le Publications, vol. 3, no. 2.

Sisters in Study, 1988. 'From the Inside Looking In: a reappraisal of *Heart of the Race*'. In Grewal *et al*, pp. 91–96.

Smart, C. and B. Smart (eds), 1978. *Women, Sexuality and Social Control.* London: Routledge and Kegan Paul.

Smith, Barbara (ed.), 1983. *Home Girls: A Black Feminist Anthology.* New York: Kitchen Table, Women of Colour Press.

Snitow, Ann, Christine Stansell and Sharon Thompson (eds), 1984. *Desire: The Politics of Sexuality.* London: Virago.

Spender, Dale, 1985a [1980]. *Man Made Language.* London: Routledge and Kegan Paul.

——, 1985b. *For the Record: The Making and Meaning of Feminist Knowledge.* London: The Women's Press.

Stanko, E., 1985. *Intimate Intrusions: Women's Experience of Male Violence.* London: Routledge and Kegan Paul.

Strathern, Marilyn (ed.), 1987. *Dealing with inequality: Analysing gender relations in Melanesia and beyond.* Cambridge: Cambridge University Press.

——, 1988. *The Gender of the Gift: Problems with Women and Problems with Society in Melanesia.* Berkeley and Los Angeles, CA; London: University of California Press.

Suttles, G. D., 1968. *The Social Order of the Slum.* Chicago: University of Chicago Press.

Talai, V., 1986. 'Social Boundaries Within and Between Ethnic Groups: Armenians in London'. *Man* Vol. 21 (N.S.), pp. 251–270.

Tatchell, Peter, 1990. *Out in Europe: A Guide to Lesbian and Gay Rights in 30 European Countries.* London: Channel 4 Television.

Taylor, Marilyn, 1988 (April). *Into the 1990s: Voluntary Organisations and the Public Sector.* London: National Council of Voluntary Organisations and Royal Institute of Public Administration.

Tingle, Rachel, 1986. *Gay Lessons: How Public Funds are used to promote Homosexuality among Children and Young People.* London: Pickwick Books.

Tobin, Ann, 1990. 'Lesbianism and the Labour Party: the GLC experience'. *Feminist Review* No. 34 (Spring), pp. 56–66.

Travers, Tony, 1984. 'Local Government Finance in Greater London'. In *Governing London* (6 April), pp. 1–18.

Trebilcot, Joyce, c. 1986. 'In Partial Response to Those Who Worry That Separatism May be a Political Cop-Out: An expanded definition of Activism'. *Gossip* no. 3, pp. 82–84.

Tress, Daryl McGowan, 1988. 'Comment on Flax's "Postmodernism and Gender Relations in Feminist Theory"'. *Signs* vol. 14, no. 1, pp. 196–200.

Turner, Victor, 1968 [1957]. *Schism and Continuity in an African Society: A study of Ndembu village life*. Manchester: Manchester University Press.

Tuttle, Lisa, 1987. *Encyclopedia of Feminism*. London: Arrow Books.

Vance, Carole S. (ed.), 1984. *Pleasure and Danger: Exploring Female Sexuality*. London: Routledge & Kegan Paul.

Ward, Elizabeth, 1984. *Father-Daughter Rape*. London: The Women's Press.

Warren, Carol A. B., 1974. *Identity and Community in the Gay World*. New York: Wiley.

Waters, Chocolate, 1977. 'A Lesbian Fable (To Be Read Quickly and without Feeling'. In *Take Me Like a Photograph: Writings by Chocolate Waters* Denver, CO: Eggplant Press, p. 15.

Weedon, Chris, 1987. *Feminist Practice & Postructuralist Theory*. Oxford: Blackwell.

Weeks, Jeffrey, 1983 [1977]. *Coming Out: Homosexual Politics in Britain*. London: Quartet.

——, 1985. *Sexuality and its Discontents: Meanings, Myths and Modern Sexualities*. London: Routledge & Kegan Paul.

——, 1987. 'Questions of Identity'. In Pat Caplan (ed), pp. 31–51.

Wheelwright, Julie, 1989. *Amazons and Military Maids: Women who Dressed as Men in Pursuit of Life, Liberty and Happiness*. London: Pandora.

Wilson, Elizabeth, 1990. 'Deviant Dress'. *Feminist Review*, no. 35 (Summer), pp. 67–74.

Wirth, Louis, 1956 [1928]. *The Ghetto*. Chicago: University of Chicago Press.

Wittig, Monique, 1980. 'The Straight Mind'. *Feminist Issues* (Summer) pp. 103–111.

——, 1981. 'One is Not Born a Woman'. *Feminist Issues* (Autumn) pp. 47–54.

Wolf, Deborah Goleman, 1979. *The Lesbian Community*. Berkeley: University of California Press.

Young, Ken, 1984. 'Governing Greater London: The Political Aspects'. In *Governing London* (6 April), pp. 1–32.

Young, M. and P. Willmott, 1962. *Family and Kinship in East London*. Harmondsworth: Penguin Books.

Zorbaugh, Harvey W., 1929. *The Gold Coast and the Slum*. Chicago: Chicago University Press.

Index